TASTING THE GOOD LIFE

WINE TOURISM IN THE NAPA VALLEY

GEORGE GMELCH AND
SHARON BOHN GMELCH

Indiana University Press
Bloomington and Indianapolis

This book is a publication of

Indiana University Press
601 North Morton Street
Bloomington, Indiana 47404-3797 USA

www.iupress.indiana.edu

Telephone orders	800-842-6796
Fax orders	812-855-7931
Orders by e-mail	iuporder@indiana.edu

Library of Congress Cataloging-in-Publication Data

Gmelch, George.
    Tasting the good life : wine tourism in the Napa Valley / George Gmelch and
Sharon Bohn Gmelch.
        p.   cm.
    Includes bibliographical references and index.
    ISBN 978-0-253-35644-4 (cloth : alk. paper) — ISBN 978-0-253-22327-2
(pbk. : alk. paper) 1. Wine and wine making—California—Napa Valley.
2. Wine tourism—California—Napa Valley. 3. Wine tasting—California—
Napa Valley. 4. Anthropology. I. Gmelch, Sharon. II. Title.
    TP557.G595   2011
    641.2'20979419—dc22
                                                              2010047691

1 2 3 4 5   16 15 14 13 12 11

TASTING THE GOOD LIFE

To the Napa County visionaries, community leaders, and advocates of the Agricultural Preserve whose foresight has protected the valley's character and agricultural heritage.

CONTENTS

TASTING THE GOOD LIFE

INTRODUCTION / *Tasting the Good Life*

Say "Napa Valley" and most people think "wine country." Although some Napa residents cringe at this description, it is accurate. The valley, located in northern California a little more than an hour's drive from San Francisco, is carpeted with vineyards and home to more than four hundred wineries, the densest concentration anywhere in the world. The fine wines they produce account for one-third of the economic impact that wine has on the economy of California. The valley's wine industry and its first cousin, wine tourism, employ seventeen thousand people. Local street and business names signal wine's dominance: Zinfandel Lane vies with Zinfandel Inn, Zinfandel Ranch, and Zinfandel Restaurant; Grapeleaf Graphics with Grapevine Placement Service; Vineyard Dental with Vintage Concrete. Each year about five million domestic and international tourists arrive to "taste" the good life—to enjoy Napa's natural beauty and climate, to drink fine wine and eat fine food, and to indulge their other senses.

Despite the size of its reputation and tourist flow, the Napa Valley is actually quite small, just thirty miles long and a few miles wide. It could fit easily into a corner of California's Central Valley or the Bordeaux region of France. Compact and visually stunning, it is encircled by mountains that rise 2,500 feet above the quiltwork of trellised vines on the valley floor. Not only scenic, Napa's mountains are largely responsible for creating the soils that permit the growing of premium wine grapes. The valley's Mediterranean climate also plays a role. During the hot growing season from May through October, the lush green vines contrast dramatically with the dry oak-covered hillocks and knolls. With the onset of rain, the colors reverse, with the grasses on the hillsides becoming green and the leaves on the dormant grapevines changing to yellow or red and then brown before dropping. As beautiful as the agricultural landscape is, take away the surrounding mountains or cover them in houses and it is hard to imagine the Napa Valley having quite the same tourism appeal, no matter how good its wine and food.

Locals conceive of the valley as having two parts: the wider and more populated southern end, where the small city of Napa is located, and "up valley," which refers to everything from Yountville north. The valley's population is unevenly distributed between the two. Napa city has a population of about seventy-seven thousand, while the up-valley settlements of Yountville, St. Helena, and Calistoga each have populations under six thousand and revel in their smallness. The difference is more than demographic; it is also economic and cultural. The up-valley towns are wealthier and have more style: fine restaurants, big-name wineries, and spas. This distinction, however, is becoming less pronounced as Napa, once a blue-collar town well past its prime, has spruced up its waterfront and downtown. Once ignored by wine country tourists eager to get to more picturesque and chic up-valley destinations, the city of Napa now finds itself a tourism player and is becoming an increasingly popular stopping-off point.

Wine tourism is not an entirely new phenomenon. As early as the late 1600s, visits to vineyards were part of the European "Grand Tour" undertaken by young British elites to absorb high culture and finish their education. Individual wine connoisseurs also traveled to their favorite wine-growing regions: John Locke toured France's wine regions in the 1670s, as did Thomas Jefferson in the 1780s. Wine did not become an organized and specific travel interest, however, until 1855, when the wines of Bordeaux were classified and a guide was published for visitors to the Paris Exhibition. France's wine-growing regions then acquired an identity as a tourist destination, and specific chateaus began attracting visitors. Germany had well-established tourist wine routes by the 1920s. Today, some form of wine tourism can be found in virtually every wine-growing region of the world.

Since the 1980s, visits to American wine regions have become increasingly popular. In part this is due to Americans' growing appreciation and consumption of wine, but it also reflects trends in tourism itself. More people today are interested in actively engaging with the places they visit and in supplementing the tourist gaze (passively looking at historic sites, art, or natural wonders) with other sensory or bodily experiences. Wine tourism satisfies these desires. It offers the sounds of nature and the visual beauty of a rural landscape— enhanced by vineyards, winery architecture, and landscaping—with the opportunity to concentrate on other senses, particularly smell and taste. In Napa, tourists can also indulge their sense of touch—beyond the "mouth feel" or textural experience of wine and food—through spa treatments, body massages, and thermal baths. Some characterize the valley as a sophisticated and hedonistic Disneyland for adults.

Visiting wine regions also satisfies other tourist quests. For those just developing an interest in wine, it offers the opportunity to learn about this artisanal product and how it is made. For regular wine drinkers and connoisseurs it offers the opportunity to expand their knowledge and appreciation through "tasting," the quintessential wine tourism activity. Wine regions are also appealing because they contrast with most visitors' familiar surroundings, which are typically urban, thus providing one of tourism's central experiences—difference of place. Because wine is branded on the basis of its geographical origin, visiting the Napa Valley means traveling to the source, the real and only place where a particular wine or wines could be made. Thus, wine tourism also appeals to many tourists' unconscious quest for authenticity, which is also enhanced by the nostalgia that rural, agricultural environments evoke.

Our initial interest in the valley stems from family connections. As a teenager in the early 1960s, George visited the valley many times to stay with friends in Yountville. In 1971 his parents left the Bay Area and moved to Oakville, purchasing an old ranch from the Christian Brothers Winery. By then we were married, and the valley became the home to which we returned on holidays. George's younger sisters attended high school in St. Helena, while his mother ran a seasonal, mostly weekend bed-and-breakfast. We inherited the family property along with George's siblings in 2005, and today divide our time between Oakville and San Francisco, where we teach cultural anthropology at the University of San Francisco.

Tourism is also an academic interest of ours. Many of the places where we have lived while conducting research or to which we have taken college students on terms abroad are popular with tourists. Whether Tasmania, Ireland, Japan, or Barbados, we have seen firsthand the changes that tourism can bring. We began to study, write, and teach explicitly about tourism in the 1990s, focusing initially on Barbados and later Tasmania. Embarking on a study of wine tourism in the Napa Valley was a logical extension of this work; it was also a wonderful way to learn more about the valley—the place which had become our second home. In this book we look at wine tourism as a particular type of tourism. Who are Napa's wine tourists? What do they do in the valley and what do they take away from their experience? What work goes into supporting this form of tourism and what perspectives can people who work in wine and wine tourism offer? What impact is wine tourism having on the Napa Valley, its residents, and the wine industry?

To answer these questions, we adopted a multi-method approach. As cultural anthropologists we relied primarily on participant observation and informal and formal interviewing. The former included hundreds of hours spent visiting wineries to observe and participate in tours and various kinds of tastings, including those led by wine educators that pair food with wine. We also spent many hours standing at tasting bars conducting informal interviews with servers and tourists and steering casual conversations onto our research questions. To get behind the scenes, George worked for a time as a server at a local winery, and we both put in a grueling day as volunteers on a bottling line. To verify and quantify some of the patterns that emerged in these forays, with the help of two students we administered a survey to 161 visitors outside various wineries.

To assess wine tourism's many impacts on the Napa Valley, we interviewed Napa County officials, town planners, local mayors, chamber of commerce staff, business owners and tour operators, winery owners and winemakers, vineyard managers and workers, wine educators and tasting bar staff, chefs and restaurant workers, art dealers and local artists, spa owners and masseuses, local historians and longtime residents of the valley. A major shortcoming in the literature on tourism has been the lack of insiders' voices. To begin to fill that void, and because we believe that narratives are particularly compelling and insightful, we collected oral histories from seventeen people who work in different areas of Napa's wine and wine tourism industries. We selected them in various ways. Some we already knew. Others we met through chance encounters. Most, however, were recommended to us as being especially good at what they do.

The narratives in this book, derived from the oral history interviews, are organized into four sections that reflect the different settings and workplaces in Napa Valley tourism: vineyard and winery, tasting room and tours, food and fine dining, and other recreational venues—the wine train, massage, hot air ballooning, bike tours, and art. The narratives reveal in an intimate way the many paths that have led people to the valley, the work which underpins Napa's wine and tourism industries, and the perspectives of insiders on tourism and the changes it has brought. These stories also show the expertise that goes into making the Napa Valley North America's premier wine region and wine and culinary tourism destination.

1 / The Napa Valley—a Brief History

Native Americans arrived in the Napa Valley at least four thousand years ago. Because of Napa's mild climate and natural bounty, their numbers were large for a foraging people. Kit Carson reported seeing "thousands" of Indians in the valley in 1829, but just thirty years later he found a fraction of that number.[1] Referred to as "Guapos" by the Spanish and "Wappos" by the white settlers who followed them, their actual name has been lost in time, although some have suggested that they called themselves the Onastis. They were subdivided into localized groups like the Mayacomas, Ulucas, Callajomanus, and Caymus.

The Wappo or Onastis lived in small settlements on the valley floor, moving seasonally to camps in the mountains. According to Robert Heizer, who led the University of California at Berkeley's archaeological excavations in the 1940s, the largest villages had up to forty houses, each usually occupied by two families, and one or two sweat lodges (a ceremonial sauna).

The Wappo did not keep dogs or other domestic animals. They hunted deer and game and also fished, making several trips a year north to what is now Lake County for this purpose. At least once a year some journeyed to the coast to dig clams. They also gathered acorns, horse chestnuts, berries, and roots, and used stone mortars for grinding them. They worked high-quality obsidian—available near St. Helena—into scrapers and spear and arrow points and also traded it to other groups. Several of our Napa interviewees showed us some of the many Indian artifacts they had collected along the banks of the Napa River and in fields being prepared for vineyards.

The encroachment of white settlers into the valley in the 1830s brought tragic changes for the Wappo as they were pushed off their land, their game stocks were diminished, and they succumbed to diseases to which they had no immunity. A cholera epidemic in 1833 and smallpox in 1838 killed an estimated two-thirds of central California's Indians, though no figures specific to Napa are available. The few Indians who escaped disease and other hardships might still be "murdered in cold blood," noted the historian C. A. Menefee in his 1873 *Historical and Descriptive Sketch Book of Napa, Sonoma, Lake and Mendocino Counties;* into the 1850s, "whites, to avenge cattle stealing or murder were surrounding Indian sweat houses and killing the occupants as they emerged from

Photograph of Wappo woman by Edward S. Curtis, c. 1924.
Courtesy of the Library of Congress.

the door." Most settlers referred to local Indians derisively as "diggers" who dug in the dirt for food, in contrast to the more romantic Plains Indians who hunted buffalo from horseback.

In 1856 most of Napa's remaining Wappo were moved onto a reservation in Mendocino, 140 miles to the northwest. It was abandoned a decade later and many of its survivors found their way back home to the Napa Valley, where they took up work as field hands, wood choppers, herders, and domestic staff on the ranches of the land's intruders. In 1861 the visiting British agriculturalist

William Brewer encountered Indians on George Yount's ranch who were living in "mere sheds covered with bushes or rushes" and squatting around fires . . . some with bright red blankets around them. . . ."[2] By the end of the nineteenth century, white settlement had virtually obliterated the aboriginal life which had flourished just seventy-five years earlier. Today, Napa's rich Indian heritage is seldom acknowledged, and unlike many parts of the nation where places have been named after the local Indians or where their own place-names have been retained or reinstated, few Wappo names are evident in the Napa Valley today. In contrast, many places—Yount, Rutherford, Chiles, and Conn—are named after Napa's early Euro-American settlers.

The First Settlers

Napa's first settler was George Yount, who arrived in 1836. (After his death, the town of Sebastopol was renamed Yountville in his honor and in doing so avoided confusion with the town of Sebastopol in the Sonoma Valley.) Yount had been a farmer when he left his wife and two daughters behind in Missouri in 1826 to join a mule pack train heading for Santa Fe. He became a hunter, trapper, and "Indian fighter" in the Southwest before moving in 1830 to California which was then a Mexican territory. While on a hunting trip the following year Yount entered the Napa Valley and allegedly exclaimed, "This is a paradise. It's here I want to live and die." While wintering in Petaluma in the Sonoma Valley, he was employed to make wooden shingles for the Sonoma Mission and, later, for the home of the Mexican general Mariano Vallejo, who would later grant him land.

In 1834, Mexico secularized the Franciscan missions in Alta California and began disposing of their property; within eight years three hundred land grants had been given to Mexicans and foreigners alike. The land grants were intended to increase Mexico's influence over the region to counter that of the Russians, who were expanding their Alaskan colony south to northern California. Through Vallejo's patronage, Yount received two square leagues (11,814 acres) in the center of the Napa Valley, encompassing all of what is today Yountville, Oakville, and Rutherford.

In 1850, fourteen years after Yount's arrival, the first official census of the newly created Napa County showed a population of just 405, with women a small fraction of the total, as was the case in most early frontier settlements. Many of the new residents, including Yount, listed Missouri as their previous residence. Although the valley was still in a natural state, it was fast being brought under cultivation. "A road had just been laid out through its centre," noted one observer in the 1850s, "and . . . ploughs were cutting up the virgin soil in all directions."[3] Even after the road was built, locals still traveled by horseback on trails that crisscrossed the valley, connecting one rancho to another. As communities emerged, stagecoach routes were developed; traces of their tracks can still be seen in remote parts of the valley. By 1860, the county's Euro-American population had grown tenfold. From the top of a mountain the following year, one visitor described what he saw: "San Pablo Bay gleams in the distance; the lovely Napa Valley lies beneath us, with its pretty farms, its majestic trees, its vineyards and orchards and farmhouses. Its villages, of which three or four were in sight, the most picturesque of which is St. Helena, are nestled among the trees at the head of the valley."[4] In 1866, a newspaper account noted, "No part of the State can boast so many pioneers."

From Ranching to Farming

Ranching began to fade in importance following the extreme cold and heavy rains of the winter of 1861, which killed many of the valley's cattle. A severe drought between 1863 and 1865 eliminated much of the available grazing, forcing ranchers to sell their remaining livestock and often their land. Between 1850 and 1870, the size of the average land holding in Napa dropped 90 percent. Cattle ranching was dealt a further blow in 1872 when Congress passed the federal "no fence" law, which made ranchers liable for any crops their free-ranging herds destroyed. Soon after, visitors to the valley began to comment on the number of fenced fields they saw. As cattle and the hide and tallow trades they supported declined and as wheat prices also slumped in the 1870s, Napa's settlers began to plant apple, prune, and olive orchards. By 1910 the Napa Valley had over five hundred thousand fruit trees.

Many of the farmers who arrived in California as overland immigrants brought experience from years of farming in the midwestern and eastern United States. What worked well in the regions they came from, however, often did not apply to California agriculture. Napa's farmers had to develop a working knowledge of new soil types, new insect and plant diseases; without summer rains, they had to learn to irrigate to get through the annual six months of drought. Most succeeded through experimentation—for a time growing a wide variety of crops and then concentrating on those that grew best in their locality. Early diversification gave way to specialization.

Vineyards were part of this early agricultural diversity. Wine had first been made in California in the 1780s by the Franciscan priests at Mission San Juan Capistrano. It was made from black Mission grapes and was not very palatable. Without crushers or winepresses, the grapes were put into troughs, where Indians trod on them in their bare feet. The resulting pomace (crushed fruit) was then poured into cowskin containers to ferment, and later decanted into casks. Since the Franciscans' production exceeded their sacramental and medicinal needs, a small local wine trade developed. In Napa, George Yount made wine from Mission grapes grown on his property using the same process. In 1857, Yount made his first commercial shipment of wine, consisting of six casks and six hundred bottles. But, curiously, none of the many visitors to Yount's home who describe his hospitality ever mention being served wine; historian William Heintz has suggested that because so many of the valley's residents had strong religious beliefs, they regarded the consumption of alcohol to be a sin.[5] It was the gold rush that began in 1848 which increased the demand for wine and spurred many of Napa's farmers to plant vineyards. The demand for wine became so great that it outstripped the supply available from southern California and encouraged the importing of foreign wine. Napa's farmers could see the profits to be made.

From the 1850s onwards, the Napa Valley became a wine-producing area. The pioneers in this new industry were mostly European immigrants from areas with wine-making traditions: Charles Krug (from Prussia), Jacob and Frederick Beringer (from Germany), Jacob Schram (from Germany), and Gustave Niebaum (from Finland). They planted improved grape varieties, devised ways to plant more vines per acre, and introduced wine-making innovations that improved the quality of Napa's locally produced wines. Growing grapes and orchard crops like prunes also suited Napa's weather; farmers had learned that wet years often alternated with dry, making annual crops like wheat and corn unreliable. By the mid-1860s, Napa had fifty recognized vintners; some of them organized viticulture clubs for the exchange of information and lobbied for the emerging wine industry. Reflecting the prosperity of many of Napa's new wine-makers, brothers Jacob and Frederick Beringer built a seventeen-room mansion, the now famous Rhine House, in front of their cellar. It remains an important part of a tasting room complex at Beringer Winery.

These European vineyardists planted vineyards on the hillsides following the Old World tradition in which the valley floor was reserved for food grains and gardens. Some, like Jacob Schram, also believed that the well-drained soils of mountain vineyards produced superior grapes, and they understood that grapes planted at elevation were less susceptible to frost damage during the critical days of new vine growth (since cold air sinks to the valley floor). They pioneered a new style of architecture, building imposing stone wineries, like Greystone, which when it was built in the 1880s was the largest stone winery in the world. It served as a winery for over a century and now houses the West Coast branch of the Culinary Institute of America (CIA).

Most of the laborers who built these impressive wineries, the hillside caves used as storage cellars, and the stone fences that snake across Napa's landscape were from China. After the completion of the transcontinental railroad, for which many Chinese laborers had been recruited, they looked elsewhere for work. In Napa they found it in mining, tanning, factory work (a local cigar factory), and viticulture. "Chinese laborers are employed in all parts of the business," wrote the author of a guidebook for "Travellers and Settlers" to California in 1873. "They quickly learn to prune and take care of the vines, and their labor is indispensable."[6] Small "Chinatowns" emerged in Napa, St. Helena, and Calistoga. St. Helena's was located near the present-day site of Gott's Roadside café (formerly Taylor's Refresher). Calistoga's was the largest and once had over a thousand people, but Napa's was the most influential within the Chinese community since it housed the temple of Pei-ti (god of the North). Although their labor was indispensable, as is that of Mexicans and Mexican Americans today, all but a few Chinese were eventually driven out of California. Beginning in the late 1870s, Napa businesses and landowners began receiving threats against hiring Chinese labor, and individual Chinese were robbed and beaten. The historian Linda Heidenreich reports that "bands of white laborers roamed from field to ranch driving Chinese laborers from their places of employment."[7] In 1882 Congress passed the Chinese Exclusion Act, which prohibited further immigration from China. St. Helena citizens formed an Anti-Chinese League; by 1894 Calistoga had a White Labor Union. It wasn't long before few Chinese remained in the Napa Valley. They were replaced by immigrant workers from Italy and elsewhere in southern Europe.

New markets opened up for California wines in the 1870s after France's vineyards were struck by phylloxera, a vine-destroying root louse. By the end of the decade grape growing and wine production employed more workers in Napa than any other type of agriculture. The phylloxera scourge that destroyed French vineyards, however, hit California in the 1890s with the same disastrous effects. Eventually, a louse-resistant rootstock was found—a native grapevine from the eastern United States to which Napa's (and France's) varietal vines were thereafter grafted. By the middle of the decade, California's wine industry had begun to reestablish itself, and several Napa wines received medals in a world-class competition in Paris. In less than a century, the Napa Valley, like most of California, had gone through major cultural and economic transformations: from Indians and a natural landscape, to the Spanish mission system and Mexican pastoralism, to American ranching and wheat, to a more diversified fruit-based agriculture, including viticulture, and the emergence of real towns.[8]

Early Tourism

Napa's earliest tourists came not for agriculture or wine but to "taste the waters"—to enjoy the valley's hot springs and mineral-water spas. The White Sulphur Springs resort, comprising a hotel, cottages, and a bathhouse, was built

Chinese laborers in Napa, c. 1884. Photograph by LeWelling. *Courtesy of David Kernberger.*

in 1852 at the site of a sulphur spring in a narrow canyon west of St. Helena. It became a popular destination for San Franciscans. White Sulphur Springs was not only the first resort in Napa, it was the first in California and marked the beginning of a flamboyant resort era that would last fifty years.

But the best known of Napa's nineteenth-century resorts was one founded by Samuel Brannan, a former Mormon missionary who turned his energies to starting a newspaper and buying businesses and real estate in San Francisco. After visiting several fashionable European spas with his wife and children, he decided to build a spa that would rival all others. When he learned that a place in the upper Napa Valley variously called Agua Caliente and Hot Springs Town, which had hot springs and even an "old faithful" geyser, was for sale, he bought all two thousand acres and laid out his resort. It featured an elaborate hotel with bathhouses, guest cottages, a skating rink, a dance pavilion, an observatory, and a distillery—an odd choice for a former Mormon missionary. He christened it Calistoga. According to the apocryphal story, Brannan, having had too much to drink, rose to announce the construction of his new Saratoga of California and muddled the comparison with the well-known New York resort, calling it the "Calistoga of Sarafornia."

Unfortunately for Brannan, although the name stuck, the resort never attracted the numbers he hoped for. Even the railroad he constructed from Napa to Calistoga, which made it easier for guests to reach the resort, was not

Napa Soda Springs, c. 1900.
Courtesy of the Napa County Historical Society.

enough. His divorce, in which the court awarded his wife half his fortune in cash, sealed the resort's doom by forcing Brannan to sell. He left Calistoga in 1877, the same year a guidebook extolling the virtues of its mineral springs was published: "Their waters are much used, both for drinking and bathing, with good repute for curative results."[9] The property was then purchased by Leland Stanford, who, for a time, considered building his university there. Several small hotels and bathhouses were later built in the vicinity of the hot springs. Some bottled and sold carbonated spring water, which in the nineteenth century was valued as a tonic and aid to digestion. Over a century later, Calistoga is still the primary destination in the Napa Valley for tourists who wish to soak in hot mineral water or mud baths and to receive associated restorative or beauty treatments, including massage.

In the late 1880s, Napa Soda Springs was developed into a luxurious resort, the so-called Emerald Gem of the West. Its circular central building was topped by a glass cupola from which guests could peer down seventy-five feet into its immense lobby. Its stone Castle Hotel had crenellated parapets and a turret; the grounds contained a separate dining hall, bathhouse, and fanciful pagodas. Guests could go hunting, fish in a stocked stream, ride horses, bowl, play tennis, swim in a 150-foot-long pool, or just stroll on its thousand-acre grounds.[10] Like Napa's contemporary resorts, it provided many jobs for locals.

Most visitors to Napa's resorts at this time were wealthy families from San Francisco, located just across San Pablo Bay. Napa's pastoral landscapes, clean air, and dry, sunny climate have long attracted fog-weary urbanites. They crossed the bay by ferry and then made their way north by train or stagecoach. The trip took about half a day. In some cases, families rented a cottage at a resort for the summer with husbands joining their wives and children on the weekends or at less frequent intervals. Writer Robert Louis Stevenson was one of the many people who sought health in the valley. He first went to the Hot Spring Hotel in Calistoga but could not afford to stay there and so moved into a bunkhouse in an abandoned mining camp on Mount St. Helena. He squatted there with his new bride for two months in the summer of 1880. It was Stevenson who first referred to wine as "bottled poetry," but apparently he was not referring to Napa's wine making at the time, which he described as still at a "raw" stage of development. When a reporter from the *San Francisco Call* was sent to the Napa Valley in 1895 to do a feature, the article barely mentioned wine and focused instead on the natural beauty of the valley.[11]

Tourism to the Napa Valley declined after 1900, in part due to the automobile which expanded the range and ease with which people could travel and brought competing vacation sites within reach. The automobile and new oiled roads meant many people could drive to the Sierras, Lake Tahoe, or Yosemite. Some tourists now traveled straight through the valley to spend their time and money in the newly opening resorts of Lake County, to Napa's north. Southern California destinations also became attractive, and tourist dollars began slipping away.[12] The great 1906 San Francisco earthquake also played a role, shifting the geologic formations underlying the valley's hot springs and reducing or cutting off their flow. The earthquake also damaged many of the valley's venerable old buildings and knocked down nearly all the chimneys in the town of Napa. The devastation in San Francisco destroyed fortunes and reduced the number of residents able to afford a resort vacation. By World War II, most of Napa's nineteenth-century resorts had virtually disappeared.

Prohibition and the Wine Industry

The wine industry was facing its own challenges. Americans had long debated the effects of alcoholic beverages on human actions and morals. Led by pietistic religious denominations like the Methodists, prohibitionists viewed drinking as personal sin and argued that the only way to prevent its evils was to ban its consumption altogether. They were supported by many tea merchants and soda and soda fountain manufacturers who reasoned that a ban on alcohol would increase their sales. While the central concern of the prohibitionists was hard liquor, wine was vilified too. At the time it was still a luxury for most

Americans, although wine appreciation was on the rise. As debate between the "drys" and the "wets" heated up in Washington, D.C., and in the country's editorial pages, Napa's winemakers became increasingly alarmed. "Good, well-meaning, but misguided people," wrote the editor of the *St. Helena Star* in May 1909, "have suddenly determined that the viticultural industry is all wrong and must go with the rest. In their zeal the agitators would prohibit the manufacture and sale of wine, have the grape vine pulled up by the roots and the great cellars left empty."[13]

California's winemakers worked to separate themselves from the liquor and "saloon" trades, but ultimately they failed. With the passage of the Eighteenth Amendment and the Volstead Act of 1919, the manufacture, transport, and sale of all alcoholic beverages was prohibited. A few of Napa's wineries were able to survive by producing wine for medicinal or sacramental purposes; other wineries and independent growers were able to market their grapes in the eastern United States, where they were purchased for the home production of wine. (The law allowed Americans to make two hundred gallons of wine per head of household per year.) A few wineries continued to illegally produce wine and to sell it out the back door. For a time, auto traffic from the Bay Area to Napa increased as people traveled to buy bootleg wine and whiskey; Crane Park in St. Helena was said to be swollen with people camping with their cars waiting to purchase. But most of Napa's wineries were forced to close down. Many ripped out their vines and planted other crops, particularly walnuts, prunes, and Christmas trees. Others turned to dairy and cattle. Some former vintners became prune farmers on a scale that rivaled their previous cultivation of grapes. Former wineries and vineyards disappeared behind a profusion of fruit trees, whose white and pink blossoms in the spring presented a dazzling spectacle. Fruit dehydrators soon proliferated in the valley, causing the *St. Helena Star* in 1924 to tout the prune as "one of Napa County's greatest resources."

After repeal finally came in 1933, it took decades for California's wine industry to revive. Many former customers had switched to bathtub gin and cheap cocktails during Prohibition and never returned to wine; those still drinking wine often preferred sweet to dry. Napa Valley's high-quality grape varietals had been replaced by lower-quality vines like Alicante Bouschet and Petit Sirah which grew thicker-skinned grapes and could be more easily transported by rail to the East. Much of the craft knowledge of viticulture and wine making had also been lost when winemakers left California for other wine-producing regions or left the business altogether.

As recently as 1950, Napa's wine industry was still in the doldrums, with grapes ranking fourth—behind cattle, prunes, and poultry—in value. Grape growers earned less money for their crops than did farmers of any other fruit. Only 25 wineries were in operation, compared to 109 on the eve of

Mid-valley Napa ranch during prohibition, c. 1925.
Courtesy of David Kernberger.

Prohibition. Napa's only remaining major wineries were Beaulieu Vineyard, Beringer Brothers, Louis Martini, Inglenook, and Charles Krug. In the 1950s, most California wineries outside of the Napa Valley produced bulk table wines in huge fermenting tanks and shipped it in railroad tank cars. Their wines were marketed under generic names like "Sauterne" or "White Burgundy," which were blends of any white grape varieties available; "Burgundy," "Claret," and "Chianti" were blended from an assortment of red wine grapes. In Napa, wineries were beginning to label their finer wines with the grape's varietal name: Sauvignon Blanc, Chenin Blanc, Cabernet Sauvignon, Pinot Noir, and the like. Varietal labeling (indicating a wine made primarily or exclusively from a single grape variety) did not become widespread in Napa, however, until the 1970s.

The recovery of Napa's wine industry in the 1960s was greatly aided by the leadership and marketing of winemaker Robert Mondavi and by the watershed designation of the valley as an "agricultural preserve." It was sealed by the triumph of two Napa wines in a blind tasting at a special Paris competition in 1976, loosely portrayed in the 2008 movie *Bottle Shock*.

Robert Mondavi

In 1962 Robert Mondavi and his wife, Marjorie, made a grand tour of Europe's major wine-producing regions, visiting nearly fifty renowned wineries in Bordeaux and Burgundy in France, Tuscany in Italy, and the Moselle Valley in Germany. Mondavi was deeply impressed by how hard European vintners worked to bring out the natural character and flavor of each grape varietal. He took note of their use of small oak barrels to add depth of flavor and complexity to their wines. Back home, California's vintners were still using large redwood vats and focused more on mass production than on producing quality wines. There were two basic methods of making wine: one for reds and one for whites. Among the American public, sweet wines were still more popular than dry table wines, and California's wine industry was dominated by the Central Valley's bulk wine producers, notably Italian Swiss Colony and Ernest and Julio Gallo.

Mondavi returned from Europe convinced that Napa vintners could produce wines with the same subtlety and complexity as those produced by the Europeans and that the valley had the necessary climate, soils, and varietals to grow top-quality grapes. He believed that his winery—Charles Krug—should abandon the jug wines they mostly sold and strive to produce fine wines. Mondavi was determined to lead the way by adapting the techniques he had seen in the Old World and implementing new technologies such as stainless steel tanks, gentle presses, and quality bottling.[14] In 1966, after breaking with the rest of his family, he established the Robert Mondavi Winery in Oakville, the first major new winery to be built in the Napa Valley since Prohibition. Perhaps Mondavi's greatest contribution to the valley was his conviction that Napa wines could only be placed in the company of the great wines of the world if the quality and image of all Napa wines was raised, not merely his own. Mondavi was known to say "One bad wine in the valley is bad for every winery. One good wine in the valley is good for everyone." Acting on that principle, he encouraged Napa's winemakers to cooperate and to share ideas, equipment, and facilities, just as others had helped him with his first crush in 1966. It was that cooperation, coupled with Mondavi's relentless promotion and marketing of Napa wines, that, notes Julia Flynn Siler in *The House of Mondavi,* "fueled the valley's explosive rise to fame."[15]

Something else happened on Mondavi's trip to Europe that would have a lasting effect on the valley's development. He and Marjorie sampled the way aristocratic European wine families lived, with their chateaux, manicured vineyards, gardens, fine food, and devotion to art and music. A meal at La Pyramide in Vienna, one of the world's great restaurants with its graceful pairing of foods and wines, was for the Mondavis a revelatory experience. A decade later, Robert and his second wife, the Swiss-born Margrit, would bring chefs from France to cook and teach classes at their winery. They contributed to a budding culinary movement, which paired fine wine with the best available ingredients prepared to perfection, which also elevated the valley's renown and encouraged both wine and culinary tourism.

The Agricultural Preserve

In 1968, Napa County's board of supervisors created the Agricultural Preserve Zone. The "Ag Preserve," as it came to be known, replaced one-acre zoning with a minimum lot size of twenty acres, which soon was doubled to forty acres. The agricultural preserve was a radical idea, designed to preserve open space, prevent overdevelopment, and protect agriculture and the valley's foundation industry—wine. Nothing like it existed elsewhere in California, or anywhere else in the United States. And it was achieved despite vigorous opposition from developers and some citizens who wished to profit by subdividing their land for house lots and commercial activities, or simply to divide their property among their children.

The fight over growth in the valley had began almost a decade earlier, in 1959, when a local newspaper, the *St. Helena Star*, revealed that the California Highway Commission planned to build a freeway through the middle of the valley, cutting right through its vineyards. Environmentalists, vineyardists, and some winery people rallied the local population and succeeded in stopping it at the last minute. Their efforts highlighted the importance of the valley's agricultural integrity and also showed the power of protest. The Ag Preserve flew in the face of the pro-growth ethos prevalent in the state. Its passage altered the future of the Napa Valley profoundly by successfully protecting it from the urban sprawl that was spreading out from San Francisco in all directions. It has enabled Napa to avoid the ugly fates that have befallen other once-beautiful California valleys like the San Fernando and Santa Clara, whose farms, small towns, and main-street society are now paved over, choked in traffic, and shrouded in smog. The Ag Preserve has enabled Napa to retain its agriculture and rural atmosphere—the bedrock of its wine and wine tourism industries. In the course of preserving the valley's agricultural land and open space, historic and cultural resources such as stone bridges, rock walls, and barns have also been protected. Without the Ag Preserve and the refined, yet countrified, lifestyle it has made possible, the valley would never have become the highly desired tourist destination that it is today.

The Paris Tasting

In 1976 Steven Spurrier, British-born wine expert and Paris wine shop owner, came up with the novel idea of organizing a blind tasting of California and French wines to celebrate the bicentennial of the American Revolution. He personally came to California, including the Napa Valley, to select wines for the tasting. In Paris there were two rounds of judging. In the first, judges tasted the finest white wines of Burgundy, all world-class vintages, and California white wines. In the second round, they appraised the finest reds of California and Bordeaux. The results were a shock. A Napa Valley 1973 Chateau Montelena Chardonnay, made by winemaker Mike Grgich, edged out the best French whites, and a Napa Valley 1973 Stag's Leap Wine Cellars Cabernet Sauvignon, made by vintner Warren Winarski, took first among the reds. *Time* magazine trumpeted the results in a full-page story headlined "Judgment of Paris." The Paris tasting inspired winemakers not only in Napa but in newer wine regions from Australia to Chile. Napa's success against the world's renowned French wines is said to have convinced its vintners that they could make top-quality wine on their own soil. It also caused Napa wine prices to rise and tourists to stream into the valley to sample or "taste" what were now clearly America's finest wines. Entrepreneurs arrived, too, wanting to own a vineyard and in some cases to find a new vocation. *Forbes* magazine ran an article with the title "California Wine: Everybody Wants It," commenting that the potential for growth in the Napa Valley was "breathtaking."[16] Speculators began buying valley property. Some large corporations also moved in, purchasing some of Napa's best-known wineries, including Inglenook, Beringer, and Beaulieu. Foreign investors arrived as well, beginning with French-owned Moët-Hennessy, which bought acreage near Yountville in the mid-1970s to build the Domaine Chandon winery and restaurant. By 1983, there were 107 wineries in the valley, about the same number that had existed prior to Prohibition but double that of the mid-1970s.

The Rise of Wine Tourism

Before Prohibition there had been some attempt to attract visitors to Napa's wineries by creating spaces where they could sample locally made wines. Charles Krug Winery opened what was probably the first public tasting room in California in 1882. Illuminated with gas lights, it was set up among large redwood casks in the cellar. It lasted only a few years, however, before financial difficulties forced the sale of the winery. Inglenook Winery opened its "sampling room" around 1890; according to wine historian William Heintz, it was well appointed with "walls made of solid oak and adorned with costly pictures and plaques of bronze and porcelain."[17] Inglenook's founder, Gustave Niebaum, was a Finnish sea captain who had made his fortune in the Alaskan fur trade and intended his sampling room to impress winery visitors, the media, and his personal guests. Its furnishings were made to order in Germany, its stained glass windows in the Netherlands. The restored room is now part of the Rubicon Estate winery.

At the end of Prohibition in 1934 Beringer Brothers began offering public tours of the winery, marking the beginning of wine tourism to the valley. In the late 1930s and 1940s Beringer's manager, Fred Abruzzini, invited Hollywood celebrities to visit the winery. Among them was radio personality Janet Lee, who praised the valley and the winery on the air. She encouraged other celebrities to visit, including actors Carole Lombard and Charles Laughton, comedians Bud Abbott and Lou Costello, boxers Rocky Marciano and Gene Tunney, and singers Louis Armstrong and Roy Rogers. For San Francisco's Golden Gate Exposition in 1939 Abruzzini produced a colorful tourist map showing the main routes to the winery and interesting points along the way; he personally stood outside the gates of the exposition to hand them out. He succeeded in attracting "sizeable crowds" to the winery, according to Beringer chronicler Lorin Sorenson; by 1940, twenty-five thousand people were visiting each year.[18]

In the 1950s, Beringer Brothers turned its historic Rhine House into a hospitality center so that visitors would have "a place to linger and explore after a tour of the cellars and an opportunity to enjoy the architecture of the fine old home in St. Helena while also sampling some of the Beringer vintages."[19] Beaulieu Vineyards in Rutherford also opened a tasting room in the 1950s. The top wineries attracting visitors during this period were Christian Brothers, Beringer Brothers, Martini, and Beaulieu. Between 1957 and 1959 Christian Brothers Winery had an average of 57,000 visitors, while Beringer Brothers received 50,000. Martini and Beaulieu wineries (which were not open to visitors in 1957) reported receiving 10,000 and 17,000 visitors, respectively, in 1959. Clearly, the late 1950s was an important period for Napa's growing wine tourism.

The Mondavi family, owners of the Charles Krug Winery, also opened a visitor center in the late 1950s, placing a sign on Highway 29 welcoming visitors in. A few years earlier, Robert Mondavi had introduced tastings at the winery to encourage wholesalers to handle Krug wines, and later he organized concerts. He believed that good wine was part of good living and that activities at the winery should reflect this. A well-connected bon vivant from New York, Francis "Paco" Gould, was hired to handle public relations. He produced a quarterly publication called *Bottles and Bins,* aimed at publicizing Napa wines and encouraging people to visit. The Mondavis hoped that when people saw someone of Gould's sophistication extolling the merits of the valley and its wine, they would be enticed to come too.

Despite these efforts, when William Ketteringham, a Stanford University geography student, studied the settlement history of the valley in 1961 he found that only a few wineries were "well-equipped to handle large crowds, having parking lots, guided tours, special tasting rooms. Visitors come in private cars and in guided tours on Gray Line and Greyhound."[20] At this stage, the volume of wine tourists to the valley had not yet reached the point where

Postcard of Christian Brothers Winery indicating early wine tourism, c. 1955.
Courtesy of David Kernberger.

it was particularly noticeable to locals, unless they happened to live near one of the few wineries that had tasting rooms. Instead, what old-timers recall is the stream of cars that headed up-valley on Friday evenings and returned on Sunday on their way to and from Lake County, where they went boating, fished, and camped. "The valley was just not a desirable or fun place to visit in the 1950s and 60s," noted local historian Lin Weber. "There were no restaurants of any quality, few places to stay, and few things to do. Sure, people came to visit their Aunt Susie, but what else were they going to do—look at the cows?"

In the 1960s, per capita wine consumption in the United States was still low, but it was beginning to grow as more Americans discovered wine's pleasures and began to view wine as a symbol of status and culture. Some people were also taking up gourmet cooking, which often paired food with wine. By the end of the decade, wine consumption had accelerated to the point that in one three-year period (1969–72) Americans increased their wine purchases 12 percent per annum. Americans were also becoming more affluent, had more leisure time, and enjoyed taking Sunday or weekend drives in their new cars, which in northern California often meant trips to the Napa Valley.

When the Swiss chocolate firm of Nestlé bought the Beringer winery in 1971, many of the changes they introduced were aimed at attracting visitors. (They also had a long-term strategic plan to improve the quality of their wines from the vineyards up.) They refurbished the Rhine House, using the main floor as a tasting room and gift shop and the upper floors for private tastings. New landscaping and footpaths connected the old estate to the old cellar buildings and impressive aging caves, which had been dug by Chinese laborers in the nineteenth century. Guided tours were conducted throughout the day. Beringer also hired a public relations person to attract visitors.

During the 1970s, Napa's tasting room clientele included many young visitors—including many graduate students from Berkeley and the University of California at Davis—who were attracted by free wine tastings. Most of these wine tourists were newcomers to wine and showed a marked preference for sweet wines such as rosés, French Colombard, and Chenin Blanc. Today, few visitors ask for such wines, and even fewer wineries produce them (although dry rosés have made a comeback).

Despite the success of the tasting rooms at Beringer, Beaulieu, Mondavi, and Charles Krug, most Napa wineries were slow to embrace tourism. Many were torn between delight and irritation: "Are we in the wine business or in the tourist business?" they asked. A survey commissioned by the nonprofit Napa Valley Foundation in 1984 found that only one-fifth of the valley's wineries had a "fully open-door policy" for tours, tastings, and sales. Some wineries offered tours "by appointment only" and typically scheduled one or two each day for a limited number of people. Most wineries discouraged tour buses, which disgorged forty to fifty people at a time and swamped their tasting rooms. Some did so by levying a charge of up to $10 per bus passenger, while not charging those who arrived in their own cars or in limousines. In 1977, Yountville's Domaine Chandon became the first winery to charge for tastings. They did so mainly because the high excise tax on the sparkling wines they served made it prohibitively expensive to give free tastings. This started a trend of charging for tastings, a practice that is nearly universal today.

A study of local tourism and its impact that was commissioned in 1983 by the town of St. Helena described the typical visitor to the valley as someone coming to the "wine country via private auto for the day only. Bay Area residents and out of the area visitors usually arrive in Napa around 10 AM, visit one or two wineries, have lunch and return to home or hotel by dinnertime."[21] In the early 1980s there were still few first-class restaurants, accommodations, or activities that would entice visitors to stay the night.[22] Altogether, 1.7 million people visited Napa wineries in 1983. If the estimated 25 percent of visitors who didn't stop at any wineries are added in, the number of tourists then visiting the valley exceeded 2 million.[23] By way of comparison, the San Diego Zoo drew nearly 3 million and Yosemite National Park attracted more than 2.5 million at the time. In a little more than a quarter century, by 2010, the number of visitors to the Napa Valley had more than doubled, to over 5 million, and most were staying one or two nights.

The Wine Train

The Napa Valley Wine Train is a nine-car vintage train that travels up the valley from Napa to St. Helena several times a day, offering three-hour lunch and dinner excursions. Painted in the distinctive wine colors of burgundy, Champagne gold, and grape-leaf green, the train has parlor and lounge cars, a vista dome, and a Chef de Cuisine kitchen car. Most of the train's cars, which date to the early 1900s, were purchased from museums in the southeastern United States for about $2,500 apiece, after which another $200,000 was spent stripping and refurbishing each car. The interior decoration—crystal chandeliers, brass trim, mahogany paneling, woolen carpets, and upholstered chairs—recalls an earlier, more elegant style of travel à la the *Orient Express*. Passengers sit at elegantly set tables or in comfortable lounge chairs as the train glides slowly out of the city of Napa and travels north at eighteen miles per hour, allowing them to gaze leisurely at the valley's famous vineyards and wineries.

The train follows the route established by Samuel Brannan in 1868 to carry San Franciscans to his Calistoga resort. After his resort failed, the Southern Pacific Railroad took over the line and used it to bring farm equipment into the valley and haul out fruit and bulk wine in an era when wine was an agricultural commodity rather than an art form. Being able to transport wine easily and inexpensively by rail was a boon to the development of Napa's early wine industry. When the Southern Pacific ended its service in 1987, a group of investors led by Vincent DeDomenico—who had made his fortune building up and then selling his Golden Grain Macaroni Company and its famous Rice-a-Roni label as well as the Ghirardelli Chocolate Company to Quaker Oats—got the idea of using the track to run a tourist train which would stop near the major wineries. At first several influential winery owners supported the plan, but as they thought more about the likely impact of four or five large groups of train passengers descending on their tasting rooms each day, they got cold feet. They had already discouraged tour buses. Other residents were concerned about the train's potential impact on traffic since the tracks crossed the valley's major artery, Highway 29, several times. Some also feared the "Wine Train" would increase tourist traffic on the roads as well as deposit thousands of tourists weekly in downtown areas. The Wine Train, many thought, would mark the valley's turning point from a working agricultural community to a tourist trap.

St. Helena residents were especially vocal opponents. They were concerned about traffic and tourist numbers, but also about what they saw as inevitable pressures for the development of tourist services and the conversion of local-serving businesses to tourist-serving ones. The compromises that were finally reached prohibited passengers from disembarking along the way. Even so, when the Wine Train opened in September 1989, protesters lined the tracks carrying anti-train signs; a flatbed truck with a large "No Train" poster was parked on the tracks. Today the scaled-back but quite successful Wine Train makes twelve excursions each week and carries over 100,000 passengers each year on its thirty-six-mile round trip from Napa to St. Helena.

By the 1980s the Napa Valley had become a magnet for wealthy San Franciscans and others who could have a second home there and still be only an hour and a half from the city and an international airport. Living in "Wine Country" had become part of the idealized California lifestyle. Some newcomers also wanted to own vineyards, and a few aspired to produce wine with their own label. Many of these new vineyardists were men who had made their fortunes in other industries—manufacturing, electronics, real estate, or the run-up of the stock market. The director of the Napa Valley Grape Growers Association caustically pronounced, "This is no longer just a farming area. It's a label, like Calvin Klein."[24] The prime-time television soap opera *Falcon Crest* was set in Napa and centered on the misadventures of a wealthy family dynasty; it aired on CBS for nine seasons (1981–90) and also contributed to the valley's celebrity image. As journalist James Conaway wrote in *Napa: The Story of an American Eden,* the valley had begun to "take on a gloss that had more to do with money than with the product for which it had become famous." And as in an earlier era, the valley attracted celebrities like Robert De Niro, George Lucas, Robert Redford, Robin Williams, and Joe Montana, not just to visit but to buy homes. Developers also became eager to cash in, and enormous homes—derided by some as "starter castles"—began to appear on the hillsides. How this flood of newcomers and tourists has changed Napa's landscape and towns, its local culture, and the wine industry will be explored in later chapters, but first it is important to understand the phenomenon of wine tourism itself.

2 / The Tourism of Taste

Miles: Let me show you how this is done. First thing, hold the glass up and examine the wine against the light. You're looking for color and clarity. Just, get a sense of it. OK? Uhh, thick? Thin? Watery? Syrupy? OK? Alright. Now, tip it. What you're doing here is checking for color density as it thins out towards the rim. Uhh, that's gonna tell you how old it is, among other things. It's usually more important with reds. OK? Now, stick your nose in it. Don't be shy, really get your nose in there. Mmm . . . a little citrus . . . maybe some strawberry . . . [smacks lips] . . . passion fruit . . . [puts hand up to ear] . . . and, oh, there's just like the faintest soupçon of like asparagus and just a flutter of a, like a, nutty Edam cheese . . .

Jack: Wow. Strawberries, yeah! Strawberries. Not the cheese . . .

Sideways, *2004*

As the popularity of the film *Sideways* suggests, wine has become a central component of a sophisticated lifestyle for a growing number of Americans. It is intertwined with the way they dine and entertain, how they travel, and even how they enjoy a quiet evening at home. Yet Americans still lag far behind Western Europeans and the citizens of many other countries in the degree to which they integrate wine into their lives. Robert Mondavi, who did so much to advance Napa's reputation as a fine wine region, experienced this connection to wine while growing up in an Italian-American household. His visit to Europe in 1962 confirmed his belief that wine—like music, art, travel, and good food—contributes to a gracious and "civilized life," and many of his later initiatives in the Napa Valley, such as the Mondavi Winery concert series and the Great Chefs program, were aimed at cultivating this.[1]

During the 1960s, as America's middle class expanded and the age of jet travel began, more people started traveling abroad. Like Mondavi, many were exposed to cultures where wine was consumed regularly and not restricted to special events. Partly due to this exposure, as well as their own rising affluence, more Americans began to experiment with wine. Between 1969 and 1972, wine consumption in the United States grew 12 percent annually compared to less than 3 percent for each of the preceding 20 years.[2] Much of this growth was driven by baby boomers (Americans born between 1946 and 1964) who were coming of age and whose tastes and lifestyle choices differed significantly from those of their parents. Today, aging baby boomers still form the largest group of core wine drinkers (people who drink wine more than once a week) and of wine tourists to the Napa Valley. Fortunately for the future of the wine industry, drinking-age members of the large "millennial generation" (Americans born between 1977 and 1994) are also interested in wine for a host of reasons including affluence and familiarity, many having grown up in wine-drinking families. Industry publications note that millennials are more interested in consuming wine than in cellaring it and describe them as "fearless in matching food and wine."[3] In 2008, Americans consumed just over 11 liters of wine per capita, a quarter of the amount consumed by citizens of France (51 liters) and Italy (44 liters).[4] Industry representatives claim that the demand for wine in the United States reached a tipping point the previous year when for the first time "core" wine drinkers outnumbered "marginal" drinkers (those who drink wine as infrequently as once every three months). Despite a softening of demand for expensive wines during the financial crisis that began in 2008, Americans' interest in wine appears recession-proof and consumption has continued to grow.

Wine Tourists: From Neophytes to Oenophiles

Who are Napa's wine tourists? According to a large-scale survey by Purdue University's Tourism and Hospitality Research Center, published in 2006, most are well-educated.[5] Nearly three-quarters are college graduates; one-third hold master's degrees or doctorates. They are also well-off. Over half (58 percent) had annual household incomes of $100,000 or more; a quarter had incomes over $150,000—in contrast to just 16 and 5 percent, respectively, of the general population.[6] This privileged profile matches that of wine tourists in most other parts of the world. The majority (61 percent) of Napa's wine tourists are forty-five and older. Over 90 percent are Americans, with Californians—many from the San Francisco Bay area—making up over half. Most people (64 percent) who visit the Napa Valley come with a partner; others travel with a few friends or family members. (The average group size is 3.5.) The valley is promoted as a romantic getaway for adults, and very few people bring their children. Wine tasting is not especially compatible with children, a point discussed by Ellen

Flora in her narrative in chapter 5, although some wineries do minimally pre-pare for them by having coloring books and crayons on hand. The Napa Valley Vintners website enables visitors to search for "family-friendly wineries," but the list of "dog-friendly wineries" is longer.

Despite some basic similarities such as high educational level, in other respects Napa's wine tourists are a diverse group with different reasons for visiting the valley and widely different levels of wine knowledge—like Miles and Jack in *Sideways*. Although most visitors do come for the wine, whether to buy or simply to sample and learn, they also come because Napa is a desir-able destination. It is beautiful and, for northern Californians especially, a convenient place to celebrate a birthday, anniversary, promotion, or wedding. (Groups of similarly dressed young women entering or exiting a limo is a fairly common winery sight.) Still others come to Napa to unwind. They may visit wineries, but their primary purpose is to relax, eat out, and perhaps get a mas-sage. For international visitors, Napa is a must-see California destination; it has name recognition and cachet, like Tuscany and Provence, to which it is often compared. Those who grew up in wine cultures are curious about America's version. But even non-drinkers will visit wineries to tour their wine-making facilities or aging caves, enjoy their architecture or art, and stroll through their gardens or enjoy the view.

When we conducted our own survey of 161 wine tourists and asked them to rate their knowledge of wine, only 7 percent considered themselves to be very knowledgeable, 59 percent thought they were moderately knowledge-able, and 34 percent said they were not at all knowledgeable.[7] Studies of wine tourists in New Zealand and Victoria, Australia, found similar self-reported levels of prior wine knowledge. When we asked tasting room servers, tour guides, and wine educators to classify Napa's tourists on the basis of their wine knowledge, three groupings emerged. One category, commonly referred to as aficionados or collectors, comprises connoisseurs who are very knowledgeable about wine and often keep well-stocked cellars. They typically come to Napa several times a year, sometimes by private plane, specifically to buy wine, and they often spend thousands of dollars. According to one tasting room server, the aficionados she encounters typically belong to several wine clubs, tend to do only reserve tastings (of a winery's more expensive, limited-production wines), and enjoy engaging in "wine talk" and receiving "VIP treatment" at the winery. Hobbyists or "middle-of-the-road wine drinkers" make up a second category. They are less knowledgeable about wine than the connoisseurs, but they enjoy wine and the wine tourism experience. They tend to be younger; they want to learn more about wine to enhance their enjoyment of it and, for some, to acquire a form of cultural capital—knowledge that confers social status. When they speak to servers at the tasting counter, they sometimes describe themselves by varietal, as in "I'm a Cab [Cabernet Sauvignon] person." They are likely to belong to a wine-tasting group at home and to one or more wine clubs in the valley. They do not come specifically to buy wine, although they typically buy a bottle or two at each winery they visit.

Novices or neophytes constitute a third category of wine tourist. They are not knowledgeable about wine but are sufficiently interested to want to learn more and curious to see what the Napa Valley is all about. They tend to visit wineries whose brands, like Mondavi or Sutter Home, they are familiar with from their local liquor or grocery store. Most are value conscious and usually have a price point above which they will not spend. Napa's novice category in recent years has included more Asians (especially Japanese, South Koreans, and Chinese), which reflects the boom in interest in wine in those countries. Wine sales in Japan increased after the publication of the comic-book sensation *Kami no Shizuku* ("Drops of the Gods"), about a son's heroic odyssey to find the world's best wines and claim his inheritance. A growing number of South Asians, many of whom live in the San Francisco Bay area, are also visiting the valley. They tend to arrive in larger, mixed-age groups comprising family and friends. The younger among them are interested in trying wine, while members of the older generation tend to be non-drinkers and come to enjoy the scenery and overall experience instead.

Napa's Tourism *Terroir*

Cradled by mountains, just over thirty miles long and a few miles wide at its widest, the Napa Valley has an intimate feel. It is also perfect for touring, with more wineries within easy reach than in any other wine region of the world. What tourists see is a true winescape: row upon row of trellised grapevines advancing across the narrow valley floor and up the lower slopes of the Vaca and Mayacamas mountain ranges.[8] This natural and viticultural beauty is enhanced by the meandering Napa River, which cuts through the middle of the valley and is best appreciated when viewed from the hillsides or above from a hot air balloon.

The valley is beautiful at all times of year, and the services and amenities tourists expect are always available. From January to March, wild mustard blooms between the dormant vines, turning the hillsides and valley floor an iridescent yellow and green. The tourism industry has capitalized on this with its annual Mustard Festival, which combines food, wine, art, and entertainment, to attract visitors during this less active season. In April the wildflowers are in bloom and the vines experience "bud break" when new shoots emerge.

Tourists begin to arrive in numbers in May as the vines bloom and set fruit. In summer the valley is carpeted in green as the grapevines leaf out and the vines grow. By late July the berries begin ripening and in August most grapes change color from green to yellow or purplish-red, a developmental change called veraison. Three-quarters of Napa's grapevine acreage is planted in black wine grape varieties ("reds"). Cabernet Sauvignon dominates in terms of value, followed by Merlot, Pinot Noir, Zinfandel, Cabernet Franc, Syrah, and small amounts of a dozen more varietals. Chardonnay is the primary white varietal, followed by Sauvignon Blanc, and far lesser quantities of a dozen others.

Crush or harvest usually occurs in September and October; the exact timing depends upon the variety of grape, a particular vineyard's location, and that year's weather. This is when the second influx of tourists arrives, adding to the heightened activity of harvest when the fields are filled with the sight and sound of workers hand-picking the ripened clusters and the roadways are busy with tractors ferrying grape-filled gondolas to the wineries for processing. By November, as winter dormancy and the end of tourist season approaches, the vines' foliage transmutes into autumnal golds, red, and orange before dropping.

Beauty is definitely a significant part of Napa's natural and viticultural appeal. When the Purdue researchers asked tourists to describe Napa as a wine region in their own words, their most frequent response was "beautiful scenery." "We've been here once before," a retired academic told us, "but we decided to come back because it is so beautiful and peaceful." Environmental psychologists like Rachel and Stephen Kaplan have found that the places that impart a sense of well-being, at least for Americans, typically have a balance of trees and pasture, clear borders, and vistas that curve out of view; people like "spatial definition, coherence, legibility, and mystery (the promise of learning more through exploration)."[9] Most of these characteristics are prominent in the Napa Valley and have been enhanced in a very deliberate way by the wine industry. Many vineyard owners, for example, have outlined their vineyards with trees or stone walls and planted rose bushes at the end of each row of vines. Many wineries are picturesque, perhaps situated at the end of a winding lane. Others are designed to be imposing with fountains and grand landscaped entrances. Most longtime residents preferred the valley when it was grittier, before it evolved from agriculture into today's agro-tourism. But to most visitors, Napa—despite such deliberate beautification and the growing number of wineries and tourists that now flock to it—still seems authentically rural and appealing.

"We read guidebooks and picked out certain wineries," an engineer explained to us, "because they said the view across the valley was very, very beautiful. The architecture of the wineries also appeals to us. Basically, we wanted views, interesting architecture, and maybe one good tour." Winery architecture serves two functions: to facilitate production and to put on a show. The pioneer showcase winery built in the modern era—since Prohibition—is Robert Mondavi's Mission-style winery, which was designed in the 1960s by architect Cliff May. Since then many noted architects, among them Michael Graves (Clos Pegase Winery), Jacques Herzog and Pierre de Meuron (Dominus Winery), and Howard Backen (numerous wineries), have put their stamp on the valley. An early example of modern design is Domaine Chandon, built in the mid-1970s, with its stripped-down forms and rhythmic, scalloped roofing that blends into the landscape. But Napa's wineries come in all styles, from historic buildings (including original stone winery buildings from the 1860s and '70s) to neo-rustic barns or ranchlike structures, from architect-designed showplaces to replicas from other eras and places. The latter include a castle (Castello di Amorosa) built from stones taken from an Italian monastery, a replica Monticello (Monticello Vineyards), a Persian temple (Darioush Winery), a Venetian estate (Del Dotto Vineyards), and a Cape Dutch farmhouse (Chimney Rock Winery)—some of which are disparaged as inappropriate to the history of the valley and contributing to its "Disneyfication."

Most wineries are carefully landscaped in a style that befits their architecture and "story"—the narrative they have created to distinguish themselves from other wineries in the valley. Some are planted with California native plants like poppies and valley oaks. Others evoke the Mediterranean with grasses, olive trees, and fountains. Still others suggest wine's Old World heritage with European-style formal gardens of roses and boxwood hedges. More than a hundred wineries on the Napa Valley Vintners' website list gardens as one of their special features, clearly cognizant of their tourist appeal. Other wineries eschew all decorative trappings and highlight this fact in their advertising:

> Unlike the many lavish and imaginatively themed new wine facilities
> . . . the inspiration for Rutherford Ranch comes from the hard-
> working early settlers of this region. Instead of image and spin, the
> success of our efforts relies exclusively on tangible results—wine qual-
> ity so good it speaks for itself. Rutherford Ranch favors substance
> over pretense. We don't waste our resources on fancy wine centers
> or fanciful stories.[10]

As the numbers of Napa Valley wineries and tourists have grown, pressure has been placed on local government to control development in order to preserve the valley's agriculture. In 1984 there were 120 wineries, of which about 90 offered some sort of tasting or tour to the two million tourists who then visited the valley each year.[11] Today, there are over 400 wineries and five million tourists visiting each year. The exact number of wineries is difficult to pin down. Some wineries are not open to the public; others are wineries in name only in that they lack "bricks and mortar" and produce their wines at other facilities using their own or purchased grapes. Still others have been approved by the county but are not yet producing.[12] In some wine regions—Tuscany and Australia, for example—wineries are considered to be in the hospitality business as much as in wine making. Many have restaurants, extensive gift shops, and even inns and wedding chapels and derive much of their revenue from corporate dinners, parties, wedding receptions, and other non-wine retail sales. In 1990, after a hard-fought battle in response to local fears about similar developments in Napa, the county passed the Winery Definition Ordinance (WDO), which prohibits wineries from engaging in such ancillary activities. This ordinance explains why Napa's wineries—with the exception of Domaine Chandon—lack restaurants. It also explains a phenomenon that some tourists find confusing and mildly annoying, namely, the signs they often encounter at many winery entrances which state that tastings are "by appointment only." This restriction does not reflect snobbery as some suspect but rather was mandated by the WDO for all wineries opened after 1990; in practice, it sometimes is loosely applied. In 2010 the WDO was modified slightly to allow wineries to serve food with wine (as long as the charge to customers for such tastings does not exceed the cost of doing so) and to hold business meetings and retreats (as long as at least half their content focuses on wine making or education).

With so many wineries to visit, how do tourists decide where to go? There is no shortage of information. Many people consult guidebooks. A book search on Amazon.com for "Napa Valley" yielded 887 entries; a search for "Napa Valley wineries" resulted in 387. The internet itself is an invaluable resource. The Purdue researchers found that half the tourists they surveyed had used the internet for information, especially for lodging. The valley's towns—Napa, Yountville, St. Helena, and Calistoga—and their chambers of commerce all have websites, as do most wineries and the industry's trade organization, Napa Valley Vintners. Wine blogs are another important source of information for some Napa tourists. Reflecting the importance of wine tourism to Bay Area residents, the *San Francisco Chronicle* carries a regular column called "The Tasting Room" in its weekly "Wine and Food" section. It reviews area wineries, including descriptions of the "vibe" of their tasting rooms and the overall quality of the visitor experience. Word-of-mouth is also important, especially for "boutique wineries"—those with small production that typically do not advertise or distribute their wines through regular wholesale and retail channels. Many tourists, of course, visit the wineries whose brands they are already familiar with and regularly buy.

The Tasting Room

While architecture suggests what lies inside, the tasting room is the real public face of wineries. Most are handsomely appointed, featuring a lot of wood, stone, and other natural materials. They impart an air of sophisticated yet casual elegance—a fitting environment for imbibing wine, the ultimate artisanal agricultural product. Napa's tasting rooms vary in size from intimate to spacious. At Elizabeth Spencer Wines in Rutherford the tasting room is tiny and feels claustrophobic with ten people in it. But because it has been created inside a historic stone building (1872), the community's original post office, it seems quaint instead. The people who can fit at its bar (the rest can spill out into its garden patio) feel special, as if they have discovered an authentic hidden gem. The tasting room at Black Stallion, another boutique winery, is large befitting the property's original use as an equestrian center. A large oval bar stands in the center of a spacious, high-ceilinged room where visitors can stroll around, enjoy the architecture, or peruse the gift area. It also includes, as many wineries do, an outdoor patio with comfortable seating and a separate members-only wine club lounge.

Some facilities seem designed primarily to impress. Darioush's tasting room has an indoor fountain, columns, and a large sky light evoking a boutique hotel lobby more than a winery. At Hall Winery in Rutherford those visitors who choose to sample the winery's "exclusive" wines do so in an equally exclusive setting: they sit at a long table in a fourteen-thousand-square-foot aging cave lined with handmade Austrian bricks, under a massive chandelier depicting a vine's root system and adorned with hundreds of Swarovski crystals.[13] Other Napa wineries, however, are surprisingly modest and take a no-nonsense approach to the tasting experience. Saddleback Cellars in Oakville has wedged a tiny bar and wine-barrel table into a storage area and hung some western memorabilia on the wall. Most of its visitors choose to taste at the picnic tables outside. Tasting experiences like this appeal to those who want to feel that they are in the know and have discovered Napa as it used to be, before tourism took off. A wine blogger who has been visiting Napa since 1966 described his experience at the Smith-Madrone Winery this way: "You won't find a fancy tasting room or barrel room, or any merchandise for sale. The only thing you will find is just pure, honest, old-fashioned conversation and a passion for making good wine. . . . The good old days of the Napa Valley."

As important as setting is—the valley, winery architecture, tasting room décor—most wine tourists' experiences are made or broken by the people who

Cathy Chase, who has served wine at Raymond Winery since 1994, provides knowledgeable and personalized attention.

serve them. As tasting room consultant Craig Root explains in his narrative, "Next to wine quality, the most critical part of a successful tasting room is staff, staff, staff." Good tasting room associates, or servers, through their words of welcome, friendly smiles, and attentive but not oversolicitous service, create the special experience wine tourists seek. "We wrap them up in a genuine welcome," explains server Jim McCullough. When visitors approach a tasting counter, they are usually invited to look at the list of wines being poured and briefly told about the types of tastings available. Once they reach a decision, he begins pouring a flight of wines—typically one-ounce servings of four to six wines. Most tastings begin with some of the winery's whites, move to the reds, and often end with a dessert wine or port. As the server pours each wine, he announces the vintage and varietal: "This is a 2008 Cabernet Sauvignon." Most servers will then describe the wine's characteristics in terms very similar to the winemaker's tasting notes which are usually printed on the wine list placed in front of each customer. Different Cabernet Sauvignons, the valley's dominant wine, have been described as possessing the "distinctive flavors of chocolate, berry and mineral," as having a "noticeable mintiness," as being "a lush, fruit-forward wine with balance from beginning to end," and as having "intense black fruit flavors, grip to its tannins and a long finish of concentrated fruit." If the wine is a blend, the server will usually describe the different varietals used to create it: "This 2001 Arcturus is a blend of 62 percent Cabernet Sauvignon, 21 percent Merlot, 15 percent Cabernet Franc, and 2 percent Petit Verdot."

Good servers gear their conversation and the amount of wine talk they engage in to the interest level of their customers. Many today will mention some of the foods that a wine complements. "This is our salad and sushi wine," a server at Raymond Winery told our tasting group. "It's one of the few we make that doesn't see the inside of an oak barrel." The best are adept at making wine tasting enjoyable and wine making understandable, using analogies and metaphors such as "a winemaker selecting barrels is like a chef selecting herbs" and "an oak barrel adds flavor to the wine, like a cinnamon stick adds flavor to your hot chocolate." They can also answer such questions as "How many bottles of wine does a vine produce?" (four to six) or "How many grapes are in a glass of wine?" (about a half pound per five-ounce glass).

When we asked tourists what their most memorable experience in the Napa Valley had been, they ranked their winery experience just after Napa's scenery and the company of the people they were with. When we asked what they liked about their favorite wineries, most talked both about the quality of its wine and its friendly staff. "Our server was very funny," one woman related. "I really enjoyed listening to him and tasting wine with him. He was good at explaining what to look for in the wine. Wine can be so intimidating." Many wine tourists seem surprised by the friendliness they encounter in Napa. At Mumm, which produces sparkling wine, we overheard a tourist ask her server to explain how the "bubbles get in the bottle." After listening to the answer, she remarked, "You know, I didn't think people would be so nice here [in the valley]." When we later asked the same server how common such comments were, she said, "I don't know what people expect. That we're going to be mean? Lots of people tell me they're surprised how friendly people are here. Why shouldn't we be friendly?" When the Purdue researchers asked tourists to rank ten statements about the Napa Valley in terms of their impressions before arriving and then after, the largest positive gain was in response to the statement "People I encountered in the Napa Valley were friendly." Since wine is still culturally defined as an elite product, it may connote aloofness to many visitors and hence their surprise.

Servers often talk about where a wine's grapes were grown: on the winery's own property, within a single vineyard, in a famous vineyard like To-Kalon, or within a prestigious appellation. If prompted, they may go on to discuss what distinguishes a particular vineyard or appellation's *terroir* from others in the valley. *Terroir*—a term most Americans struggle to pronounce—

refers to the physical features of soil, slope, and microclimate that interact to give the grape varietals grown there unique characteristics. (Some people add tradition and culture into the *terroir* mix.) The Napa Valley comprises a single American Viticultural Area (AVA), or appellation, which is divided into fifteen sub-appellations meant to reflect physical differences in *terroir*. Atlas Peak, located in the foothills of the Vaca Mountains, for example, is described by Napa Valley Vintners as having volcanic soils that often require irrigation and as being 10–15 degrees cooler in summer than the valley floor largely because of its elevation. The Cabernet Sauvignon vines grown there are said to produce "bright berry and cherry fruit," while its Chardonnay grapes are described as "crisp, floral, aromatic, with distinctive pear-mineral flavors and bright acidity."

While a few of Napa's sub-appellations relate quite closely to soil type and microclimate, marketing concerns and past land usage also have shaped where appellation boundaries have been drawn. Most of Napa's AVAs are too big and diverse to offer a truly unified *terroir*. In describing the Oakville appellation, which runs across the middle of the valley between Yountville and Rutherford and up the hillsides on both sides, Craig Williams, former director of wine making at Joseph Phelps Vineyards, has said, "To be honest, I don't know how meaningful the phrase 'Oakville appellation' is. There are tremendous differences [within it] in exposure, soil, and elevations."[14] Nevertheless, some of Napa Valley's appellations have acquired distinct reputations which affect the price of wine. Because of its reputation, Cabernets and Chardonnays produced from Rutherford AVA grapes fetched prices that were 45 percent and 34 percent higher than those produced from an average of all Napa Valley's appellations. The Oakville AVA brought the next-highest premium for Cabernets and Chardonnays, with prices that were 41 and 33 percent higher than the average.[15] Whether tourists purchase wines from these appellations because they know or believe that they actually produce better wine, or simply because buying them implies that they are sophisticated consumers, is unclear.

Conversations between wine servers and tourists may cover many facets of the wine-making process as well as interesting facts about the winery. This is when terms like "Brix" (one way to measure the degree of ripeness and sugar content of grapes) and "malolactic fermentation" (a secondary fermentation sometimes used to reduce the acid content of red wine and the sharpness of some whites) may be introduced. At Newton Vineyard the tasting groups we participated in were told more than once that Newton's wines are "unfiltered and unfined [nothing was done to remove suspended solids] to avoid stripping the wine of its distinct aroma and flavor." At Frog's Leap Winery, one of forty-two "green" wineries in the valley, servers inform visitors about its sustainable farming philosophy and environmental features such as solar panels. These are developments the wine industry is encouraging which also prove useful in marketing, especially among younger consumers. Some wineries promote the fact that they employ "biodynamic" farming methods, which carefully consider the energy and natural interrelationships of organisms within the vineyard based on the tenets of Austrian philosopher Rudolf Steiner. If a winery's winemaker is well-known—like Mike Grgich, who made the 1973 Chateau Montelena Chardonnay that won first place in the Paris Tasting of 1976—this is certainly mentioned. Most servers and tour guides will also impart a little of the winery's history and lesser facts deemed interesting; for example, that Swanson Vineyard's signature Cabernet Sauvignon blend Alexis is named for one of the owner's three daughters.

If a winery is family owned and operated, the server will highlight this fact; it also will be a featured part of the winery's story on promotional materials. At a tasting at Raymond Vineyards, the server assured our group that the family—which has Napa connections extending back five generations—"really does the jobs listed for them" even though they sold a majority interest in the winery to the Japanese conglomerate Kirin, who later sold it to the Australian brewer Fosters. Family ownership contributes to the image the wine industry wishes to project, namely, that wine is an artisanal product lovingly produced by people whose lives are devoted to it. Common expressions like "a great wine springs from love and humility" and "it takes a great poet to make a great wine" convey this romantic view of wine making. Words like "passion," "quality," and "handcrafted" recur on winery websites, as does language that stresses a winery's lengthy wine-making tradition: "6th generation Napan," "California roots," "French heritage," or "Italian heritage." But as one middle-aged tourist who has been coming to the valley for years told us, "It used to be you'd come up here and taste wines while talking to the people who have made them instead of those who just pour them. Now, you're removed from the people whose passion and love is making wine." Family owners are aware of such feelings, and some make a point of periodically showing up in the tasting room or on tours. Their presence does make a difference. When one of ZD Wines' family owners, Brett de Leuze, unexpectedly appeared at a small tasting that was part of a Wine Train excursion we participated in and chatted with our group, the event did seem more exclusive and memorable.

Taste and "Taste"

Wine tastings should proceed at a leisurely pace. Only the most popular brand wineries during the height of tourist season discourage visitors from lingering at the tasting counter since having people crowded together, some-times three deep, is antithetical to their individual enjoyment as well as to wine sales. Wine is meant to be enjoyed—swirled in the glass and held up, its color admired; swirled some more to open it up and then smelled, its "nose" or aromas inhaled; sipped and held in the mouth, its "mouth feel" appreciated; moved about the tongue, its tastes discerned and savored; and then swallowed or spit into the provided container. The flavor and enjoyment of wine emerge out of a complete sensory experience that melds sight, smell, and taste with a person's prior experience and memories and a host of situational and psycho-logical factors.[16]

Taste is largely odor, and as Diane Ackerman notes in *A Natural History of the Senses,* "some chemists have gone so far as to claim that wine is simply a tasteless liquid that is deeply fragrant."[17] Seventy percent of our ability to distinguish flavor is derived from smell. Before we can smell something, it has to be airborne, which is why it is so important to aerate wine by swirling it in the glass (or by decanting it into a larger container or by using a Venturi).[18] Some experts distinguish between a wine's aroma (odors emanating from the grapes) and its bouquet (odors stemming from aspects of the wine-making process such as fermentation or aging). Chemist Ann C. Noble, while in the Department of Viticulture and Enology at the University of California, Davis, developed the Aroma Wheel, a visual graphic that breaks wine aromas into twelve basic categories like spicy and woody, which are further subdivided: licorice and anise under "spicy," vanilla and coffee under "woody." Its goal is to standardize the terminology used by professionals and amateur tasters. While our tongues and soft palates can only detect five basic tastes—sweet, salty, bitter, sour, and umami (also called savory, a meaty or brothy sensation)—our nose is capable of recognizing thousands of odorants. When we hold and swirl wine around in our mouths, the warmth helps vaporize the wine, sending its flavors around the palate and up into the nasal cavity. Some tasters suck air in through their lips and teeth while holding the wine in their mouths to acceler-ate aeration and aid them in picking out a wine's components. But it is actu-ally in the brain (in the orbitofrontal cortex) that taste and smell are brought together to form the sensation of flavor.[19]

Everyone responds to wine differently. One reason is physical. How we react is partly determined by our genes, which dictate the number of taste buds we possess (most of us have about ten thousand), the amount of protein in our saliva, the rate at which it flows, and our sensitivity to hot and cold. How we sense taste is also influenced by the state of our health: whether we are stressed, or have a cold or a serious illness. But learned and associative fac-tors are equally, if not more, important. Sensations are socially constructed;

we learn to fully perceive, appreciate, and interpret what we sense based on our experiences and cultural milieu. These include the social environment in which we consume wine—such as the people we are with and the ambiance of the setting—as well as our cultural and ethnic backgrounds. Smells and flavors that are familiar to one person may not be to another; someone used to eating lychees might perceive this aroma and taste in a wine, while others would not. The Aroma Wheel itself reflects the smells most Americans are familiar with and may therefore have a cultural bias. Some aromas and tastes trigger positive memories and associations for individuals, while others trigger bad ones.

Expectations and suggestion also play a role in how we perceive taste. The more we learn about wine, the more our responses to a particular wine are conditioned by that knowledge (sometimes overriding a genetically programmed aversive reaction to a taste). If you are told that a Cabernet Sauvignon contains herbal tastes, you will search for those tastes when you next sample it, and if motivated enough, you will probably perceive them. Component tastings, in which different amounts of the same flavoring (e.g., black cherry) are added to a series of glasses containing the same wine, reveal that even experienced wine drinkers from similar backgrounds vary in their perception of which glass contains the strongest concentration. As one wine educator told a group we were with, "The learning curve with wine is not bell-shaped, it keeps going up."

Many wine drinkers swear by the ability of Riedel stemware to improve their perception of the flavor and aroma of wines. The shapes and sizes of Riedel's glasses were designed to enhance the character of specific varietals. Controlled laboratory experiments on the effect of the glasses on tasters' appreciation of wine have found that they do not make a difference in any physical sense.[20] Yet, as one winery president admitted: "My highly skeptical tasting group tasted the same Chardonnay blind in seven or eight high-quality crystal wine glasses, all of different manufacture, and damned if the Riedel glass didn't 'win.'" In cases in which tasters know they are drinking from a Riedel glass, they may perceive that the glasses "work" because they have been convinced through masterful marketing that they do make a difference. Moreover, they are beautiful, delicate, and expensive, and they have become part of the culture of wine drinking—factors which all exert their own influence on perception.

People do vary in their physical sensitivity to the components of wine—its tannins, bitterness, and acid. In 1991 experimental psychologist Linda Bartoshuk coined the term "super taster" to refer to the 25 percent of people who are very sensitive to these components because they have more taste buds than the average person. They experience alcohol as harsh and hot and, as a result, tend to enjoy drinking lighter wines and sweeter varietals. At the other end of the continuum are "tolerant tasters," the quarter of the population with fewer taste buds than the average person. They rarely notice tannins and bitterness in wine and find alcohol to have a sweet taste. They tend to like bolder, higher-alcohol wines—usually reds. In between are "sensitive tasters," about half the population, who are only moderately sensitive to the tannins, bitterness, and acid in wine and therefore are open to a broad range of wine styles.[21] A good server will attempt to understand each individual's palate by asking questions about their likes and dislikes. Between pours, especially when switching from whites to reds, some wineries change the taster's wineglass or rinse it out. Visitors also may clean their palate with water or bland crackers or breadsticks, though not all wineries provide these.

Being able to discern and name the subtle aromas and flavors within wine—to recognize dried currants, sage, raspberry jam, black tea, vanilla, soy sauce, cedar, and the like—is not a natural skill, yet many people are sufficiently curious about wine to work at it. Moreover, being knowledgeable and discerning about wine has become a sign of sophistication. "It is knowledge a person seeking upper-middle-class status should have," explained cultural anthropologist Kenji Tierney in an interview:

> Because social class in America is less based on heredity than in Europe, we rely more on displays of "taste" and acts of consumption. My students [at an East Coast liberal arts college] all say, "Oh, you have to know about wine." What they mean is they need to know about wine so they can talk intelligently about what they're drinking and create the right impression with future clients and in-laws. This may not be the conscious motivation people have for going to the Napa Valley, but it lurks in the background for many and helps explain why so many wine tourists are college educated and affluent. For the working class, knowing about wine is less socially "useful"; it doesn't bring the same social rewards and fewer are motivated to go wine tasting.

As French sociologist Pierre Bourdieu argued, our "dispositions" to value certain things and to behave and think in certain ways are based on our family, class background, education, and the social arenas we operate in during our adult lives.[22] Members of different classes or social groupings value different things, including types of food and drink, entertainment, and art, yet a culture's dominant aesthetic—the cultural standard of what "good taste" is at a given point in time—is always defined by its elites and those in power. "Many people who feel they didn't acquire the 'tastes' appropriate to their aspirational social class at home or in school experience 'class anxiety,'" continues Tierney:

The Napa Valley Appellation and its Sub-Appellations

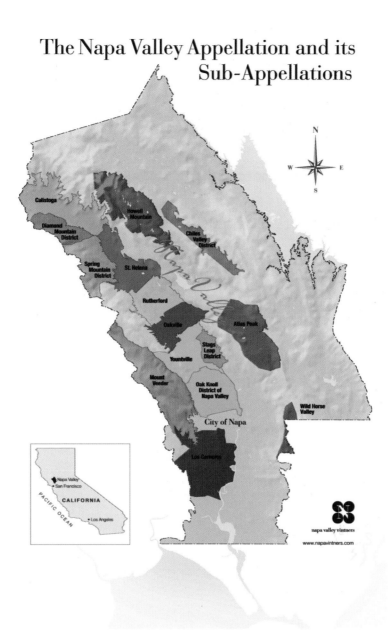

The Napa Valley, appelations, and sub-appellations.
Map courtesy of Napa Valley Vintners.

Mustard in vineyard.

Vines.

Nouveau Medoc Vineyard and Wine Cellars

Lithograph of Nouveau Medoc Vineyard and Wine Cellars by V. Duhem, c. 1890. The winery was located in Oakville while most of the vineyards were on Howell Mountain on the east side of the valley. *Courtesy of the Bancroft Library, University of California, Berkeley.*

Fieldworkers.

Vineyard view, Chicken Palace.

Domingo Uribe and a fellow worker remove excess foliage to expose the forming grape clusters to the sunlight.

Night harvesting of Chardonnay in Carneros. Photograph by Jason Tinacci. *Courtesy of Napa Valley Vintners.*

One reason people go to art museums is to see what taste
has been culturally approved, what artwork is appropriate
or "the good stuff." It's very similar with wine tourism. The
experience of wine tasting is pleasurable, but acquiring wine
knowledge and having made trips to Napa are also forms of
social capital that are useful in their lives back home. This is
a subtext to wine tasting and wine tourism at this moment
in American culture.

In the film *Sideways*, the character Jack apparently is not afflicted with class
anxiety, while Miles may well be:

Jack: Man! That's tasty!

Miles: That's 100% pinot noir. Single vineyard. They don't even
make it any more.

Jack: Pinot noir?

Miles: Mmm-hmm.

Jack: Then how come it's white?

Miles: Oh, Jesus. Don't ask questions like that up in wine country.
They'll think you're some kind of dumbshit, OK?

All tourism is a form of consumption through which people acquire intan-
gibles like experience and status. In his 1899 classic, *The Theory of the Leisure
Class,* economist Thorstein Veblen coined the terms "conspicuous consumption" and "conspicuous leisure" to describe two ways by which people gain and
signal status. Wine tourism combines both. Knowledge, experiences, and products that signify status can be used by people in two ways: exclusion and inclu-
sion. Drinking fine wine and traveling to Napa, which is difficult to do cheaply,
can be used by individuals in an exclusive sense to differentiate themselves from
others. It can also be used by individuals in an inclusive sense, as a form of self-
classification, by which they ally themselves with others whose interests and
lifestyle they share or wish to share. The vineyard communities that emerged
in the United States in the 1980s are one form of such self-classification. Sited
adjacent to vineyards or with enough land for residents to plant their own small
vineyards, they offered residents the opportunity to attend wine classes, dinner
lectures, and harvest parties with fellow oenophiles. Much like those based
on golf, these communities unite people around a high-prestige, social-capital
amenity.[23]

While no planned communities of this type exist in Napa, the Napa Valley
Reserve—an invitation-only private winery and club—affords its members

"access to an ultra-private world of premium winemaking, cultural studies of wine, private gatherings and seasonal celebrations. It's luxurious, unpretentious, and totally insider. No wonder accomplished people all over the world are vying to become members."[24] Established by H. William Harlan, founder of the luxury Meadowood resort and Harlan Estate winery, members work with the latter's viticulture team to make, name, and custom-label their own wine. The Reserve is an exclusive club which for a membership fee of $165,000 (in 2010) and the agreement to buy a certain amount of wine offers inclusion in the inner workings of Napa's wine culture. It also can be argued that some of the Napa Valley's newer residents were drawn to live in the valley for similar reasons—to be surrounded by viticulture and feel like a wine insider.

Market researchers have coined terms like "Veblenian" and "snob consumer" to describe people who value luxury consumption because of its exclusivity.[25] Such consumers undoubtedly fueled the cult wine phenomenon that burst on the Napa scene in the mid-1990s. Much of the appeal of cult wines is that relatively few people know about them. They are expensive, highly rated wines that are produced in small amounts and sold only to those consumers who have managed to get on the winery's mailing list. The wineries that produce them seldom have tasting rooms and do not market their wines in conventional ways. Some lack bricks-and-mortar facilities and instead rent space and equipment at an established winery, provide top-quality grapes (either their own or purchased), and hire a great winemaker or consultant to produce their wine, which they then bottle and label. Two of Napa's best-known cult wineries are Harlan Estate and Screaming Eagle. When the latter's 1992 Cabernet was released in 1996, a standard bottle (750 ml) cost $50; four years later a six-liter bottle was purchased at Auction Napa Valley for $500,000. Since the wine was bought at a renowned wine auction which funds local health and youth service nonprofits, the high bid reflects altruism and, perhaps, a second layer of status concerns—being known as the high bidder. The true quality and value of many cult wines has been questioned. "They are commonly over-ripe, over-concentrated, and generally over-the-top," claims wine journalist Larry Walker. "They are also undrinkable when young and of questionable ageability. . . . They attract way more attention than they deserve."[26]

Another indicator many wine drinkers use to assign value to a wine—besides price, appellation, and reputation—is its rating. If a wine has received a high rating from *Wine Spectator* magazine or the wine critic and oenophile Robert Parker, tasting room servers will usually point this out; it will certainly be featured on the winery's tasting notes and in its promotional materials. *Wine Spectator* rankings are used by many Americans as an index of quality and sophisticated judgment. A score of 95–100 is intended to indicate a "classic: a great wine," while a score of 90–94 signifies "outstanding: a wine of superior character and style." Since relatively few Americans are directly connected to places where wine grapes traditionally have been grown, few have developed the same appreciation for local wines that many continental Europeans possess. They tend, instead, to think about wine in a national or global context, and ratings help them come to terms with the whole constellation of wines that exist. A single point increase in a *Wine Spectator* score has been found to raise a wine's price by 6 percent.[27] Robert Parker claims that his own influential rankings have created a democratic way of tasting and have leveled the playing field for wine consumers. Critics contend that he has standardized taste (a taste that reflects his own palate and interaction with wine) and encouraged the development of globally accepted wine styles. (Parker is said to prefer powerful, fruity, high-alcohol, and oaky wines.) By doing so, they maintain, he has contributed to the suppression of local *terroirs* and the freedom of winemakers to ignore the styles preferred by critics in order to create truly unique wines.[28]

Tasting Economics

Visiting the Napa Valley increases most tourists' interest in wine. Over half the people we surveyed (53 percent) agreed with the statement "I am more interested in wine after visiting the Napa Valley"; another 29 percent said that this "may" be true. Similarly, 81 percent of the tourists participating in the Purdue study said that their visit was "very likely" or "likely" to affect their future wine purchases. Without tasting rooms, however, there would be much less wine tourism and far fewer direct sales. Tasting rooms allow people to learn about and sample wines in beautiful and congenial settings, thereby creating positive memories and associations that will transfer into future sales. Early tasting rooms were mainly places to showcase a winery's wines; today they are important profit centers. The tasting room is the largest source of revenue for many small and medium-sized wineries. Some wineries, such as V. Sattuti, only sell from the tasting room. Seventy percent of the tourists we surveyed had already purchased wine at a tasting room, and another 13 percent said they planned to. The profitability of the tasting room becomes clear when compared to that of the normal three-tier distribution system. A hypothetical case of wine retailing for $240 (or $20 per bottle), for example, is first sold to a distributor for about $130. The distributor in turn sells it at wholesale to a retailer for about $180. Finally, the retailer sells it to the public for $240. Winery tasting rooms bypass both the distributor and the wholesaler, selling at retail prices. In 2006, Napa's wineries earned $184 million in direct tourist spending at the tasting room.[29]

Once, wine tastings in the Napa Valley were free. No longer. In 2010 only a handful of wineries, including Heitz Wine Cellars and Frank Family Winery, continued to offer free tastings. Wineries began introducing tasting fees in the late 1970s as the number of tourists grew in order to offset the cost of the wine and tasting room labor. Some may have been influenced by research which indicates that people will buy more wine if they have had to pay to taste it.[30] Most winery tastings in 2010 cost between $10 and $25, but twice that if special wines or wine and food pairings were involved. Far Niente, for example, charges a $50 fee to taste its library wines (a winery's library wines are its older vintages, of which there are limited amounts). The tasting fee is waived if six bottles are purchased. Some tastings are quite lavish and even more expensive. At Swanson Vineyard's "salon," described in Shawn LaRue's narrative, eight people sit around a table beautifully set with flowers and Riedel stemware and enjoy wine, small portions of food, and conversation guided by a knowledgeable and witty host. Unlike the nineteenth-century Paris salons after which it is styled, however, the conversation typically revolves around wine rather than the literature, art, and politics of the day; the winery advertises the experience as "decadence with a wink."

Wine clubs first appeared on the scene in the mid-1980s. Domaine Chandon is said to have been the first to establish one. It emerged as a marketing tool to build the winery's relationship with its customers; no wine transactions were involved since the direct-to-consumer shipping of alcohol was virtually prohibited (and still is prohibited or restricted in many states). Today, wine clubs are an important and profitable adjunct to cellar door sales and the tasting room experience, and Domaine Chandon now has a five-person staff devoted to running its club. Most clubs ship two bottles of wine to their members three or four times a year. Having a tasting room but not a wine club has been likened by tasting room consultant Craig Root to "building a car without a fuel injector." Tasting rooms normally operate at a 30 percent profit margin and are the largest source of income for many, if not most, small and medium-sized wineries in the valley. If a winery has a tasting room and a wine club, this profit margin can increase to 50 percent. Wine clubs are especially important to wineries that do not sell their wines to brokers or distributors for resale to restaurants and retail outlets. They are valuable in another way, too. Club members become ambassadors for Napa's wineries, serving their wines in homes across America and talking to their friends about their membership. They also allow winemakers to experiment with new varietals or blends since wine club members, who expect to receive diverse offerings, provide an automatic market. Wine clubs also increase the job satisfaction and paychecks of tasting room staff since servers typically receive a small monetary incentive for each new member they sign up.

Tourists are motivated to join a winery's wine club if they like its wines and have positive feelings about the winery, which often hinges on the rapport they have developed with their server. There is also an economic incentive to join. Members typically receive a discount of 15 to 20 percent (before shipping and sales tax) on the wine they receive.[31] Their tasting fees are also immediately subtracted from the cost of the first shipment, effectively eliminating them. Belonging to a wine club allows visitors to stay connected to their favorite wineries and to memories of their Napa experience. Back home, they enjoy the luxury of having a wine shipment arrive at their door, the pleasure of drinking it, and possibly the social cachet of serving it to guests. They can also continue their wine education by consulting the accompanying tasting notes and information—winemaker notes, wine-food pairings, and recipes—contained in the club newsletter. Moreover, membership brings perks including access to limited-edition vintages and library wines, complimentary tastings and tours on their next visit to the valley, a comfortable members-only lounge, invitations to members-only open houses and vintner dinners, and free entry to release parties. Silver Oak's release parties take place each August on the winery grounds under a huge tent and draw as many as three thousand enthusiastic "lovers of Silver Oak," in the words of one employee. In 2006, 150 cases of Cabernet were poured as guests sipped and sampled tri-tip steak, beef chili, venison, and other foods. They could also have a complimentary photograph taken next to a display of Silver Oak bottles with vineyards in the background or have their wineglass signed by the winemaker. There was wine to buy, of course, and wine accessories, books, and logo apparel. Wine club names typically include words like "ambassador," "select," "connoisseur," "premier," "preferred," "signature," and "classic" to reinforce the idea of exclusivity; the word "club" itself suggests privileged membership.

3 / Consuming Place: Napa's Culinary Terroir

*F*ood is an essential part of the tourist experience. Not only do people need to eat when they travel, but cuisine is a fundamental expression of local culture. When folklorist Lucy Long coined the term "culinary tourism" in 1998, she defined it as "the intentional, exploratory participation in the foodways of another." Eating local foods gives tourists the opportunity to discover and participate in heritage and identity, whether their own or somebody else's. As sociologist Barry Glassner has pointed out, many tourists today "would be ashamed to come home and say they . . . didn't taste the national dish." When we encounter an unfamiliar cuisine or engage in a novel culinary experience like dining in a famous chef's restaurant or attending a cooking school in a special locale, what we know or think we know about food is also challenged, extending our knowledge and discernment.[1] Acquiring a refined sense of taste and an appreciation of fine cuisine are also attributes of cultural capital that were once restricted to wealthy gourmets, but no longer.

This interest in culinary experiences reflects national and international trends in both tourism and food. More tourists today seek direct sensory experiences over passive forms of sight-seeing and entertainment. In 2007, one in six Americans who traveled for leisure had either taken a food tour, enrolled in a cooking class, toured a winery, or participated in another culinary activity as part of their vacation.[2] For many visitors to the Napa Valley, food experiences are another form of "tasting," which like wine tasting bring together a complex set of sensory and social experiences. Because eating involves all our senses it has a special capacity to capture a time and place. Part of what makes culinary tourism so appealing and memorable is consuming foods in the place where they are grown or created. The tourism industry recognizes this and promotes each destination's unique culinary attractions through advertising copy and images and by organizing food events like the Napa Valley Mustard Festival, which combines food and wine with art and music.

Today, the Napa Valley is a recognized culinary destination. But unlike some parts of the United States which are known for particular foods or distinctive dishes—think Cajun andouille, Hawaiian poi, or New England clam chowder—Napa is known for specific restaurants and for the diverse range of fresh ingredients available, the skill with which they are prepared, and the chic yet casual pastoral setting in which they are served. The tourists who visit Napa are, on the whole, a sophisticated set who appreciate both fine wine and fine food. As sociologist Gary Alan Fine has noted, "It has become common-place to suggest that you are what you eat. However, it is equally appropriate to suggest that you are *where* you eat."[3] The Napa Valley is "the only place in the country," says chef Thomas Keller, "where people come specifically to drink excellent wines and eat fine food. But there's more to its appeal . . . it is American bounty itself." Jeffrey Longenecker, former executive chef of the Meritage Resort, agrees: it is the "availability of ultra-premium, local artisan ingredients that make the Napa Valley a one-of-a-kind epicurean destination."[4] Napa Valley restaurants actually receive more direct income from tourism than does the wine industry; of course, a significant proportion of their revenue comes from wine sales.[5]

Americans are also becoming increasingly knowledgeable about food and concerned about what they eat: from concerns about confined animal-feeding operations and genetically modified foods, to dismay at the standardization of food tastes and choices, to alarm about environmental pollution and the loss of biodiversity and worry about the long-term sustainability and moral implications of industrial agriculture. Their disenchantment is both reflected in and has been reinforced by a spate of recent books about the sources and quality of our food.[6] This "uneasiness over where food comes from," writes historian Paul Freedman, "coupled with a periodic shift toward simplicity, has led to a cuisine of authenticity in which quality, naturalness, seasonality and local ingredients are paramount."[7] This is what Napa offers.

The organic food movement, born in northern California and part of Napa's contemporary agriculture and food culture, is a reaction to concerns about our food supply. True organic farming means eschewing synthetic pesti-cides and fertilizers, practicing crop rotation and composting, supporting plant diversity (such as growing heirloom varieties of fruits and vegetables), and selling locally. Although the production of organic foods still lags far behind the amount of food produced through industrial agriculture nationwide—it accounted for less than 1 percent of all U.S. agriculture in 2008—organic *is* steadily becoming mainstream. The USDA's first survey of organic farmers, conducted in 2008, discovered nearly fifteen thousand growers in all fifty states. It also found that their sales had increased between 14 and 21 percent annu-ally during the previous decade, showing its growing popularity.[8] The closely related "slow food" movement, more often referred to today as "farm to table," is also picking up speed. One of its goals is to preserve endangered agricultural products and practices. But it is also devoted to improving the culture of food by reasserting the role that food plays in creating community; it also argues that taste is a sensation capable of development.[9]

Both movements support sustainable farming practices and the consumption of local, seasonal foods, organically raised livestock, and handmade artisanal foods (such as cheeses, breads, olive oils)—all of which are becoming more available. As one measure, since 1994 the number of farmers' markets operating in the United States has nearly tripled. All Napa Valley communities have them. A growing number of Napa Valley vintners are also farming organically. Eighteen percent of all the certified organic vineyard acreage in California is found in Napa, even though the county produces just 4 percent of California's wine. Napa Valley Vintners lists 184 wineries as sustainably farmed and 42 vintners and grape growers as members of its voluntary "Napa Green" winery and land programs, which certify best practices in wine operations and farming.[10]

Americans' growing interest in food quality, preparation techniques, and new taste experiences is reflected in television programming. In the 1960s and 1970s Julia Child (*The French Chef*) and Graham Kerr (*The Galloping Gourmet*) had popular cooking shows, but the viewership for such programs increased enormously in the 1980s and 1990s. The Food Network was launched in 1993, and there seems to be no end to the current demand for television shows devoted to cooking and food. Series like Chef Anthony Bourdain's *No Reservations* on the Travel Channel explicitly link food to tourism, as do magazines like *Gourmet Traveler* and *Food and Travel* and specialist guidebooks like Lonely Planet's World Food series. Popular books such as Bourdain's *Kitchen Confidential* and Ruth Reichel's *Garlic and Sapphires* as well as films like *Julie and Julia* and the animated feature *Ratatouille* also demonstrate the public's heightened interest in the workings of restaurants and the role of the chef. The restaurant business has been transformed, in the words of Bourdain, from "food service industry" to "glamour profession." The Napa Valley today undoubtedly has the highest concentration of "celebrity" chefs of any rural area in America, largely because of tourist demand.

California is often in the forefront of food and lifestyle innovations. A study of place-names found that "California" appears on more food labels, on a greater variety of food products, and on more gourmet foods than the name of any other state.[11] None of this is surprising given the state's climate and flourishing agriculture. The Napa Valley is particularly blessed in this regard. The valley has also benefited from its proximity to the San Francisco Bay area, which has incorporated new waves of immigrants (among them Japanese, Chinese, Vietnamese, and Mexican) over the years who have introduced new ingredients and cuisines. The Bay Area is also the home of such food pioneers as the late writer and gastronome M. F. K. Fisher, whose culinary essays celebrated food's evocation of place, time, and memory as well as the fundamental humanity of savoring and sharing meals with others. Bay Area chefs Jeremiah Tower and Alice Waters are credited with originating "California cuisine" with the goal of bringing the finest and freshest ingredients to the table.

When Waters opened Chez Panisse in Berkeley in 1971, she stressed the importance of using seasonal and locally grown produce and of cooking with a light, improvisational touch to let the taste and inherent qualities of the ingredients shine through. She also encouraged the production and use of artisanal foods like bread and cheese. "A significant component of the counter-cultural movement of the 60s was resisting industrial agriculture," cultural anthropologist Kenji Tierney reminds us, "with hippies going on to communes and growing organic produce." Cooking and eating wholesome food became a form of self-expression and sensual experience. What emerged was a new generation of cooks and eaters who demanded healthy and organic foods, and incorporated previously eschewed "ethnic" foods into their food repertoire. Before becoming a restaurateur, Alice Waters had been part of this movement.

At the time Waters opened Chez Panisse, however, the food scene in the Napa Valley was still "steak or Eye-talian."[12] According to one guidebook author, visitors to Napa then could expect to find nothing to excite "culinary passion."[13] Although a century earlier spas like Napa Soda Springs and White Sulphur Springs had offered that era's fine dining to visiting San Francisco elites, they were long gone. In the early 1970s, dining "was very limited," remembers one resident. "There was a little Mexican restaurant in Oakville and an awful diner in St. Helena called Vern's Copper Chimney. Going out to dinner meant going to the Grapevine or to Jonesy's Steak House at the County Airport." When chef Philippe Jeanty arrived in the valley from France in 1977 to work at the new French-owned Domaine Chandon winery and restaurant, he felt like he had entered "the Wild West. . . . The biggest obstacle was to bring the quality of raw ingredients up to what I was used to."[14] Many of the fresh ingredients common in France, like chanterelle mushrooms (*girolles*), were not available. But Napa Valley's food scene was beginning to change.

In 1973 JoAnne Lincoln started working at the Oakville Grocery, a hundred-year-old general store purchased by winemaker Joseph Phelps which evolved into the valley's first gourmet food provisioner. At that time, says Lincoln,

> it was still more of a local store. We made sandwiches for the winery workers, but we also had ingredients for winery staff that were cooking for special events. We carried specialty items like French cheeses

and truffles and things that are everyday items now, like dried tomatoes and arugula, which were exotic then. We had a floor-to-ceiling section of imported mustards and jams which really appealed to tourists. In the early '80s we began to place a lot of emphasis on chefs' ingredients and specialty produce like Chinese long beans. We had a store in San Francisco and I would split orders with them so we would just go into the city once or twice a week to pick up produce. We also had a very interesting wine cellar with hard-to-find wines.

One of the earliest restaurants in the valley to offer the lighter, fresher food now known as California cuisine was The Diner in Yountville, which opened in 1976 and became very popular with locals. The first to offer fine dining were the restaurant at the Domaine Chandon winery and the original French Laundry, which was opened in 1978 by Don and Sally Schmitt in a stone building in Yountville that had previously been a residence, a saloon, a brothel, and a French steam laundry. Sally Schmitt has likened her own cooking to "Chez Panisse cuisine," which focused on simple preparation and fresh ingredients.[15] "For the era it had the same qualities, the same reputation" as the current French Laundry, remembers JoAnne Lincoln, who worked there after leaving the Oakville Grocery. "Its cuisine is on a different level now because I think dining generally is on a higher level. But in the '70s and '80s the Schmitts' French Laundry was a special place to eat in the valley. It was a relaxed whole evening prix fixe event."

Napa's food and restaurant scene emerged fully during the 1980s and 1990s. French-trained chef Bruce LeFavour opened Rose and LeFavour in St. Helena in late 1982, followed the next year by chef Cindy Pawlcyn's Mustard's Grill. It is Pawlcyn who is most often credited with shaping the culinary landscape of the valley; she has been referred to by some as Napa Valley's Alice Waters. Napa also benefited from a strong economy and the "Silicon Valley" technology boom of the mid- and late 1990s, which gave more people the money to focus on refining their taste, fueling the demand for fine dining and fine wine. Many top chefs opened restaurants in the Napa Valley, taking advantage of its growing public appeal and the resources it offered—fresh ingredients, fine wine, and scenery.[16]

Several organic farmers also began business in the Napa Valley in the late 1980s, including Forni Brown Gardens in Calistoga and Long Meadow Ranch in Rutherford, which grow heirloom and specialty vegetables and herbs, often at a chef's request. The latter also produces extra virgin olive oil, grass-fed beef, organic eggs from chickens that are truly free-range, and wine. When the Napa Valley Wine Train began running in 1989, gourmet lunches and dinners made from fresh high-quality ingredients were marketed as one of its principal draws. In addition to its refurbished vista dome and parlor and lounge cars, from which passengers could gaze at Napa's passing winescape, tourists could also watch their meals being prepared through the glass observation wall in the Chef de Cuisine car and later enjoy them.

The valley's importance in the world of cuisine was solidified in 1995, when the country's most prestigious school for professional chefs, the Culinary Institute of America (CIA), based in Hyde Park, New York, opened a branch in the former Christian Brothers' Greystone Cellars in St. Helena. It quickly attracted top chefs to teach and give public cooking demonstrations; its restaurant remains a popular tourist destination. The former executive director of the Napa Valley Conference and Visitors Bureau, Daniel Howard, has credited the valley's restaurant scene with being the "catalyst" for the dramatic increase (46 percent) in tourist revenue in Napa County between 1992 and 1996. Today, fine dining is an integral and recognized part of the Napa Valley tourism experience; fully 82 percent of the tourists we surveyed considered "food and dining to be a special part of the Napa experience." When asked to characterize Napa's cuisine, they most commonly used words like "worldly," "sophisticated," and "fresh."

Napa's wine industry has actively promoted culinary experiences. One of the earliest initiatives was Mondavi's Great Chefs program, which beginning in 1976 brought internationally known chefs, including Julia Child, to the winery each year to give cooking classes and demonstrations. A couple of years later, Beringer Vineyards started bringing young American chefs to their winery to design dishes whose flavors would balance and complement its wines. In 1989, Beringer established the influential School for American Chefs with French master chef Madeline Kamman teaching its annual two-week program. Today a number of wineries, including Cakebread Cellars, offer cooking classes, and many wine club newsletters and winery websites and tasting rooms provide recipes. Robert Sinskey Vineyards' website, for example, includes the "Vineyard Kitchen" with seasonal menus designed by Chef Maria Helm Sinskey. Food also figures prominently at major wine industry events, including the annual Auction Napa Valley.

While tasting room staff once confined themselves to discussing their winery's wines, today most servers suggest some foods that go well with them: "This Cabernet is the classic accompaniment to rack or leg of lamb" or "This sparkling [wine] has muscat added which gives it a peachy taste that goes well with spicy foods and pâté." The Robert Mondavi Winery provides a printed "Matrix of Wine and Food" which matches their wines with different foods and seasonings and makes menu recommendations. Seated tastings which pair

Ellen Flora and Étoile restaurant staff discuss wine and food pairings.
Courtesy of Domaine Chandon Winery.

food with wine have become common. In some cases, the pairing is limited to cheeses, but others provide caviar, nuts, dried fruit, chocolates, and other foods. The elaborate salon-style tasting provided at Swanson Vineyards is discussed in detail in Shawn LaRue's narrative. Wineries like Frog's Leap, Cakebread Cellars, Fetzer Vineyards, Robert Sinskey Vineyards, and Round Pond Estate have large organic gardens which serve seasonally available estate-grown vegetables and fruit. This is very appealing to tourists, and the practice is also found in wine regions in Italy.

Many wineries have chefs on call to prepare food for special tastings and community or trade events like vintners' or wine club dinners. Ten percent of Napa's wineries have culinary directors and resident chefs on staff and have fully integrated food programs into their operations.[17] Wineries were hiring chefs to prepare food, explains Chef Laura Lee, "but having to pay an outside caterer didn't make as much sense as putting in your own kitchen and providing that service yourself. If a winery has a beautiful garden where it can hold events, so much the better." Unlike other wine regions, Napa wineries—with Domaine Chandon as the single exception—do not have restaurants. They are precluded from doing so by Napa's Winery Definition Ordinance which seeks to keep the industry's focus on agriculture and wine production.

Today the availability of locally grown organic produce and artisan purveyors of poultry and eggs, grass-fed beef, lamb, cheese, mushrooms, olive oil, vinegar, honey, and chocolate as well as the presence of many great chefs makes the Napa Valley a premier culinary destination. The valley is also close to the Pacific Ocean which supplies fresh fish and shellfish like Hog Island Oysters from Tomales Bay. According to Chef Ken Frank, "The wine country is the best non-urban place in the country to eat today. . . . There's nowhere other than Napa where the focus on food and wine is so intense."

Most Napa chefs obtain their produce locally. Chef Perry Hoffman of Domaine Chandon's Étoile restaurant, for example, gets quail, squab, duck, rabbit, lamb, heirloom potatoes, grapeseed oil, greens, and eggs from local providers in Napa, Calistoga, Sonoma, Petaluma, Pope Valley, Sebastopol, Novato, Vacaville, and Penngrove. According to Ellen Flora,

> The majority of our foods, meats, and fish come from local providers. It's so easy now. Forni Brown will grow a custom salad for you, so why wouldn't you do it? We have trucks coming every morning. In the fish category we do bring in some unusual things like from New Zealand that gets flown in through a specialty company. Fifty percent of the vegetables served at Étoile were grown here at the winery—all our tomatoes, all our citrus. We raised five thousand pounds of lemons alone. All our honey comes from bees on our property—a specialty company manages this for us. Don Watson, another service, will bring animals to your property to graze. We've had sheep graze on our vineyards and later served them in the restaurant.

Growing their own organic produce or buying directly from organic growers and artisan producers guarantees that chefs are able to obtain the best ingredients. Restaurants like the French Laundry and Mustard's Grill, as well as Domaine Chandon's Étoile, have large organic gardens which also allow them to experiment with unusual varieties of vegetables, herbs, and edible flowers. The French Laundry's garden is likely to include *ficoide glaciale* lettuce, which is actually a succulent, and yacon and oca, two South American root crops. At the beginning of each season Tucker Taylor, the restaurant's gardener and horticulturalist, gives the chefs seed catalogues to select from, and at regular meetings he lets them know what is becoming available so that they can better plan their menus. As Thomas Keller points out in his narrative, the French Laundry's garden is as much a teaching opportunity for young chefs as it is a source of high-quality and novel produce for the restaurant. The Napa Valley Cooking School and Culinary Institute of America also have large organic teaching and restaurant gardens.

Part of the new food ethic—much like the fair trade movement—is that organic and specialty food producers should be justly compensated for their labor. Many of the people working in Napa's food industry agree, which explains in part the high cost of dining in many of Napa's restaurants and the

Chef Perry Hoffman of Domaine Chandon's Étoile restaurant. *Courtesy of Domaine Chandon Winery.*

cost of purchasing artisanal foods. "Many tourists are shocked" by the cost of artisanal cheese, Napa cheese purveyor John Raymond explains,

> but nobody making cheese is being paid nearly enough for what they are doing. I've got two cheese guys right now who almost quit last year because they weren't getting any money. I'm determined to pay them the right amount for their product and that means I have to charge more. If I charged what their labor's really worth, I'd be paying one guy $92 a pound. Obviously, I can't do that, but I try to be fair. Tourists help me do this.

Americans need to learn to pay more for high-quality food, says anthropologist Amy Trubeck, and to develop a "food view" that places value "on where food comes from, how it is grown or raised, and how it tastes."[18] This appears to be happening, and it explains part of the appeal of fine dining in a place like the Napa Valley, where the best quality produce is used and beautifully prepared to extract its full and essential flavors. In a society where time is a valued commodity, it is also a luxury to be able to linger over a meal which itself has taken considerable time, care, and creativity to prepare. For some tourists, dining in the Napa Valley in a famous chef's restaurant, being familiar with the language of cuisine and with unusual foods and, in some cases, with advanced cooking techniques (such as *sous vide*) imparts status as well as pleasure. Not without reason, travel and lifestyle writers have christened the Napa Valley "the Tuscany of America." It has become that romanticized place envisioned by Robert Mondavi in the early 1960s where life revolves around fine wine and food and where tourists can experience "the good life."

4 / From Vine to Wine

Vineyard Foreman / Juan Martinez

"Sometimes you are like a father, sometimes you are a teacher, sometimes you are a counselor."

Napa's viticulture is labor-intensive. Roughly 75 percent of Napa's grapes are picked by hand in order to ensure perfect fruit—minimally bruised, no broken berries, no mildewed bunches. In contrast, about 75 percent of the rest of the state's wine grapes are picked by machine. Mechanical harvesters are rough on the fruit and add too much MOG ("material other than grapes"), such as leaves and stems, into the bins. With Napa wine grapes fetching nearly ten times more per ton than Central Valley grapes, growers can afford the extra labor costs of harvesting by hand.

There are about seven thousand farmworkers in Napa County during the peak summer months. Two-thirds live permanently in Napa or neighboring counties; the rest arrive seasonally, mostly from Mexico.[1] The valley's shortage of affordable housing forces many to crowd together in rented apartments or to commute long distances from neighboring Lake and Solano counties. Low-cost accommodation for 180 people is also available in the valley at three farmworker camps funded by the wine industry and operated by the Napa County Housing Authority. For $12 a day the farmworkers get a bed and three meals of traditional Mexican food, although the camps have strict curfews and do not allow drinking. Some migrant farmworkers sleep al fresco along the riverbank, under bridges, in vineyards, and in cars along the back roads. Despite a large increase in the number of farmworkers required by the valley's expanding vineyards and wineries, the number of beds in farmworker camps has actually declined from four hundred in the 1980s.

Many farmworkers, like Juan Martinez, were raised in poor villages in central and southern Mexico and came to the United States for work, borrowing money to make the long journey by bus, train, or foot. Napa is a desired location. In the vineyards they can earn considerably more than their compatriots who harvest strawberries or lettuce in the Central Valley or

Vineyard foreman for Opus One Winery, Juan Martinez. *Courtesy Opus One Winery.*

———

apples and pears in Oregon. Few are promoted to equipment or tractor operator, and even fewer reach supervisory or management-level jobs like Juan Martinez. He is one of the "can-do guys" vineyard manager Jim Lincoln refers to in the following narrative.

———

I was born in the village of Piocalpichi in Jalisco in January 1957. My father was taking care of an hacienda, a big ranch of two hundred acres, for a French guy who had all kinds of businesses. My three sisters and I were born on the ranch. I grew up there until I was eight, when my father sent me to the city of Aguascalientes to go to school. When I was sixteen and got out of high school, my father and mother had an idea about immigrating us to the United States for a better life. My dad started getting the papers [green cards] for me and my brothers and sisters. He could do that because my mom, although she was Mexican, had been born in Illinois and was a U.S. citizen. Her father had taken her back to Mexico during the Depression, and that's how she met my father and got married and had us. After we put in the application to the consulate, it took six months before we got our green cards and papers.

We came to Napa because one of our uncles was already established here. His name is Felipe Moran. He invited us to come to the Napa Valley to see if we liked the area. My father had to quit his job with the French man to come to the United States. We had to leave my mother behind in Mexico to take care of the younger kids for a few years. I was seventeen when I arrived and very shy, so the idea of going to school here made me nervous.[2] I didn't know much English and I thought everyone would make fun of me. Also, I knew that my father needed help supporting the rest of my family and my mom in Mexico, so I started working as soon as I got here. I had to get a permit from the high school in St. Helena to be able to work because in those years you needed a permit to work if you were not yet eighteen years old.

My first job was in the hills in the place that is now Hess Winery. When I started there, they were knocking down trees and clearing land to develop vineyards. So my first job was loading logs, branches, rocks, and stuff on the trailer of a big Caterpillar so it could be removed. The wood was taken to a burn pile and the rocks were piled up. Picking up rocks and all that heavy stuff was pretty hard for me, being just seventeen. I was working ten hours a day and getting $2.25 an hour. I thought this would be really hard, really tough for me, if I had to do this kind of job my whole life. So I said to myself that the first opportunity I had I'd go back to school and learn something, at least the language or some viticulture classes or something. Doing well in school in Mexico and then coming here and going into one of the toughest jobs was pretty hard for me.

I worked up there in the hills for two years, but I had a bad experience. Let me tell you. Coming from Mexico, you don't know how to drive, so you have to learn on your own. My father had purchased an old station wagon and I was giving rides to about ten people. Every morning at five or five thirty I was driving up those hills. It was dark and foggy with woods and wet roads and all that. Coming up one morning I forgot there were some sharp curves and I took one too fast and with the wet ground the car went out of control and into the embankment. It totally ruined the car, destroyed it, and one of my riders was in really bad shape. He was yelling and said he couldn't see anything for about an hour. The other guys had bruises and little cuts. It was a bad experience and it really scared me. I thought I was going to be jailed. We didn't have car insurance and I didn't have a driver's license. Luckily no police car came by. We just called a tow truck and pulled the station wagon back to my house. That tow truck guy actually gave us a ride back to work and took some of us back home. My father had purchased a car with a lot of sacrifice with what he was earning, and he wasn't able to purchase another one for six to eight months.

After two years working up there [Hess], my uncle Felipe brought me over to a job with the Napa Valley Vineyard Company, which is now called Beckstoffer. My uncle was a foreman and the head of the local United Farm Workers Union, so it was pretty easy for him to get me that job. It was a lot nicer work, and they were paying me fifty cents more per hour. I think they liked the way I worked because they started teaching me tractor work, truck work, pesticides work, a lot of stuff.

In the late '70s, the Napa Valley Vineyard Company had about twelve crews with eight guys on each crew. In those years they were managing probably two thousand acres in the valley. During the harvest we were sometimes short hands, so we would work Monday through Saturday right through the eight weeks of harvest. It was really tough at times, but you did it because you had to make a living and the money was better than anywhere else. We worked piece rate, which means you get paid for what you do. Different growers used different systems. Some paid by the bucket. Some paid by the box or picking pan, but most companies paid by the ton. Today workers earn, depending on the [grape] variety and the tons per acre the vineyard produces, between $80 and $150 per day.

Many companies now like to pick at night, starting at 2 or 3 AM and working until eleven in the morning. In cooler temperatures of night we can double the amount of grapes that we would pick during the heat of the day. The companies like that because it means they can hire fewer crews and having fewer people makes it easier to manage. It also means less housing is needed and less services.

We split the money evenly among the crew, and that was not too much of a problem because the company would let us choose our crew members. We would choose people that would pick at our pace. I was usually picking in the second- or third-best group out of ten or twelve groups. Everyone knew who the best crew was. If you weren't comfortable or not capable of keeping up with the guys in the number one crew, then there was no sense of trying to get into the best group. There is a big difference in the speed of the work between the number one picking crew and the number ten picking crew. Sometimes the best crew would pick almost double the slowest crew.

Later I got a job with Robert Mondavi working on the new vineyards they were developing in Carneros. I knew the field supervisor there and I asked him if he needed workers. He told me to check back in a week, and when I came back they hired me. I was a vineyard worker, or in Spanish what we call *trabajador general* or *trabajador general de la vineyard*. I helped develop all of Mondavi's Carneros range, which was 310 acres. It had been nothing but grazing land for cattle before, so we had a lot of work, putting in drainage and reshaping and grading the land. The experience I had from working at Hess and the Napa Valley Vineyard Company helped a lot and started opening doors for me. Since I knew what to do, Mondavi gave me a small crew of six guys. We laid out where the vines were going to go, put in the trellises, and then after planting the vines, we also did the irrigation system and cultivation—the whole thing. In one year alone we planted close to a half million vines.

Two years later they made me a foreman at the Carneros ranch. I was thirty-eight years old. I did that for three years, and then my supervisor retired and they put me in his position. The job of a crew supervisor can be fun, but it can be hard too because you're the guy right in the middle. You're between the company and the crew. If the guys are doing something that is not to the satisfaction of the company, you have to straighten them out. If the company is pushing a little too much on the crew, working them harder than what their capabilities are, then you've got to say so. But it can also be good in that you're able to help your people. You're able to teach them what you have learned over the years. You're with the crew all day and you have to play a lot of personalities. Sometimes you are like a father. Sometimes you are a teacher. Sometimes you are a counselor. They ask you for your opinion on something, you have to help them. If they're sick, you may have to take them to the hospital or the doctor because some of them can't drive or don't have a car. You tell them which doctors are good and try to help them as much as you can because some of them are away from home and don't know enough to decide by themselves.

In 2001 Mondavi hired a new winemaker, Michael Silacci, for their Opus One winery. Mr. Silacci was looking for a supervisor for the Opus vineyards. I knew him from the 1980s when I worked for the Napa Valley Vineyard Company. He told me that when he looked at the list of Mondavi workers available and saw my name, he knew that I was going to be his man. He wanted Juan Martinez. That made me very proud. He told me to think of fourteen guys [vineyard workers] that would be really good for Opus. So, that's what I did. I looked at all the guys that I had worked with and I chose the best. All fourteen came. They were really proud to be working for Opus. They saw how well Opus treated their workers with good wages, much better than what any of the guys had before. One bonus at Opus is that every quarter of the year, they give us a few bottles of wine—different wines from Mondavi and some from France. You see, 50 percent of Opus is owned by a French company. Best of all, in December they give us some of the really good, top-quality wine.

Can you talk about how your work changes during the year?

Vineyard work changes as the year goes around. In January, February, and half of March we prune and tie the vines. There is trunk tying, cordon tying, and cane tying. Trunk tying supports the trunk of the vine on a trellis stake so the vine won't fall down in the wind or with the weight of a lot of grapes. Cordon tying attaches the cordons [the branches or "arms" of a grapevine] to the foot wire of a trellis for the same purpose. And with cane tying, you tie the canes [shoots] on each end to the trellis. In pruning you want to leave three to five canes on each plant, with fifteen to twenty buds on each cane. If you get big, massive vines you won't have much fruit. Pruning takes skill and not all field hands are allowed to do it. The pruning can be pretty hard too, especially on your wrist. Every time you cut a shoot you are putting pressure on your wrist. To prune a vine you have to make about fifteen cuts, and you might be cutting fifty vines an hour, so in a nine-hour day that's about 450 vines and about 7,000 cuts. That's a lot of repeat motions. Sometimes guys' wrists get swollen really big, and some guys get bumps or bubbles on their wrist tendons. Luckily, most go away in a month or so after we stop pruning. But not always.

Then in spring and early summer, when the vines are leafing out, we remove the excess foliage. [This is done to increase air circulation around the developing grape bunches and ensure that the right amount of sunlight reaches the fruit so that it can develop its sugar in the weeks ahead. Taking account of the sun's trajectory, workers remove the leaves that block the gentle morning rays, and leave others to shade the grapes from the scorching afternoon sun.]³ After that we prepare the equipment for frost-protection work. At the same time there is some replanting of vines and some trellis repair. Then we wait for suckering time, which starts in June. Suckering means getting rid of the unwanted shoots; you only want to keep the shoots that are going to produce grapes. Suckers grow all over, from every direction. You need to get rid of them in order to preserve the good fruit-bearing shoots and open up the fruit zone to sunlight.

July is probably the busiest time of the year for the vineyard workers because there are a lot of different activities. If you have vines to be grafted, it's the time of the year to do it. Irrigation starts. Cultivation with the tractor starts. Pest management starts. And heat protection starts. We have a sprinkler system in the vineyards to protect the vines in really hot weather. In July and August you protect them from heat; April and May you protect from frost.

As we get close to harvest, the only thing left is crop thinning, which means removing clusters that you don't want. You have to knock off some of your crop so that the rest of it can grow evenly, mature, and get good coloring. After crop thinning you are into harvest and this, too, is a really busy time of the year. You only have a small time frame to get the crop in once the wine-maker, who goes from block to block tasting and testing the grapes, decides the crop is ready. Then we have to pick them as fast as we can.

For me the only time to take a vacation is November and December. That's the slowest time of the year. The rest of the months are really super busy. I often go to Mexico on vacation. It takes me thirty-eight hours to drive there. I stop in El Paso for a few days to see my in-laws. Then it's another fourteen hours' drive to my father's rancho in Jalisco. Every time I go, I spend about a week taking my kids to see different parts of Mexico, so that they can get to know the country.

Do you think people in the wine industry appreciate the work of Mexican laborers?

Today I see the growers and companies are better at appreciating the efforts that the Mexican people are making for this valley. I see some companies putting money into worker housing, trying to assist them. When I hear people talk about vineyard workers, I think they do it with more respect today because they know how much we Mexican people have given to developing the wine industry. But I'm not sure they really know much about the lives of the migrant workers.

> *When we asked grape growers and winery owners this question, most readily acknowledged the enormous importance of their Mexican labor force; but when we examined 120 Napa winery websites we found only one that gave much attention to their Mexican workers. That was Spottswoode Estate Vineyard & Winery, a family-owned winery on the edge of St. Helena, which devoted an entire page to the families of three of their Mexican workers, noting, "We are highlighting these men because we realize that we could not possibly achieve the quality of our fruit and wines—and thus, our success— without their expertise and commitment. . . . They truly are the foundation of the Estate Vineyard and Winery—and we look forward to many more years of working with each of them!" When we asked tourists if they knew who did the vineyard work, we discovered most had little awareness of the importance of Mexican laborers to the wine or tourism industries.*

At the end of the day in the vineyards what do the workers do?

A lot of them have different lifestyles. Some of them go back and play on a soccer team and try to practice a little bit. Some of them go to school at night to learn more English. Some of them go back home and help their wives, and maybe drink a few *cervezas* [beers] and try to rest a little bit before the next day. The guys that are pretty established, who have permanent jobs, have their wives here, and some of them have bought their own houses. So at the end of the day they have homes to go to. But the seasonal workers who only work six to eight months out of the year come by themselves from Mexico. They leave their kids and their wives down there.

Have your workers had many problems with immigration?

A lot of guys don't have papers, so for them Immigration [the Immigration and Naturalization Service (INS)] can be a big problem. Every day when they leave their houses for work they don't know if they're going to return in the evening. If a policeman stops them, they're going to be checked to see if they have a driver's license, and if they don't, the police are going to ask them for IDs. The police or highway patrol report these individuals to the INS, or they arrest them right there. So, guys without papers try to be as careful as they can. They try not to drive too much. If they can walk from where they live to the grocery store, they will do it. In the '70s and '80s, when the INS was really active and sent lots of workers back to Mexico, we had some incidents. When the INS would come by, the guys would run off and there'd only be three or four of us left in the field. The guys without papers would try to hide under bridges or up in the hills. There was this one guy who had his green card and was really nice to people. Once, when he saw some INS cars and vans coming he called the guys that he knew who didn't have any papers and got five or six into his car—a big car—and drove them down Highway 29 all the way to Calistoga where he let them loose at the bottom of the hills so they could go up in the hills and hide. But the INS saw the whole thing from a helicopter. The guys were able to get out of the car and hide, but the INS caught the driver and arrested him. They threw him on the ground and kicked him a lot and then took him to the detention center. When he would not confess to what he had done, they kicked him some more. When he was released—because he had a green card—he went back to work for the same company, but his body was never right after that. I think he later hired a lawyer and fought the INS.

In those years, the border was pretty easy to cross, so the guys who were arrested and sent back to Mexico would be back in the valley on the third or fourth day. It was that easy to cross. People were so familiar with the border areas that they could cross by themselves. The ones that didn't have any experience would pay somebody to guide them.

But these days you have to be really careful about workers not having papers. The companies that are pretty established have regular crews that come back every year. These guys have permanent job positions and most of them have their wives here, especially if the company gives them health benefits. But in the small companies, where the seasonal workers only work six to eight months out of the year, the guys come up from Mexico by themselves. They leave their kids and wives at home. They come from all over Mexico, but most are from five or six different states—most of all from Michoacán. It doesn't matter to me where my workers come from as long as they are good workers. Right now, I have guys from Michoacán, Oaxaca, and Zacatecas.

Do you have any contact with tourists?

Some visitors see the different systems in the vineyards, like different spacing of the rows and the different types of trellises, and want to ask you about it and to take pictures, especially when we are working closer to the winery where the tourists are visiting. Sometimes they ask where we come from, how many hours we work a day, if we like what we do, and questions like that. I enjoy answering their questions. If I have the time to spend, I answer as much as I can. If they ask one of my workers, he will usually direct the questions to me. But there are a few guys from the crew that can speak some English and will try to answer the tourists themselves. Also, as you probably know, quite a few tourists speak Spanish today. So sometimes they ask their questions in Spanish. Most people who ask questions are women.

Even though it's really hard work at times, I still love what I do. I really enjoy working outside and seeing how the vines develop. My connection to the vines and to the wine is so big that I will probably never try to find another job that is not related to growing grapes and the wine business. I really feel proud of what I have accomplished and what I have learned about growing grapes. And when I think of my success in the United States, I think it has been due to a few things. One is being an honest and hard worker. Two, I know that to be able to do something in life you have to sacrifice at times. I've tried to learn, not just by going to classes at night, but learning from the people I am around at work who know a lot about grapes and wine making. I try to get close to them and ask them questions, their opinions, to learn as much as I can.

Have you ever considered resettling in Mexico?

I love Mexico, but I don't think I would ever go home to live. All of my brothers and sisters are here in the Napa Valley. There are ten of us, and we're all here, so I really don't have much reason to go to Mexico other than to see my father's friends or my parents when they are down there. My parents go to Mexico for two or three months and then come back to Napa for two or three months; they keep going back and forth. There are two of us [brothers] who when we retire will probably do what my parents do, going back and forth. But to live there permanently, probably not. To return permanently you need a lot of money to get a good business going and to make sure that you're not going to fail. It's been about thirty-five years now since I've lived there and I've lost how things go down there—how the laws go, how you get into business, and all that. So for me, to go back and start a business would be pretty hard. And even if I could leave, I would miss a lot of things about the Napa Valley besides my family. I would miss the vineyards where I've been working my whole life. I would miss the beautiful weather. I would miss the comfort we enjoy here. This valley is probably one of the best places in the whole United States to live. Right now, I'm really happy here and happy with what I do. I make good wages. I'm able to take my kids out to dinner when I want to. Plus, I really like wine, and if I was in Mexico, I would probably miss the wine a lot. Mexicans, you know, are still mostly beer drinkers.

Vineyard Manager / *Jim Lincoln*

"Although I don't like to admit it, there is a romantic side to wine that you just don't get from farming broccoli."

A vineyard manager oversees all the labor and resources necessary to grow wine grapes. This includes preparing an annual plan for every vineyard, managing vineyard crews and all "material inputs" (pruning, suckering, leafing and other canopy management, fertilization, irrigation, and fungicide spraying programs), organizing the harvest, and keeping costs down while striving for the optimal combination of quality and quantity of wine grapes. Jim Lincoln is a manager for Beckstoffer Vineyards, the largest owner of vineyard land in the Napa Valley—over a thousand acres. He oversees Beckstoffer's southern region, which includes five ranches, from Oakville in the north to Carneros, bordering San Pablo Bay, in the south. Jim is also a two-time president of the Napa County Farm Bureau. With a youthful appearance that belies his more than twenty years' experience, Jim says the heart of his job is "keeping my vines happy and balanced."

———

When I was in high school in the late 1970s, I had no intention of working in agriculture. I didn't mind working in our family vineyard, but we were told by our St. Helena High School counselor that agriculture was dead, that it was for rednecks, and that to get anywhere we needed to go into computers or electronics. I started college looking at electrical engineering, but that didn't really appeal to me. So I stumbled around a few years thinking that agriculture and farming weren't good enough. Back then I didn't know of any rich farmers either, so grape growing didn't seem like a wise career choice. Then I took a geology class as a general ed requirement and found it interesting. After several more classes, I transferred to the University of Alaska at Fairbanks, which had a strong geology program. My father had always thought I should go to school in Fairbanks, probably because he used to fly there for Pan Am. They refueled in Fairbanks on the way to Tokyo. But after my first semester, I knew that I didn't want to spend my life looking for oil and that's when I decided to return to California, go to UC Davis, and get my degree in agriculture, which is what I should have done right out of high school.

I chose agricultural science and management which seemed the perfect blend of agriculture and business. The science and technology of new farming methods especially appealed to me. I also liked the idea of being outside and

Vineyard manager
for Beckstoffer
Vineyards, Jim
Lincoln.

not behind a desk all the time. When I got to Davis and started taking classes in water science, irrigation, and soil science, everything fell into place.

My first job out of Davis was as a viticulturalist with Swanson Vineyards. Swanson Vineyards wasn't very big, only 130 acres, so there was a lot of "hands-on." When I started there in January 1987, they were redeveloping 80 acres of vineyard. I spent my first two weeks on the job picking up rocks in the open fields with the crew and trimming rootstock on rainy days. It was a great opportunity to learn field Spanish. When the vineyard manager, Anne Kraemer, took a job at Domaine Chandon in the spring of 1990, I became vineyard manager. But this still involved a lot of hands-on time with the field crew. We were removing old vineyards and replanting them, building trellises, training vines, installing frost control and irrigation systems. Swanson had two ranches: one in Oakville and the other on the Silverado Trail. We completely redeveloped them both, and I became really good at vineyard redevelopment. [*Laughs.*]

In 1996 I left Swanson to become the vineyard manager at Atlas Peak Vineyards. It's a long way from everywhere but it's a magnificent setting—a sweeping uplifted valley high in the eastern hills. I was responsible for about seven hundred acres, and like at Swanson, we did a lot of redevelopment, planting about sixty to seventy acres of new vineyard every year. It was wild and isolated up there with a fair amount of "Wild West" or cowboy attitude. There was just a lot of work going on all the time. Atlas Peak is also prone to frost and to fire. Because of the threat of frost, we had a tremendous water system that included a lake with over a thousand acre-feet of water. I have a great picture of a CDF [California Department of Forestry] helicopter pulling water out of our reservoir to use on a fire further up the mountain. Because we had to get things done in a viticulture-timely manner and under a tight budget, we often had to have a lot of guys [fieldworkers] do work quickly rather than try to get things done exactly right. This was especially true when we were planting significant acreage. I sometimes had crews of over a hundred guys.

Decisions at Atlas Peak often had to be made fast. Sometimes you got caught and sometimes you were a hero. I remember one time we had a frost situation, and because the phone lines were unreliable, the frost alarm was not reliable. To be on the safe side, I sent a guy up there at midnight every night—it's about a ten-mile drive. Martin would spend the night up there watching for frost. If it looked like it was getting too cold, he would start the sprinkler system. A mixture of ice and water will always stay just above 32 degrees because when water freezes it releases a good deal of heat [thus protecting the grapes]. One day I had Martin doing another job down at William Hill Winery and it was late in the day when he finished, so I told him, "No point in driving your truck all the way back up to Atlas Peak now, coming back down, then going back up at midnight. Better to go home and get some rest, and just make one trip." So wouldn't you know, halfway up the hill at midnight his company truck died in the canyon. We had junky old utility trucks which had been purchased at auction. Martin was caught where there's no cell phone or radio service. So he decided to run down the hill to the Soda Canyon store where there's a pay phone and call his assistant to pick him up. By the time the two of them got up to Atlas Peak it was about 3:30 AM and the temperature had already dropped to 26 degrees. They quickly started all the pumps and at about 5 AM he called to tell me what had happened and that everything was now running. But because I had told him to go home in order to save a trip up and down the hill, we burned up [through frost damage] five acres of vineyard. That was significant money. Actually, I thought the junky company truck was equally to blame. But when I mentioned that to the general manager, he said, "Don't even go there. You're not going to blame this on a company truck. That was just a bad decision." So we agreed to disagree and let it go.

Up there, everything was less forgiving and on a larger scale than I was used to. I had to adapt and be superorganized. It usually took us eight nights to get the vineyards sprayed, and because it was always windy it was always difficult. When I was developing new vineyards, there was so much rock up there that we'd have to call a blaster to come up with dynamite to blow it up for us. These rocks were so big they couldn't be moved using a D8 or D9 [large Caterpillar tractors]. There were also lots of rattlesnakes. It's a hot, dry, rocky environment—perfect for rattlesnakes. I had a crew training vines once, and one guy reached down into the grass at the base of the vine on a cool morning and a rattlesnake bit him on the tip of his finger. I ran him down to the Queen of the Valley Hospital, and we were thinking it's no big deal. The doctor came in and used a ballpoint pen to mark how far the swelling had developed and wrote the time on the guy's hand. At first, my guy was okay. I stayed with him until about 4 PM, at which point I assumed he was fine, but around nine that night he started to have a reaction, and they gave him the anti-venom. Apparently it's very nasty and it really messed him up. He was out for several weeks with nerve damage and was real shaky when he came back. His reaction to the anti-venom was probably worse than the snakebite.

There is also some element of danger when you work on hillsides with tractors. Some of our terraces had a 30-degree slope. You couldn't just put anybody on a tractor; you had to have experienced guys. During harvest I watched one driver make a wrong move which caused the brakes to lock up. The tractor slid all the way down to the bottom of the hill. The driver was too scared to jump off, which was lucky. If he had, he might have rolled the tractor and gotten hurt. Fortunately, I had guys who'd been working at Atlas Peak for ten years and really knew their stuff. I'll give you an example. One hot day in July, a twenty-one-inch main line [water pipe] blew. It literally disintegrated and took most of the dirt with it, leaving this giant hole. How do you go about fixing a twenty-one-inch main line? [*Laughs*.] The guys said to me, "Don't worry about it. We'll fix it. We've got some pipe over here." And they started in with a backhoe. They dug a hole big enough to put a semi [truck] in. Then they cut out a section of pipe, put a slipcover over it, and slid another new section in. They had it fixed by 10 AM the next day, which was just astounding to me. They had a can-do attitude which they took great pride in. They were really good guys, and I miss them.

It was at Atlas Peak that I developed a real appreciation for what some guys on crews can do and what other guys can't. Today I look for fieldworkers who can do things, and I give them the responsibility and the pay raises to go with it. They get promoted to tractor drivers and equipment operators. These guys are absolutely invaluable. Whatever oddball job needs doing, they can get it done. Unfortunately, some of the "can't-do guys" call it favoritism and complain to HR [human resources] about their not getting better raises.

One of the reasons I got the job at Atlas Peak was because I had experience with Sangiovese [grapes] at Swanson. Atlas Peak had a lot of Sangiovese, which was the craze in California at that time. Sangiovese is a really finicky grape to grow, and it is easy to overcrop, which means having too much fruit on the vines for quality. Sangiovese has big clusters which easily overlap other clusters, which means they don't get enough sunlight and the berries don't get color. Flavor, tannin, and wine color are all derived from the skin of the berry. Generally with overcropped vines you end up with a really weak wine, but the extra grapes improve profits for the corporation. The thing about farming that corporate winery owners often don't understand is that the cost of creating the product usually equates with its retail value. Growing crops like alfalfa hay or garbanzo beans has little to do with quality—it's all commodity pricing. If you grow better garbanzo beans than your neighbor, you're probably not going to be able to sell them for a better price. So to make more money, you have to produce more beans. This is *not* the case with wine grapes. We get rewarded for quality. We're looking for good quality and reasonable tonnage, not maximum tonnage.

At Swanson we were growing Sangiovese on relatively good soil. If we had done nothing except prune the vines, they would have overproduced at eleven tons an acre and the wine would have been weak and of poor quality. So we managed the vines and reduced the yield to around seven tons per acre. We made sure every grape cluster had good exposure, and we cut out the sunburn. We removed suckers [nonproductive shoots] and put it on a trellis system that separated the canopy. We did a lot of work which produced really nice grapes and made really nice wine. But when I got to Atlas Peak, they didn't do any of these things. They just produced. Then they would try to co-ferment Sangiovese with Petite Verdot [grapes] in the winery or put it on the skins of the prior tank in order to concentrate what was left. The winemaker was always fighting to manage color; it was always a struggle in the winery.

After four years with the corporate-owned Atlas Peak Vineyards, Jim moved down the mountain to Stag's Leap Wine Cellars, which was then family-owned; its owner and vintner, Warren Winiarski, had made the Cabernet Sauvignon that won the 1976 Paris tasting—the competition that forever changed the world's view of California wines.[4] We asked Jim what kind of contact he had with visitors to the valley.

At Stag's Leap I dealt with groups of wine distributors, collectors, and restaurateurs. I'd take them out to the vineyard and give them my spiel, tell them what we were doing, how we did it, and why we were special. In some regards,

I was the face of the product. Stag's Leap has always said that fine wine is made in the vineyard, and I agree with that completely. Decisions that I make every day in the field are as important as the decisions the winemaker makes in the winery. We're a team. I really like the exchange of ideas that takes place when talking to groups of winemakers from other wine-producing regions. I had one group from Hungary. Some of their concepts were completely backwards to ours. I'm sure they were right for their vineyards, and it was a reminder of how nuanced viticulture can be.

I always try to get across that growing wine grapes is still farming. Some of the time, it's not fun. It's not romantic. It's dirty and it's hot. Everyone has this bucolic idea, "Wouldn't it be wonderful to be a gentleman farmer growing wine grapes in wine country." Sometimes the reality is not so romantic—frost, sulphur and insect sprays, dealing with labor, the logistics of harvest. Sure, you're growing premium wine grapes—and I do love doing that—but it's still agriculture.

Has viticulture changed much since you started out in the 1980s?

There's been an explosion of technology in the vineyards. We have neutron probes and capacitance probes measuring soil moisture. We have weather stations with radio telemetry to the internet which I can instantly pull up on my laptop in my truck as I'm driving by a given block. With all the record keeping we do, I can retrieve data on how much water and fertilizer each block has received, how much it produced last year or in the last five years, how many clusters it had last year, what the cluster weights were. There is so much information now that you can get lost in it. But with all the new technology and data, there's still no substitute for going out into the field and looking at the vines with your own eyes. I put a lot of stock in that. Maybe it's because I grew up without the technology or maybe I still don't trust it, but just by looking at a given vine or block I can tell how it's doing and what it needs. Experience and years of seeing different scenarios count for a lot. For example, if you get a water stem potential pressure reading of 13 or 14 on a particular block, it's a warning. But it doesn't always correspond to what you see in the field. So I'll go out and look, and sure enough the vines are growing just fine. I walk along and feel the leaves. They're cool even though it's 11 AM on a warm day, and I can see that the shoot growth is still sufficient. Some people try to manage by the information that technology provides; they live and die by the numbers. In my opinion, you can't farm that way. You have to get out and see the big picture. I end up calibrating the numbers technology provides me based on what I see in the field and each block's history.

What do you like best about your work as a vineyard manager?

I enjoy being outside in this beautiful environment, out there in lush green vineyards early in the morning, being in nature, growing things. Maybe it's a comfort thing because it's what I grew up around. I like the annual cycle of it, too, and I think that vines are a whole lot more interesting than commodity agriculture. Although I don't like to admit it, there is a romantic side to wine that you just don't get from farming broccoli. It's also a perennial crop so you get another shot at it every year. If I wasn't in viticulture, I would probably do pomology—fruit trees—like pears or apples. Another part of the appeal of this job is doing different things every day. Except during harvest, I hardly ever do the same thing two days in a row. I enjoy seeing what needs to be done and figuring out efficient ways to do it. I also like the independence. Andy [owner Andy Beckstoffer] lets me do my job. We discuss budgets, what we expect out of certain blocks, and what our clients want. But once that's all worked out, Andy says, "Go farm." And that's a terrific thing. My favorite time of year is after harvest when we are putting the vines to bed for winter and the pressure is off. Then I'm in catch-up mode, doing all the small projects I wanted to get done during the year but never had time to.

The difficult part about being a vineyard manager is labor, primarily the logistics of labor. You're working with a crew that is from a different culture [Mexico] and speaks a different language. Many of them see some things differently. Coming from poor villages in Mexico, for example, it's hard for some of them to throw food on the ground. That's how it seems to them when we thin the vines and discard [grape] clusters. When you're disadvantaged, that seems crazy. I just try to understand the way they look at things. Sometimes I can have problems getting a crew to work together as a team. There's a tendency to want to pull down the guy who's taking more initiative, to pull him back to the level of the rest of the group. I think it's easier to do that than for the rest of the crew to mimic the fast worker. Guys that can fix things or accomplish a task that's out of the norm are invaluable to me, and, as I said, I promote them to an operator or a sprayer or I give them more responsibility. But their culture values seniority: "I've been here longer, I should get the opportunity. I'm more important." That doesn't fly with me. I want guys who can get things done, who think problems through. I tell my crews, "Look, if I'm not there and you can't reach me on my cell phone, think about the problem, make a decision, and do something. If you make the wrong decision, it doesn't matter. You made a decision. But if you stand there and do nothing, I'm going to be mad. So just think about it and take your best guess." A lot of the guys have been at this fifteen or twenty years and they're very capable, but the previous vineyard manager had not let them make decisions on their own. That drove me crazy for the first couple of years until I gained their confidence and convinced them that they could make their own decisions. I also took some heat for it because at first it came across as me not doing my job.

It's getting more difficult to manage labor here. One reason is that it's difficult for fieldworkers to find a place to live in Napa. It's just too expensive. We now have a lot of labor contractors who bring people in from the Central Valley. Others workers commute here all the way from Lodi or Stockton, almost a two-hour drive. There can be friction between outside crews and our own crews. Everybody wants to protect their jobs. I sacked a guy last week because he was telling other guys, "Slow down. Let's save the work. We don't need to be killing ourselves. We're getting paid by the hour here." He even threatened the guys on my crew who were working faster. Well, he had to go. When I told him, he couldn't defend himself because he knew he was wrong. Instead he got mad at the field supervisor for snitching on him and before he left, he told him, "I'll get you for this—just watch your back." For me, that confirmed that he was a no-good guy and that I'd made the right decision to fire him.

The unfortunate thing around here is that people make assumptions about all Mexicans based on the behavior of a few migrant farmworkers. These are young guys from rural areas of Mexico where there are not many opportunities and they work hard. It would be like sending disadvantaged, unemployed Americans who haven't finished high school to Canada to work, and then having Canadians assume that all Americans are like the worst of them. It's important to remember that if they had more opportunities in Mexico, most would stay—they wouldn't be here.

What do you remember about tourists when you were growing up in the valley?

I don't think I even heard the word "tourist" or thought about them until the mid-'70s when I was starting high school. I remember complaining about tourists driving slow, taking in the sights, and not paying attention to what they were doing. We mainly complained about their driving habits, but now I realize we do the same thing ourselves when we go to a new place. I also remember being up in Tahoe skiing and waiting in line for the chairlift, this was 1977 or '78, and somehow it came out that I was from Napa. People looked at me and said, "Wine country." They thought it was pretty cool, but I thought it was cheesy.

I didn't go on a winery tour until I was out of high school. That would've been to Beringer or Sterling. There weren't many others in those days. I think my first awareness of outsiders being interested in the valley was when a writer named Earl Roberge was doing a book on the wineries and he came to our church in Rutherford to meet the community. My parents took him around to some places like Stag's Leap. I remember that the cover of his book, *Napa*

Wine Country, had a picture of the valley through a glass of Chardonnay that was taken from the deck of Sterling Winery. We all thought that was kind of amusing.

Has tourism changed the wine industry?

Absolutely! The wine industry brought tourism. We have something like four hundred wineries now. With all the visitors coming to the valley, a traffic nightmare has been created along Highway 29. There's a big incentive for wineries to sell their products directly to the consumers at the tasting room for retail prices, rather than wholesale through a distributor. There are conservative elements in the valley that worship private property rights and think they should be able to do whatever they want. They're very much pro-development, and Napa County is challenged in trying to control them. I also think that wine tourism has made the [wine] industry more concerned about image and maybe less about product, more concerned about marketing and creating a brand than quality in the bottle. In the vast majority of Napa Valley wines the quality *is* in the bottle, but the marketing aspect has become a business on its own. Maybe this is a sign of the maturity of Napa's wine industry since our simple beginnings in the '70s.

Winemaker / *Pam Starr*

"It's a balancing act—just like wine, tourism has to be balanced."

Pam Starr is the winemaker and co-owner of Crocker & Starr Winery in St. Helena and a consulting winemaker with both Adastra and Garric Cellars. With more than twenty-five years' experience, she is one of the Napa Valley's leading winemakers. Besides being known for the excellence of her wines, Pam is a founding member of an informal group of women in Napa Valley's wine industry—Wine Entre Femme—who have recently forged links with women winemakers in Bordeaux. Charming and casual, Pam was a pleasure to interview.

———

I come from a very conservative midwestern Canadian family. My father's a surgeon, and my mother is a nurse. My parents moved to southern California when I was young, but all I could think of as a young person was "How can I get freedom?" I didn't want to be a doctor or a lawyer or the business person that my dad wanted me to be, but I was interested in science. I chose dentistry because it combined science with a form of art. I ended up going to UC Davis to study fermentation science. It may sound odd for someone who planned to be dentist, but it was a really fascinating degree that combined courses from food science, the biology department, and the brewery department. I managed to include enough other sciences to apply to dental school. But I needed money—my parents were going through this amazingly aggressive divorce while I was in college, so getting money from them was difficult. One of my professors got me a job in Sacramento at a spice company. I was taking a full load of classes and working full-time at the spice company that created seasonings for bratwurst, pizza sauce, bologna, chicken franks. It was fun, but how I graduated I don't know.

While I was studying for the dental admissions test, I took the advice of some people who told me, "Take a winery job. It's really easy, and you'll have time to study." So I did. I started working at Sonoma-Cutrer right after I graduated in June 1984 for $7 an hour. My dad was like, "Can't you get a real job?" I was still studying for the dental admissions test, but the more I got into this winery job, the more fun I had. I had a ball. When harvest came I realized what a magical world wine making is. It was exciting. It was organic. Taking fresh fruit and fermenting the juice is the oldest natural food preservation process there is. After harvest, I went back to school for a short time and took epide-

Winemaker and
co-owner of
Crocker-Starr
Winery, Pam
Starr.

miology and preventative medicine classes, but I kept reliving those harvest days. It had been so much fun. After that, I never looked back. I took my DAT [Dental Admission Test] book and gave it away.

I found a job at a winery [Edna Valley Vineyard] down in San Luis Obispo that was just getting going and that's where I learned about boys in the cellar. Girls in the cellar didn't exist back in 1984 and 1985, so I was forced to learn all about how boys work together. They had a communication style that I really didn't understand, and they would torture me, like tell me to go get devices that didn't exist. It was like cat and mouse: "Let's not kill the mouse, let's just see how far the mouse will run." They knew exactly how to do things like stack barrels and rack wine, but they were not going to give me instruction. I had to pay attention, have my eyeballs wide open, in order to learn. It was an athletic, competitive mentality. I was quite athletically inclined back then, so I had no problem picking up a barrel and sticking it on a stack myself. But I had to earn my stripes. The experience made me become better and stronger and smarter at most of the stuff they did. That was my goal. Socially, I had to learn how to sit there at lunch and feel okay with not participating. I didn't talk sports. I am not a sports fanatic. So I'd sit there and read my book, maybe read about other wines. When I brought up other wines, they'd be interested because they knew that the bosses liked it when the young fledglings running the cellar were into wine. That's how I was able to survive.

I was down in San Luis Obispo for about three months when I met a group of people who were involved with a new winery partnership which included several wineries including Carmenet. A lot of winery partnerships were emerging in the '80s. The industry was just turning. The wine business was moving away from being strictly an ag [agriculture] business to becoming big business. It had not hit the stock market yet, but it was about to happen. So this group of wineries invited me to come to Sonoma, and I ended up as part of a team. Everybody had a PhD or BS or BA, but we were all rolling barrels, connecting hoses, ripping machines apart, doing lab work, and doing sensory [evaluating the sensory characteristics of wine]. We were involved in every aspect of the business. I was out there washing and stacking and racking with the rest of the boys. I met some higher-end winemakers, got involved in the California Enological Research Association, and ended up with affiliations that allowed me to move up in the wine world. It wasn't really intentional. I just had a huge interest in how vines were planted, how the selections were chosen, and how the dirt was analyzed. We were then starting to do things that the French had done a hundred years ago, and I was very fortunate to be a part of all that research in the '80s.

Grapes really express where they are grown. So do other crops—if you plant lettuce in one kind of soil and then plant the same type in another kind of soil, and even if you pick them at exactly the same moment, they are going to taste different. With grapes you want to encourage the vines to suck up their surroundings. You have to look at the soil and see if there are components that will express well in wine. When I worked at Spottswoode [Spottswoode Estate Vineyard and Winery, from 1992 to 1997], I worked with soil consultants and organic consultants. I was developing a new block of vineyard so we could retain the character [in our wines] that had become known as Spottswoode. It's a very distinctive place.

Then I met Charlie [Crocker], and we formed Crocker & Starr in 1997. We have soil on the western half of our vineyards that comes from the "nook" that is formed at the junction of the Mayacamas and Spring Mountain. Take away Napa's mountains and you'd take away the complicated soils we have; we have fifteen different appellations in Napa. Charlie's vineyard had been conventionally farmed prior to 1997 and the soil definitely had been deprived of its indigenous organic nutrients. Vines were pumped up with water and developed to raise "grapes," rather than distinctive fruit. When I arrived, I kind of felt like Kevin Kline in that move *French Kiss* when he takes Meg Ryan out to that old vineyard and grabs the dirt and says, "See this block of vineyard. I'm going to make a great bottle of wine out of it." The first thing Charlie and I did was hire a bunch of soil and plant scientists, and we turned the whole place organic.

It took years to do it. The first thing we did was plant cover crops to aerate the soil and stimulate the organisms. I got rid of all the chemicals that would eliminate the activity of the organisms in the top three to four inches of soil, which is really important. And I cut off water. I cut off wood. Charlie and I were taking a risk staking a claim on a vineyard that wasn't really established, but I dug holes in the soil and we profiled the soil and profiled the changes. We saw the gravel streaks, and we put extra water in the gravel streaks. We planted appropriate rootstock for the soil. It has taken ten years, but I'd say the crowning achievement is this property's Cabernet Sauvignon. It grows on a really ugly old-style post trellis system that was designed for hanging a lot of fruit. But with the organic inputs we've added and because these soils are slightly acidic, our plants set themselves at an easy 2.5 tons per acre. They grow exactly a meter long, exactly pencil thickness, and have two small clusters of fruit. We rarely have to pull a leaf. Our viticulturalist likes to tell everybody that those plants make us look smart. In fact, they are a good representation of our hard work in the early years and how we've gotten those plants to suck up the soil.

This translates into a wine of distinction with a slight mineralogy to it. There is a deep broody quality to the wine. There's black chocolate. Texturally, it's very sexy. It finishes with a little bit of mineral butter, but it also has an expansive sort of soil draw to it. So it's creamy, yet savory and big at the same time. I don't expect anyone else to describe it exactly this way. I've described it as the designer who put the wine together. But it's very important to encourage the average wine drinker to have their own vocabulary. Other people's responses to wine can be extremely simple. I was showing a wine to a buyer in San Francisco on Thursday who said, "Mmm, yummy. I love this wine." Hearing this was very satisfying to me, and I thought, "Voilà! See you later! Adios! Game over! Gotta go. I've done my job!"

What do you most like about your job?

I love being outside with the vines. I love watching the seasons change. I love being able to watch the fermentations roll over without having to do a lot of inputs. I love the challenge of putting blends together. Blending is one of the hardest and most difficult yet rewarding aspects of being a winemaker. You don't just pick the fruit, put it in a tank, make one big ol' pot of wine, and stick it in a barrel. It's complicated. Five rows of vines that ripen at the same time become one piece of the final wine. When I have six pieces of Cabernet that all come from the old vine block, I look for the most powerful piece—the piece that has exactly the dark, broody, black fruit, black wine taste I am seeking. Then I'll add other components. Maybe one piece brings the wine more into the front of your mouth; another piece attacks the sides of your mouth. Wine also is changed by the barrel it's placed in. Ultimately you want the final wine to have a beginning, a middle, and an end that's pretty seamless and that leaves you with a response of pure enjoyment but also draws you back to taste it again. Your palette should respond and then clear itself, so that you'll be able to pick something else out: espresso or chocolate or maybe the mineral character of wet rock. Blending is about trying to find all those components and create an orb of flavors. I love sharing wine with people and having them walk away saying, "Look what I get to take home with me." I love that. It's my passion.

Would you say something about the wine-making community in Napa? And about being a woman in the world of wine.

When I first started in the business in the early '80s, one of the first things I learned is that farmers help other farmers. Viticulture is an ag business. Farmers sold grapes for a living, made the most they could off their land, and helped one another. When I was in the cellar at Carmenet, I remember Helen Turley at B.R. Cohn calling up and saying, "My pump is down. I'm in the middle of a racking." Jeff [Baker] said, "Come and get ours." Then he called down to the cellar and said, "Clean up the pump. Helen is going to come and pick it up." So we cleaned up our pump, packed it up in the back of her car, and she took it away. There has always been a lot of cooperation.

I think being a woman in the wine business has changed a lot. In the '80s, women were assistants. They were not directors. There was Zelma Long in the '80s. She was the highest-paid woman in the wine business and she was the president of Simi Winery. But most of the women I knew were in the lab. As the business has changed, women have become more involved in every aspect. I am co-owner of Crocker & Starr; Charlie and I have a partnership. To be successful I think women have to have a little bit more knowledge, maybe stand a little taller, and not waver on decisions.

Lately, women in the wine business in Napa have started to network. It's really exciting. It started with an all-woman tasting group. Sharon Harris got us together. She's not a winemaker but she has a lot of irons in the fire, including a winery partnership. [She is co-owner with her husband of Amici Cellars.] She also owns a home in Bordeaux, speaks French, and knows a lot of wine women over there. After a couple years of our group tasting wine together, she said, "Let's start something bigger and share our environment." That's when Wine Entre Femme was born. In January 2008 a group of French women in the wine industry came to Napa. We shared every aspect of our business with them. We had experts in business, in marketing and PR, in wine making, and in viticulture—that's an area in which there are far fewer women. Their experience here led them to invite us to France in 2009. Fourteen of us went. There could have been fifty, but timing is everything and we just decided to go. They returned to Napa in 2010. This time we also had someone from Japan, from Switzerland, and a couple from South Africa. We'd invited a couple people we know in South America, but they couldn't make it.

It's a very informal group. There are no bylaws. No set goals. No set format. We use our innate nature as women to share and learn. And we've applied what we learned from our experience in France to our businesses here. I believe we are better winemakers, marketing people, and PR people now—we have a more global sense than we would have had we not gone.

What are some of the differences between France and the Napa Valley?

It's very different there. Historically, the merchants came in and said, "You are a small little producer. I'll just buy your entire production and take it to sixteen different countries." That still exists. You can't go to any chateau in Bordeaux and say, "I'd like to buy six bottles of your fabulous Merlot blend and oh, can I also have six of your Sauvignon Blanc?" They'd just look at you as if to say, "Apparently, you don't understand." Some of the younger-generation women in Bordeaux—my age and younger—are changing things and becoming marketing gurus.[5] They are trying to bring people back to Bordeaux. France's closed-door policy has driven the public away; people are afraid to even knock on a chateau's door. They are marketing to their own country for the first time. We've already been doing that here. What they learned from us is the advantages of having an open-door policy and of sharing. We share a lot—viticulture, wine making, tasting. The reason we can do this is that we can't share the same fruit. We have a distinctive estate-wine concept here; we don't compete with each other because we don't produce the same product. What they gave us was insight into global marketing. Even if they are very small producers, their wines are in many countries. They have a much more developed sense of the global economy of wine than we do.

In what ways does tourism influence you?

When this company started in 1997, I started with one hundred cases of Cabernet Franc—not the most understood, celebrated, or known variety. So I did a lot of promotion. Part of promotion is being able to open bottles of wine in front of people and having them taste it and be able to purchase wine right then and there. That was the beginning of my involvement with tourism. Now I am involved with tourism every day. Tourists come to the winery. For them, there's nothing better than being able to directly experience what goes into a mysterious and very delicious bottle of wine. In this economic climate, it's become more important than ever for us to be able to put our wines directly in people's hands. It's a very slow, grassroots way of expanding business, of building the critical mass we need to keep the company strong and healthy.

There is something incredibly mysterious and sexy about wine. There is something even more special about a bottle of wine that's made from a single vineyard when people can experience vintage-to-vintage variation from the same source of fruit. When tourists come here [to Crocker & Starr] and see rocks in our soil, see the topography, smell the environment, see that we are located in open ag land and are part of a historic district, they leave with a sense of being part of our winery, our vineyard, and the Napa Valley. When they get home and open a bottle of our wine, they relive the experience and re-create other moments from their vacation and the feelings they had in Napa being away from their crazy work schedule.

I am a tourist too. I tour wine regions. My husband rides motorcycles and so does our friend Ren Harris. He and his wife, Marilyn, have a winery [Paradigm Winery] down the street in Oakville. We've taken trips together— the four of us—up to Oregon, parked the bikes, hired a car and driver, and done the whole tourist thing. Our driver had his idea of what we should see. And we had inside friends [in the wine business] and other wineries that we wanted to see. Everywhere we went, we learned, looked, tasted, and purchased. Oregon has come a long way, especially with their Pinot Noirs. They have more difficult growing conditions than we do, and it [wine quality] really comes down to the vineyards. They are talented. They've got equipment and all of the voodoo tools we have. It's just that they have to deal with *their* agriculture. There are pockets of really beautiful, consistently gorgeous vineyards in Oregon, and then there are the others.

What makes the Napa Valley special?

We definitely are special. Of course we're special! [*Laughing.*] We are Disneyland for adults. We offer an adult experience where people can really be kids—everything is sensory input here. But we're also special as a viticulture and wine-making region. Absolutely! This would not be the same tourist go-to place if we [the wine industry] weren't here. Hotels and restaurants build here because we are here, because we are creating these wines. Napa is beautiful, but so are other regions of the world. We're not done discovering the different soil profiles we have that can create great wines. The soils are everything to us. We are also environmentally correct, and we're working to become more correct. We want to be as green and as sustainable as possible. We are not here to reap and pillage. We realize that what we have here is special and that the possibilities are still endless.

What is your impression of tourism in the Napa Valley?

Tourism keeps us globally in the limelight. Tourism has brought in money, but it also has brought in a demand for property and elevated prices beyond what local people and farmers are able to purchase. This is sad. People who work here have to live in peripheral counties. What has tourism done to this valley? It's led to the development of hotels and bed-and-breakfasts. We have limited sewer and water here, specifically in the town of St. Helena, because there was not much proactive planning and development. The closed mentality that many people had [toward tourism]—"No, we will never allow this"—was a disservice. There's an area in southeast Napa [city] where people can shop for all the things that they need in bulk. Is that a great thing? It makes it harder for small merchants in each of our distinct little towns to supply goods and stay in business, but it has also restricted the pollution and the construction mire to areas that are not part of the "Ag Preserve." There is always the good and the bad. We have to create a balance, an environment that is sustainable long-term where people can live, get the items that they need, and supply and support local merchants and local wineries. It's a balancing act—just like wine, tourism has to be balanced.

5 / Touring and Tasting

Wine Educator / *Ellen Flora*

"Wine improves everything—food and people."

Ellen Flora—smart, stylish, and funny—began sharing her passion for wine and food with Domaine Chandon's visitors in 1992. Today, as the winery's "senior ambassador," she directs wine education for visitor center staff, teaches new employees about Domaine Chandon's wines, manages tours and presentations for the wine trade, works with the chef of the winery's restaurant and the wine team to pair wine with food, selects art for the visitor center and winery art exhibits, and travels frequently in the United States and abroad as the winery's representative.

When Moët et Chandon opened Domaine Chandon in Yountville in 1977, it became the first French-owned sparkling wine producer in the United States. Today the winery makes both sparkling and still wines from Chardonnay, Pinot Noir, and Pinot Meunier grapes—the varietals tradition- ally used in the production of Champagne. The winery is a popular venue with tourists who tour, taste, and wander its scenic grounds. Its Étoile res- taurant is the only fine dining restaurant within a working winery in the Napa Valley.

I grew up in Detroit, Michigan—not exactly wine country although grapes are grown in Michigan. I graduated from Western Michigan in 1969 with a degree in political science and English literature. I wanted to work in politics, and did some work with the Kennedy campaign. Then, when Robert Kennedy was shot, it just really soured me, and I thought I needed a break to do some- thing different. I had visited California and really loved it, so I moved there.

My original idea was to work for a while in San Francisco and then look into law schools. My brother was a lawyer in the city and a CPA. I got a job at Price Waterhouse, but every spare minute I had I would go up to Sonoma County and spend time on the coast. Not having grown up around the ocean,

Wine educator and "senior ambassador" for Domaine Chandon Winery, Ellen Flora. *Courtesy of Domaine Chandon Winery.*

I was just mesmerized by it. I took every hiking trail anyone recommended and also spent a lot of time in Yosemite and Tahoe, where my brother had a home. It didn't take long before I left the city to move to Olema, a tiny place near the coast in outer Marin County. I loved it, but within a year I moved again, up to Sonoma County. One of the things I worked on there was editing a book, a collection of Robinson Jeffers's poems about the California coast.

In Sonoma I rented a home with my sister, and we'd have Sunday get-togethers with friends. My sister always did all the cooking. Then she moved away, and all of a sudden it dawned on me that I was going to have to learn how to cook. Someone recommended that I keep my dinners simple and serve interesting wine because that would take a little attention away from the food. I thought that sounded like a good idea, so I started buying whole fish from the fishermen as they came through from Bodega Bay.

A few people were writers and one person was trying to be a filmmaker. Everybody would bring what they were working on, and we'd share our projects. During the week I'd go into Santa Rosa to this deli that had a wine shop. The very elderly man who worked there took me under his wing. I'd tell him, "I'm going to have a whole salmon, what do you think I should serve?" He'd give me two or three different wines and say, "Now come back and tell me which one you like the best." So that's really how my interest in wine started. I never learned to be a great cook, but I became really interested in how wine worked with different foods and why I liked one wine the best, while somebody else liked another.

I was living on twenty acres with a childhood friend—this was during the early '70s—and we started gardening. Being from Detroit, I wasn't quite comfortable with the idea of living on a commune or living totally off the land, but I did love the idea of growing my own food. Coming home and just going out into the garden and seeing what I could cook for dinner was pretty terrific! And because I wasn't working a nine-to-five job, we would sometimes spend a whole day gathering food for dinner, especially for the Sunday get-together. There were also markets, and many people had stands out in front of their homes. Down the road I could get fresh eggs. It was just terrific, and everything tasted so fabulous. I'd really never had that kind of country experience before. Over the next few years I really got into the idea of cooking just what was available in our area. One of my most vivid memories is getting a dozen fresh crabs and realizing that I'd never cleaned a crab before. I didn't know how you got to the meat part. It was hysterical with a bunch of us sitting in the kitchen pounding away at these huge shells, trying to figure out how to get them to look like they did in a restaurant. I'd do something like this at least once a week with a group of people, and then during the week I'd do some research so I would be ready for Sunday.

One day my friend and I met a fellow who was from a wine family, and we started talking about what kinds of wines we would make if we could. Within a year or so, we'd decided that we would try to make a Chardonnay. We didn't know much about what we were doing, but we'd heard that there were people who would sell grapes to you. We didn't have much money either, so we decided to start off really small. We made a Chardonnay with grapes from the Russian River Dry Creek area. We called it Hampton Wolmer. We made like three hundred cases. We were trying to make a Chardonnay that reminded us of some of the French wines we had tried and liked with food. This was from 1976 to the early '80s. At that time American Chardonnays were big, buttery, heavily oaked. They had this sledgehammer approach to flavor and bouquet— probably so that new wine drinkers could identify what they were. We sold a little bit of our wine in California, a lot more on the East Coast. It was just a really small project, and we disbanded by 1983 or 1984. We had different interests, but I loved being in the cellar and the whole idea of taking something from harvest to bottle. I just thought this was really terrific.

At first I thought I would raise money to start another wine project, but I went to England instead and enrolled in the Rudolf Steiner Waldorf School to study therapies for children with learning problems. I was with their program for six years. When I came back, I worked for a while at the Waldorf Summerfield School in Sonoma County. But then I got back into wine. I became a consultant for a San Francisco group that worked with hotels and wine buyers, writing reports on the styles of wines made by different California wineries. The idea was to help the restaurants' food and beverage people keep up-to-date on changes, like which winemaker had moved to another project.

This job involved entertaining, and I used to eat at Domaine Chandon's restaurant a lot. I remember telling everyone at one of our meetings that Domaine Chandon made such a consistent sparkling wine—its Bruts—that you didn't have to taste them every season. The Reserves, of course, varied from season to season. I later met the winemaker, Dawnine Dyer, and told her how impressed I was with the consistency of their style. Domaine Brut was a signature wine, and I thought she made it extremely well. When I decided to move to Napa, some friends there told me I drank more Champagne with food than anyone they'd met and that Domaine would be the perfect place for me to work. Since I had a food and wine background, it made sense. And that's what happened.

I never expected that the Napa Valley, within such a short time, would become such an important place in the world of wine. No one did a better job of bringing that to fruition than Robert Mondavi. Wine has turned a very agricultural place—a nowhere destination, really—into a really rather chic place. It's happened very quickly, and I think very dramatically. When I first came to Napa Valley, it was agricultural. But it was also a summer place for wealthy people. St. Helena, as long as I've known it, has never been an inexpensive place to buy a home. A high per capita income group was associated with the area, although it didn't appear that way when you went to functions because people dressed very informally.

Napa has a mystique. People rave about its beauty. I think it's very beautiful; if we had an ocean, it would be absolutely paradise. I've started painting again and I am seeing the valley in a new way, how dramatically beautiful it can be. The sunsets this year were just strikingly colorful. Its sounds, too. The starlings this year were so intense. I'd just open the door in the morning, and think, "Oh, my God." To me this is like Yosemite, where you look around and just go, "Whoa!" I think it's because it is so self-contained. It's thirty miles long. You have the mountains on either side. It's like a contained avenue. I've never thought about it like that before, but it's just like the Champs-Elysées. It's just this thirty-mile avenue through grapes. It's very concentrated. There's no way you could leave the valley not knowing what the physical essence of this place is.

Would you describe your work?

I travel on behalf of Domaine Chandon and Newton Vineyard's wine team and marketing department in the U.S., Europe, and Asia. I also train all our employees on wine—those in the visitor center and restaurant—as well as our distributors and major wine sales teams. I think the reason I've been here for sixteen years is because I have this wonderful position, not as a title, but because of the work it involves. I work with the wine-making team. I work with marketing. I work with the PR person. And I'm responsible for training about fifty to a hundred people a year about our wines: tasting room people, the waiters who work in our restaurant, any new employee that comes into our company. They taste the wine with the winemaker and then they taste the wines with me. I give them the history of each wine. We have nine sparkling wines for market and five that are exclusive to the winery. I also train them about the pairing of specific sparklings and still wines with food.

They should understand what foods the wines complement and how to talk about this with the public. I asked them things like, "What words would you use to describe this wine if you only have four words? What is the one word that describes the Chardonnay? What makes it unique from others, if you have only one word?" Sometimes you're in front of the camera and this can be especially important because you're only going to have about three words quoted. We do not have a strictly orchestrated public persona. The staff says what they feel comfortable saying, but we've agreed that if you are only going to have a two-minute segment with the media or if you're only going to see your distributor once in two years and you're training his staff, you'd better know what you want them to remember—the essence of that wine, what it is, what makes it unique—and who we are as a brand.

I try to train the staff to tell visitors what our winery is about as simply as possible. People are touring many wineries, and if everybody talks about how to make wine, there really isn't much that's special that you can say about it. Our winery makes sparkling. Okay, that makes us somewhat unique, but what is it about the culture of our winery that is different? In the early days, we could talk about our history in France, but our winemakers have never been French. Our first winemaker, Dawnine Dyer, was a young woman who had grown up in California. Our vineyard manager was very into sustainable farming and companion planting, which is not done in France.[1] They were hippies from the '60s, people who came of age in a state that is very conscious about how to grow things responsibly. The "stewardship of the land" idea was very big and avidly discussed when these people were studying wine making and soils. But what makes us unique, I think, is that we have been innovative. We planted wines in Carneros early, before it was a prestigious place. We were farming at the top of Mount Veeder when it was not an easy place to farm. We are probably a pioneer of Pinot Noir in Napa Valley. We were the first to bring Pinot Meunier to America, which is one of the three great varietals in Champagne. I want our staff to think about what our signatures are, what makes us different from other wine projects.

I also love training new people to understand our wines and how we got there. I'm sort of the keeper of the history. I enjoy bringing them in and sharing what I know and then seeing them become a part of it. Teaching new staff how to talk about our wines isn't always easy, politically. I want people to bring their own feelings about wine to their work at Domaine, but I want those feelings to be maybe the second layer. They also have to understand the philosophy of our winemaker—that's the first layer. They don't have to agree with everything, but they must understand it. When they drink our wine, they have to be able to say, "Okay, I know what Wayne [winemaker Wayne Donaldson] meant when he said 'What I'm looking for is . . .'" They should understand his purpose, his philosophy about wine, and that's easier said than done.

We had one winemaker for twenty-five years. I knew her wines quite well. I felt I could predict what Dawnine would say about her wines when I tasted them. I always liked her wine making and how she talked about wine because it agreed with how I felt about the wines. We had a similar language. Americans—at least the Americans I have worked with—talk more about what a wine tastes like, what it looks like, and how it smells. Since I am not a winemaker, I'm saying this rather flippantly. Then we got an Australian winemaker, and when Wayne started talking about the wine, it was different. It took me a while to shift, and that's what I mean by a different "philosophy." He talked much more about texture and feeling; he'd say things like, "How does it feel in your mouth?" That's a different way of thinking, maybe a little more Australian.

To be able to describe what something tastes like, you have to have some inner vocabulary. Both countries started out late in the game. They each had to develop a language that enables them not only to discuss wines but to compare them, and to get their wines to a certain standard. We've done things like create aroma wheels. Because of UC Davis [the University of California's viticulture program], our vocabulary has become a little more clinical, I think. Today our winemaker is Tom Tiburzi. He worked with both Dawnine and Wayne as associate winemaker. Tom's a true scientist and an artist—creative, intelligent, and thoughtful. He's an amazingly passionate man to work with. His approach is completely hands-on and he brings everyone to a very conscious or focused level of working.

Every person who starts working here will taste the whole portfolio, and I'll give them a background on the evolution of our wines. We started with one sparkling and now we have fourteen. "Why did we move to this wine? What palate is it reaching? What's its use? How do we use it in the restaurant?" That kind of thing. I'll test the tasting staff on our wines every other week. I'll do food and wine pairings and lifestyle presentations. We'll do comparison tasting because the question they get is often "Oh, I like this. What else would I like?"

Tasting wines is very personal; everyone has a different palate. Sometimes you can hit a wall trying to find a way to talk about wine in terms of something people can relate to. I started depicting our Étoile as a very elegant dancer because the wine has a lot of structure. It is very seamless. It's a very graceful wine. So I described a dancer that just moves effortlessly across the stage, probably an older dancer who is very well tuned to her craft. Someone you just love to watch, all grace and structure and finesse.

Our Chardonnays are very lush and beautiful. I described one as an opera singer, someone who is rather well endowed in maybe a low-cut dress, someone very voluptuous, full, who has a real command of the stage, privately laughs very loud. She definitely has on too much makeup, but she looks beautiful and you want to be around her and to be invited to her parties. I just started to do this and I wasn't sure where I was going to go with it, but they seemed to get it. Whenever you have a problem, try to visualize the wine as something you have an easy time visualizing—a person, a garden, a piece of art. "Is it a fun wine? Do you want to drink it alone?" Finding the personality behind the wine can help tremendously with beginning people. It opens up a door, because there is no single right answer. Everyone's palate is so different. It depends upon where you were raised, where your comfort food comes from.

When you say to a visitor, "What's your ideal dinner? Your ideal way to entertain? What ethnic dish could you eat for the rest of your life?" you learn a lot about that person. I always try to get the staff to be more technical but remain mystified at the same time, so that they can reach anybody who comes in. If a winemaker walks up, they can say, "Yes, we did that much malolactic and we didn't use all new barrels because of this or that." Or they can tell someone, "This is the best thing with chicken" or "I love this with barbecue." This is what the beginning person often wants to know: "How can I use it?" You don't know who is walking through the door. We have no appointments, except for trade people, so we don't know if a person seldom drinks wine or if they make it.

Training service people is really important. I recently had a terrible time in a Disney hotel. After every conversation I had with them trying to get them to fix the lights in my room which wouldn't turn off, they'd say, "Have a magic day." I was like, "If one more person says 'Have a magic day' one more time, I'm going to scream." There's a way to train people so that they know the philosophy behind the service. They should smile, they should greet people,

Napa Valley Wine Train in mid-valley. Photograph by Trenton McManus. *Courtesy of the Wine Train.*

A member of the millennial generation enjoys her wine, the view, and a peaceful meal on the Wine Train. Photograph by Trenton McManus. *Courtesy of the Wine Train.*

Tourists learn about the wine-making process on a Grgich Winery tour.
Photograph by Trenton McManus.
Courtesy of the Wine Train.

The barrel room at Opus One. *Courtesy Opus One.*

Two wineries illustrate the contrasting architecture of the Napa Valley: the
Rhine House at Beringer Winery and Opus One.

Tourists at the tasting bar of Silver Oak Winery.

The valley's scenery as enjoyed from the terrace of Joseph Phelps Winery adds to the wine-tasting experience.

but they should still be thinking while they're talking. When I train our staff, I don't tell them exactly what to say. They should include one or two key points in their dialogue at every station [of a tour]. But you want the uniqueness in each person to come out, and you want your staff to feel comfortable. One guide we have owns her own vineyards, so she'll talk a little more about the vineyard. Another person who's a great cook is going to talk more about food. You definitely don't want robots. Visitors are still going to leave knowing the basics—about aging sparkling, where the bubbles come from, how to open a bottle—but they'll have learned about it in the context of our wine.

Because many younger people have grown up drinking wine, the message wineries offer today is much more specific, but you still have to cover the fundamentals. You have people that are new to wine. We also have people from other countries that have moved to America but didn't grow up in a wine culture. We try to have many opportunities for them to ask questions on our tours: "Does this make sense? Is there anything else you would like to know about the fruit or vines?" It's important to communicate the quality that goes into the work and our commitment to that quality. It's science. It's art. There's a whole world behind the bottle of wine sitting on the shelf.

We've had up to two hundred thousand people [in one year] visit the winery. I've always loved meeting visitors. It's like having someone come to your home in a way. You put your best foot forward—show them around the winery and what we're doing. We used to just serve wine by the glass out on the patio. Now we do bar tastings. I think you need both. Someone who knows our wine might be traveling with friends and just want to come up and share a bottle with them or have a glass of wine. Then there's the person who really wants to be at the tasting bar because that's their idea of a wine experience. Some people know nothing about wine. They do the tour and want to have someone talk them through a tasting. Others belong to a wine club, entertain with wine, and they want to say, "We've been to Napa." If they come at harvest, it's like Christmas. It's the time of year everybody has been waiting for. You can feel the excitement, and they're just thrilled to be here then. And when they buy a bottle three to six years from now they'll have the memory of having seen how grapes in their raw form ended up in it. It's fun and that energy is really nice to share with people. So the part of my job that involves people coming to the winery—whether trade or the public—is fun. I'm shocked at times that I've hardly ever been tired of it. One reason is because you never know who you're going to meet, what they're going to be like, what they'll bring to the occasion. I love not knowing what to expect.

The person who goes into our restaurant [Étoile] is not the average person who comes to visit the winery. It's a high-end restaurant. It's expensive and you have to allow yourself two or three hours. So the restaurant is a separate destination from the winery. Ideally we'd like to see more of our visitors go into the restaurant. I love it and an important reason I work at Domaine is because I had eaten at the restaurant a lot before and always thought it was pretty terrific. They always took such good care of me. I would always entertain there because I knew that it would be something that a client would really like. But now, seeing all the younger people that are coming to the winery, I think the restaurant needs to change a bit and be more reflective of our wine. We don't make $150 bottles of wine, we make sparking wines from $18 to $50, and our still wines are around $30, which is a pretty average price. So in my opinion, the restaurant has to be a little more accessible without losing the high caliber of the food. We think our wines are fun and that they're well made, but they're not serious wines that need longer cellaring to be ready to enjoy. We want people to enjoy them, to drink them. Everything should reflect that. We've started serving more food informally in the salon [next to the tasting bar]. About ten years ago, I started bringing the Hog Island oyster people from Tomales Bay here every Sunday. I wanted to reach out to all the local providers and the artisans who make goat cheeses and the like and have a kind of food marketplace. This is what's going on in Napa [city] now.

Can you talk about the different kinds of visitors you get—nationality, gender?

We get mostly Americans, but many more young people than just five years ago. It's become a social scene for them. It's like, "Hey, let's meet at Chandon." You might have a couple of couples come from Sacramento and they'll meet their friends from San Francisco here. We also have killer concerts twice a year that they come up from the city for. Twenty percent of our visitors at most are foreign; international travel was hit pretty severely after 9/11 and now there's the recession. First the Japanese market fell out, which was something we could really see at Domaine. Germans don't seem to travel to wine country as much as they used to, unless we have a really beautiful warm year— they're always in search of sun. We see French visitors a fair amount because we're a French project. The French tend to be formal; most are shocked by how casually we dress. But there's a polarity. Some have the attitude "Umph, nothing is as good" or "Umph, if this was France." Others love it, especially the young people: "Oh, it's so free. It's so fun." Or they tell their friends, "God, we saw the whole thing. You can just go in. They take you right into their winery and they show you everything!" Everything is so guarded in France. It's one or the other. But generally, they get the biggest kick out of coming.

Most people who come to Napa come for Cabernet Sauvignons. We're not in that camp. Our winery is different, so it's skewed a bit. We have a lot of visitors from California, as all the wineries do. New York and Texas are really big draws for us. We also get a good amount from Florida, probably because Domaine Chandon is visible in Florida. The Bay Area with its changing ethnic influences also generates new groups who may just be discovering wine as part of this "California lifestyle." They are just beginning to enjoy wine and frequently come on family outings. They like to tour and taste.

Some of the men that pick grapes for us bring their families to the winery on the weekends. They're really proud. We always try to make a big deal about them because they *are* a big deal. We treat them like a winemaker. If you have ever picked grapes, it tremendously elevates your respect for those who do. Not only because of the hard work, but how joyfully they do it. I remember my sister once volunteered me and some friends to pick grapes, it must have been 1970. They were Zinfandel grapes, twenty-four acres on the Russian River, and it was a real hard year to get pickers, the crops were very big. Well, we had picked apples and cherries and things like that so we all thought, "Oh, cool. This will be great." About two or three hours later, as soon as it got hot, I was like, "This is going to be the longest day of my life." We were cut up, it was sticky, there were bees and bugs, and when we went home that night, no one wanted to go back. My sister said, "We have to go back. I said we'd pick for five days." We all said, "What?!" I remember sitting in the bathtub on the second night crying. It was the worst experience of my life. My staff always says, "Oh, we really want to go out and pick. The other wineries' staff can pick and work harvest." Then we take them out into the vineyards for our vineyard orientation in April or May, and every time it miraculously gets really hot. We're out there hiking around the vineyards and not one person comes back and says they want to do that work. It's a hard job.

There are not that many gender differences [in visitor behavior], though it's still typical for a man to say, "I don't drink sparkling." But now we can say, "Fine, we have Pinot Noir and Pinot Meunier, and Chardonnay." Some men say, "I'm just here for my wife. I don't drink sparkling wine." We always say, "Did you realize this is made from Pinot Noir grapes?" And then, they're kind of "Ahh." If they're hungry and order an appetizer, then all of a sudden the men are into sparkling: "I like it." I think women ask more questions, they're less guarded. We see a lot of women in groups because of the sparkling wine. Actually the spas have made Napa appealing for women. They can come and relax and leave their children at home. Women organize a weekend and come up to taste wine, eat at some special restaurant, maybe take a cooking class at the CIA [Culinary Institute of America], and go to a spa. That's the perfect weekend. It seems like we get a lot of teachers, too, and that's nice. They're from all fields, especially geography, science, and people interested in agriculture. They're interested in how we convey information [on tours] in thirty minutes. They're always fun because they actually listen and ask questions that you enjoy answering. The worst visitor is the person who takes the tour and then goes up to the bar and wants Zinfandel. Where did they get that idea? Some people just don't get it, the whole varietal thing eludes them—it's just so foreign to them.

How do wineries feel about tourists bringing children with them?

No one wants to talk about that to the public, but it's being discussed [among winery people] a lot. This generation is bringing their kids. They haven't learned yet that wine country is not that great for kids. Within wineries people are saying, "What do we do to keep these kids safe?" At Chandon we say things to the parents like, "We just want you to know that the grotto isn't fenced off" or "We have ponds. You really need to keep your children with you." And before they go in the winery [on a tour], we tell them, "If you have children, please take their hand." It's surprising to me. It's a bit like someone saying, "Honey, let's go down to the bar and take Billy and Suzie." I think it will change because some of them [parents] are not having a very good time. The other day I overheard this young woman say to her husband, "Let's leave them home next time."

I was talking to a woman who makes coloring books [designed for use at wineries] last night and she said, "I cannot sell them to a winery and I can't figure out why." I told her, "I think part of the problem is we're worried about the parents staying *too* long." We don't want to encourage children, and we don't want to encourage people with children to stay a long time. Andrea Immer Robinson [wine writer] totally disagrees with me on this. At vintners association events she's always saying, "You guys have got to do something about children, they're coming." But what would we do? Do we have playgrounds and man them? Say I occupy your child with a coloring book or I have a play or a film for them; you're going to stay longer and drink more. Then you'll going to leave and you'll be driving and taking care of babies and children having probably drunk more than you should. It's a worrisome thing. However, most parents are responsible and have selected a designated driver for the day.

What do you do to monitor tourists' drinking?

We use a national program called TIPS. We always have a few people on staff who are certified TIPS trainers. Basically we try to detect early. If a group walks into our building and they're really loud or they're having trouble coming up the stairs, we cut them off before they even get to the tasting room. The manager or the floor person will find the soberest person and say, "You know what? We're really sorry but we're not going to be able to serve you. A few of you appear to have had a little too much to drink." This doesn't happen often, but when it does we try to do it as nicely and as respectfully as possible. We don't want to embarrass them or say something like, "You're too drunk" or "Let us help you" or "You need to go have lunch." That's taking the mother role and it's slightly lecturing. If you do that, they're going to get angry. If people resist, we say, "My guidelines are if there is *any* appearance of intoxication, I can't serve you. The standards are if anyone in your group is slurring their words, having trouble walking, or acting out of the ordinary, I can't serve them. It's not my decision. It's the law. We can lose our license." People usually buy that. They seem to get it. What was successful for me when I was manager was to say, "You know, if we were all walking on foot, we'd pour wine for anybody all day. Then they could walk home, or in the 1800s, their horse would take them home. But we have automobiles now and the winery has responsibilities." There are usually people in the group who haven't had too much and they're grateful. They've been thinking, "This is going to ruin the whole day and probably dinner. We're here for eight hours and these two are already a problem." I've had people whisper "Thank you" to me as they are leaving. We review all our policies with the staff three times a year. We explain that if visitors get pulled over or if there's an accident, we're responsible. We could be shut down for two weeks and there's a heavy fine. So it's a big revenue loss and is taken pretty seriously.

Twenty-five percent of my job in recent years is to go on the road to introduce our new products. I have found this to be much more interesting than I expected. The winemakers and I share the travel and go with a marketing person—the person who heads our sparkling division or our still wines. This year I've been traveling with the still wine person. When we meet a distributor, their entire sales team shows up. This could be anywhere from sixteen to fifty people. They'll come in the morning and probably have a little breakfast. Then we'll give them a PowerPoint presentation about our winery—its background, where our vineyards are located, a bit about our winemakers. Although I am listed on the wine-making team, what I really am is more of a spokesperson for our wine products. I take the group through a flight of our wines. If we are doing sparking and still wines, each person will have six sparkling wines and three still wines at their seat. My part of the presentation is probably the easiest, because I'm actually talking about the reality of the wine, how it tastes, how I have used it with food, and easy ways for them to talk about it with clients. Then there are usually questions. I'm surprised at how sincere people are. You usually picture salespeople as a bit jaded. I tell them, "If you have any problem, if you go out next week and you just end up with a mental blank, call me." And they do. It's a lot of information to understand, and most people do not know how to talk about sparkling wines.

When I go into a market like New York City or Chicago, I'm generally there to meet distributors and salespeople. Of course everybody knows that the more customized any sales meeting is, the better. Distributors and sales-people see how many people a week? You want to simplify their job. I will do a seminar on our wines and will talk about how they work with certain foods, so that when they go into a restaurant they'll be able to talk about it. This is where the growth is happening now. This is the education part of it, to get people to really taste. When salespeople become knowledgeable and feel comfortable with this, they'll be able to look at a menu and talk about what role their wines can play in that restaurant. They can actually help a restaurant by saying, "These wines are going to work great with these dishes." Then the restaurant doesn't have to experiment. Until recently most restaurant people weren't really good at pairing food and wine. Now some are very, very astute. It used to be in a chef-owned restaurant that the chef made the food, then hopefully the front of the house could find the wines that would work with it. The sommelier or food and beverage person bridges the gap between the food from the chef and the table with a great wine list. This is an area where we've changed light-years. The people at the front of the house—the sommelier or their food and beverage person and the wait staff—have become savvier and savvier in terms of what they know about wine and food.

Most of the salespeople are men. A lot of the older people are now retiring and there's an influx of young people. I found the older people a little hard to work with at first because they were coming mostly from a liquor background. But if you can get your presentation to be fun, they'll come along with you because they realize they need to be savvy about wine since that's where the growth is. I don't think they like real slick presentations. I just say, "Let's drink the wine and talk about it. Let's not just talk about how it tastes, let's talk about how you can get it into an account." When I'm in that market, like New York City or Chicago, I will spend any free time I have going to visit their accounts with them—a restaurant, a liquor store. It was hard for me at first but now I like it, although I still feel more comfortable dealing with the restaurants. When they first told me I'd be going around to liquor stores, I was like, "Oh, my God." I'm still a little rough on that, but a lot of times they're just so thrilled that you would come all the way from the winery to their store in Lafayette, Louisiana, or Charleston, South Carolina. They're like, "You really work in Napa?"

Sales is not an easy job. It is a lot about relationships, except in the big modern stores like Cost Plus and Costco. They move a tremendous amount of wine. The mom-and-pop liquor stores that take the time to teach their custom-ers about wine are different. The real educators out there are the mom-and-pop liquor stores where someone comes in and says, "Hey, I'm looking for a Pinot Noir. I'm looking for a Merlot. I'm looking for a Cab, what do you think?" They hear it all day. To me they're the people that really teach new consumers about wine—"I know you like your favorite, but you should try this new wine."

Then there are the restaurants that introduce people to the way wine works with food. These people are ambassadors for your wine. So if you visit them and you do a tasting that helps them grow some new taste buds or helps them progress enough so that they can really understand what an additional barrel aging can do, they are so grateful.

I think I visited 104 accounts this year, and we placed orders in 92 or 93. After I was 100 percent for my first 50, I was, "Whoa, I like this!" But it's not always easy. Unless you go out and make a connection with people, your wine is not going to get anywhere. Once I went to an account with this young sales guy, and he kept telling me, "I don't think she understands English." I was thinking, "If she owns her own liquor store, I'm sure she understands English. She just might not speak a lot of English to you." So when we went in, I just talked to her like I would speak to anyone. At the end of our meeting, I said, "You know, my sister-in-law is Korean." She had told me she was a Kim, and I said, "My sister-in-law is a Kim. Where are you from in Korea?" And that was it. She took everything we had. Later she wrote me a note, "You're the nicest winemaker I ever met."

Some of the marketing team when I first came—not now—were not from the wine industry, and they were really clueless about what to talk about with people. When you go to a liquor store, the person you need to speak with might be with someone else—a friend or their wife. So, you need to be able to make a connection and talk to them about something other than just wine. Years ago, before we went to visit this one account, our marketing person said to me, "If you could get just one wine in that account that would be great." He'd been trying with no luck. We walked in and the owner was with his wife. The meeting didn't really go quite how I wanted it to, and I ended up talking less about our wine than about my sister who belonged to the same endangered-animal society as the owner's wife, who had a passion for animals. As we were leaving, the owner said to me, "You know, this is the first visit that anyone's really included my wife. It's been really boring for her. She's not a big wine person. If there's anything I can ever do for you . . ." So I said, "If you could just put this one wine in your account, my marketing person would be thrilled." And he said, "Done." Later our marketing person kept asking me, "What did you do?" And I said, "Well, he liked the wine. He really did." But then I admitted it was because his wife and I had talked about animals. Our marketing person said, "What? How can we teach that?" We talk a lot about this now with staff. You have to keep your eyes open and get a sense of what a visit is all about. We do it when friends come to visit us. We think, "What do they want to get out of this? Do they want to see wineries? Do they just want to sit and talk with us? Do they . . . ?" So, I think when you go into a market, you have to have that same sensibility.

When I'm on the road, I'm out the door by nine in the morning at the latest and get back about midnight. Often I do winemaker dinners at night. If I'm in a market for three days, there are probably going to be at least two. These are dinners that restaurants have usually sold to the public at which they are going to pour all of our wines, one with each course. And I'm there to talk about the wines as they have dinner, so I don't eat very much. I introduce what our wine project is all about, and then I either talk about the next two wines they're going to have or I'll get up at each course or I'll go around to the tables. A lot of restaurants like that because then people feel more comfortable asking me questions.

Food has become such an important part of wine tourism. Can you say more about food?

Sure. I remember my first trip to Europe when I ate bread and cheese and wine, and thought for maybe a few days that this was all I was going to need to eat. That was one of my first food and wine experiences, besides drinking wine with Sonoma County seafood straight from the ocean. When you go to France or Italy, you discover how important eating what is around you and drinking what is made in your area is in their food traditions. It's a simple concept, but it's not how most Americans have grown up. Unless you grew up in a food-savvy family that travels the world, you discover food in your adult life. Even though my parents drank wine and my mother cooked and baked every day, and we always had dinners together, coming to California from Michigan was a real food discovery for me. So was Europe. The foods I eat today are very different from the foods I grew up on. Now I think about what I'm going to eat for breakfast. I don't just eat the same thing every day. And I'm really excited when the apricots come into season.

Wherever I am, I'm interested in what's going on locally at the grass roots with food and wine. If I'm on Nantucket, there's an old wine project there that I always visit to see what they're doing now. In North Carolina I try finding the best barbecue. I try not to be too fanatical about it, but it's now become part of my life. I've always liked indigenous things, not just food and wine. I have a lot of friends in North Carolina, and when I visit them, we go to Jugtown, where everybody makes pottery. I just love what emerges from a place, what comes out of the soil even as an art form. Wherever you travel, someone makes an alcohol and that alcohol explains a little bit about them. Like this sorghum liquor that some Chinese officials gave me. They were in America to try to find a winery that would be interested in establishing a wine project in China. They spent about a month at UC Davis and then four days at our winery. When they left, each man gave me a gift from his province. One province had just won an award for this sorghum alcohol, which was in this vibrant aqua blue bottle with red satin ribbons. And he said, "I hope you take this home and drink some of this with your husband tonight." The translator said, "If you drink it, it will kill you." [*Laughter.*] But the bottle was so elaborate and they were so proud of it. It had just won an award, and he had traveled here with these bottles. You could tell that he felt my tasting it would teach me something about his province.

I haven't traveled nearly as much as I would like to, but I think it's important to pay attention to these things when you do—the food people eat, what they drink, why they make what they make. What is visually different sweeps you away first, but I think that food and wine have more to do with people's attitudes. I even think different kinds of drink result in different styles of rapport. That would make a very interesting study. What is it about tequila that is so wonderful? Wine slows everything down. To sit down and enjoy a bottle of wine with some friends, you have to slow down. It's not like running into a café in Italy or France ten times a day to have an espresso as I've done with friends. They go into a café, put down the money, poof, then they're on their way again. You'd never do that with wine. You have to slow down, and usually someone serves food with it. I really think there's something to this.

I don't have a great nose, but I do think that I have a palate. I know when food and wine work together. When I do training, sometimes we'll go to a restaurant where they sell our wines and I'll look at the menu and say, "Okay, let's have them with this, this, and this." I can sort of predict what will work. But the fun, exciting part of it for me now is when a perfect pairing just happens. Many things work, but there are some that are perfect—"This dish was meant to be with this wine."

There isn't one formula, but some food and wine combinations really do work. The easy thing about sparkling wine is that you have bubbles, you have delicate flavor, you have acid, and you have fruit. One of the most common things people order midday is a Caesar salad. Being heavily dressed is its signature—it's creamy, salty, anchovy. If you pair it with a sparkling Brut that's crisp, it will lift the cream off your palate and make the crisp lettuce seem even crisper. While the creamy, toasty Reserve Brut will intensify the creamy aspect and the toasted croutons will be amazing. You can eat twice as much fried calamari if you eat it with a crisp still wine or crisp sparkling. Not that we need to eat twice as much fried calamari, but it works. A lot of rich foods will be heavy after the first few bites, but with a crisp wine each bite is as good as the first. With pairings, you're finding either similarity in texture or—sometimes I really like antithesis, where you combine rich creaminess with something really light and acidic. When you get the right food and wine pairing, it just sings—the wine never tasted so good and the food alone never tasted so good. A good wine should make it all just unfold in your mouth, so you go, "Oooh!!"

Tasting Room Consultant / *Craig Root*

"Next to wine quality, the most critical part of a successful tasting room is staff, staff, staff."

Craig Root runs his own tasting room consulting firm and teaches occasional classes at the University of California at Davis on tasting room design and management. "I like listening to music and playing my drums. Besides music, I'm a pretty uninteresting guy," he claims. "I spend so much time in the public that I tend to avoid people when I am not working—not that I'm a misanthrope, I just keep my distance and harness my energy. I'm in bed by 9 PM and I get up at 5 AM, when I do most of my reading and more tedious work." The latter often includes doing financial projections for a new winery tasting room for which Craig is consulting. Despite his own characterization, Craig is one of the most personable people you could meet.

—

I grew up in San Francisco. My parents weren't immigrants, but my family was Basque. I could always tell when my grandparents were getting into a racy topic or gossiping about somebody because they'd switch from English to Basque. I suppose it's because of the Basque influence that I wear a beret. When it came to wine, my father, who was an engineer, never could seem to find a wine he liked, so he'd get two and blend them in a glass until he got the flavor he liked. I had wine and water at the family dinner table when I was five years old. When you grow up around wine, you don't think of it as a social tool to one-up people. It's just part of a meal. My parents were somewhat European in their tastes and more adventuresome than many kids' parents. When there was beer in our household, it was good quality and imported. Most people didn't eat Camembert in the '50s, but we did.

After going to a pretty good high school in San Francisco, I went to UC Davis. But not for viticulture; I majored in English. After college, I joined VISTA—the domestic Peace Corps—and worked in Tulsa, Oklahoma. That didn't work out very well because I had signed up to work with Native Americans and had trained in White Rocks, Utah. The chief and I had really connected, and he was even going to include me in some religious ceremonies if I had stayed longer. But because of bureaucratic wrangling, I ended up in a white neighborhood in Tulsa. I felt people there resented our presence since VISTA had been brought in by a black church and there was still a lot of prejudice in those days.

Craig Root.

After VISTA, I went into music. But musicians don't make a lot of money, so I worked all sorts of odd jobs. This was in the '60s. Some of my friends discovered that if you passed the civil service test, you could get a job in the post office for $7 an hour instead of the usual $3.50 that most of us were making. Since we all had long hair and looked a bit like hippies, they stuck us all on the graveyard shift—from 10 PM to 6 AM —so the public wouldn't be exposed to us. I would get up at three in the afternoon, rehearse with the band until 7 PM, get down to the post office, and work all night. Eventually I realized that I couldn't make a living in the music business and began to look for something else. However, I've continued to play professionally with a jazz trio—mostly at wineries.

My parents got a country house outside of St. Helena which I used to visit. I didn't like it that much when I was younger, because it usually meant I had to do two days of yard work with my dad and there wasn't any TV in Napa then. But I've always liked camping and nature, and as I got older I switched my whole MO and moved to the valley. I got a job at a little bar in Rutherford.

A while later I gravitated over to a job at nearby Beaulieu Vineyards (BV). I started in the tasting room for five bucks an hour. I was in my mid-twenties, and I wasn't thinking of a career in the wine industry. I just wanted to pay the rent. If I had lived in Akron, Ohio, I'd probably be working in the tire business. But I lived in the Napa Valley, which meant working in wine or something related to tourism.

BV was a formal place then, and I wore a coat and tie even if it was 105 degrees out. I mostly did tours. I figured it out once. During my thirteen years at BV, I conducted about seven thousand tours. I did just about every job there was at BV: weekend manager, special events stuff, marketing, trade relations, and eventually, I ended up being manager. I doubled their business in two and a half years—not by myself, of course. You can't do it by yourself. We restructured the training the staff received, created a wine club, and just got our people enthused about BV. Then I moved to Trefethen Winery as a manager; I increased their business by 70 percent. That's when I figured out I could get paid for what I know, not what I did. I've been a private consultant for tasting rooms ever since. I'm the only person that teaches tasting room design and management at UC Davis. I offer a one-day class every year. I've also lectured in other departments at Davis as well as at universities in Texas and Oregon. I have four standard seminars: one for owners and managers; one for sales and customer service; one for dealing with difficult situations in tasting rooms, like intoxication; and one on wine clubs.

When I started out, interacting with the public was what I liked best. I also liked the freedom and the flexibility of the job. It wasn't the kind of work you took home with you. That's one reason why tasting room jobs are great for retired people. When you leave at 5 PM, you're done for the day. Later on when I got into management, it wasn't like that. I've always chosen the path that offers the most personal freedom. I always opt for freedom over money. I met some great people working in tasting rooms, and a few of them became short-term girlfriends. In fact, that's how I met my wife. At the time, she was an untenured theater professor at Napa Valley College and working as a tour guide on the side.

I've always been a people person so working in a tasting room was a good fit for me. It's a good job for young people because you learn public-speaking skills and how to read people. In the tasting room, you could have one couple to your left who knows nothing about wine and a couple to your right who knows everything, and you have to be that chameleon that can go back and forth between them. You also learn how to use the cash register. It's a great entry-level job, and it sure beats flipping burgers. The downside to a tasting room job is repetition. You talk about the same six or seven wines over and over again to hundreds of people a week. That's why I recommend working twenty hours or less a week, because it's a burnout job. Most tasting room jobs don't pay much, maybe $12 or $14 an hour, and there are usually no tips and no medical benefits. But I do know of at least three places that pay their staffs $45,000 to $50,000 a year, but they're the exception. Tasting room jobs are also dead-end; only 10 to 15 percent of the people who start out there end up in management. After four or five years, I probably would have left to do something else, but I noticed that even though BV had a distributor in the Napa Valley, we didn't look as good as I thought we should in restaurants. So I asked permission to start going out and doing sales, which I did after my day shift at the tasting room.

Now I have my own consulting business, but to keep fresh I work one day a month as a tour guide at Hess Winery. After I've worked twenty days in a row as a consultant, driving up to Hess to do a tour is something I try to psych myself up for by thinking about the people I work with. Some of them have a wild sense of humor that I like a lot, and one is like a sister to me. If you go to work thinking, "Man, this is going to be a drag," it becomes a self-fulfilling prophecy. So as I'm driving up to Hess, I'm thinking, "I'm going to have a good time. Tom's a lot of fun, and I really like so-and-so." I remind myself of all the positives.

For years I tried to convince Hess to offer tours and now they finally have. Their tours are a combination art tour, which takes people through their art gallery, and production tour, where visitors see the winery. Hess is unusual in having an exceptional art collection with about $40 million worth of art. At the start of each tour, I ask visitors which they're most interested in and then allocate our time accordingly. One group could want 80 percent art and 20 percent production and the next group the exact opposite. Because I have lots of experience, it's easy for me to switch on a dime. I really like giving tours. There's a story behind each painting. It also helps if I can introduce some human interest and give an interesting anecdote about the artist. With production, it's best if I make the tour sequential: talk about vineyards, then the crusher-stemmer, then the fermenting area, and finally barrel storage and aging. But no matter how much you have to say, it's best to keep tours relatively short—under thirty minutes.

I try to do two things on a tour: teach people things they don't know and add human interest. One of the first techniques I use for tours and when I am pouring wine is to start out by asking open-ended questions: "Where are you folks from? How long have you been out in the valley? What restaurants did you go to? Oh, you went to Mustard's? What did you have there?" I ask these questions as a way of reading my group. It's also responsible hospitality because if my visitors are talking, it's easier for me to tell if they have had too much to drink. But the main reason I like asking questions is to engage people. I am being paid not just to take them around the winery and pour wine but to be entertaining and informative.

I should mention that there are two types of tours: one for the general public and the other for trade people, like when the buyer from the Ritz-Carlton in San Francisco visits the winery. The first is an opportunity to take wine off its pedestal and make it fun for the general public. The second is a chance to influence somebody who could put your wines on the wine list at a top restaurant, which is great not just for sales—they buy cases or pallets of wine, not bottles—but also because it becomes a billboard for your wines. Usually the tasting room manager entertains trade people. If you treated an experienced sommelier like the general public by offering Wine 101, you're going to bore and probably insult him or her as well. I like doing both types of tours.

I can usually tell in the first thirty seconds if the group is going to be a good one. I use everything you anthropologists do in observing people: body language, dress, voice tone, affability, you name it. Do they get my jokes? Do they ask questions? I always tell the staff I train that they should never judge people solely by appearance. People can get out of a limo dressed impeccably but be total cretins. Very casually dressed people may be the ones who ask great questions and later lay out $100 bills and buy five cases of your reserve wine.

I like to use lots of analogies. For example, I'll say, "An oak barrel adds flavor to the wine like a cinnamon stick adds flavor to your hot chocolate." One of my clients in North Dakota was interviewed for a television piece about wine, and the only snippet they broadcast was when he talked about oak barrels being like a cinnamon stick. Good analogies make wine so much less mysterious. I'll give you another example. When describing the effect of wine being aged in oak barrels, I'll say, "You don't want to over-oak it, because that would be like cooking rosemary chicken when all you can taste is the rosemary and not the chicken." I also say, "Like the cinnamon stick in your hot chocolate, eventually the oak barrel wears out. Not because the wood gets weak but because the wood loses its flavor." A good analogy makes it easier to understand. My goal is to take wine off its pedestal and make it accessible to ordinary people. I had a guy who said he didn't understand what the "body" of wine meant. I said, "It's just like milk. Skim milk doesn't have as much body as 2 percent milk, and 2 percent milk doesn't have as much as whole milk." He got it. When I talk about growing grapes in different parts of the valley, I say "It's like your houseplants. Some plants do better in the part of your house or garden where it's sunny and warm; other plants do better where it's shadier and cooler." In Napa, we grow more Pinot Noir and Chardonnay down-valley where it's cooler and more Cabernet up-valley where it's warmer. A simple analogy enlightens and entertains, and that's what a good tour should do. At the same time, I need to tell people the story of *our* winery and what is unique about *our* vineyards.

Safety is also an issue on tours because you're taking tourists through production facilities. When I train new tour guides, I always tell them to pretend they're taking a group of four-year-olds around. You wouldn't turn your back on those little rascals, and you shouldn't with tourists either. There have been two incidents I know of where somebody wandered away from a tour and opened a valve. At Sebastiani, it was on a really big tank. It happened on a Saturday afternoon, and because there are drains in the floor no one saw the tank leaking out. They didn't discover it until Monday morning and by then the tank was empty. That's big money literally down the drain.

I always tell the staff that by the end of the day, if they've been doing their job right, their cheerful tank is pretty low. You can start out the day with lots of enthusiasm and cheerfulness, but by the end, you're going to be pretty burned out. My wife teaches theater and speech and I work the public and clients, so by the end of the day we've had our fill of interaction. We don't entertain very much for this reason. When my daughter was young, I had to teach her that when I came home from work I needed a half hour to myself. After that I'd be all hers, but first I needed a half hour to recharge. I've found that people who work in other areas of the winery, like production or the front office, often devalue what we do in the tasting room. If you work in the cellar hauling hoses around all day or you're a general manager and have been in a union meeting and gotten beaten up, then you walk through the tasting room and see everyone standing around the tasting bar nicely dressed and chatting with the visitors, it looks like we're at a cocktail party. The work doesn't look very hard, but they don't realize that it's a performing art and exhausting.

Today most of my time is spent consulting. I do a wide variety of stuff, including design reviews with architects, income-expense projections, business plans, staff training, and "mystery shopping," where I go to a winery anonymously to evaluate staff interaction with customers. I also do some writing for *Practical Winery & Vineyard* magazine and a little teaching. When I was in VISTA in the '60s, I really enjoyed being able to help people. I think that's part of why I'm good at consulting. I'm not just doing it to make money for me but to help you make more money by helping you solve a problem. When I'm doing seminars for business people, I feel like I'm handing them practical information that they can take out and use tomorrow. One of the services I do for wineries is help them hire tasting room staff. I separate the wheat from the chaff by going through the résumés and doing the initial interviews, often in conjunction with winery management. They make the final decisions. I'd say about half the applicants have a college degree. They also tend to be people who have other income: teachers, homemakers whose partner is working, retired people, students. What I tell management is, "You can teach wine but you can't teach friendly." If I have to choose between a person who has great knowledge of wine but is kind of a downer and not very interesting and someone who isn't high on the wine knowledge scale but is outgoing and personable, I'm taking that person. I can teach wine, but friendliness is an intrinsic personality trait. All tasting rooms and tour businesses need people people—staff that are gregarious and curious and like to be around people. When I am training staff, I tell them that machines can pour wine. They're being paid to be charming and engaging and informative. The goal when pouring is to establish rapport with visitors. I usually give them my 90–5–5 rule, which is that 90 percent of the people you serve will be pretty nice, 5 percent will be jerks, and 5 percent will be absolute sweetie pies. I like to remember the sweetie pies, although they don't make the jerks any less unpleasant.

You'd be surprised how much staff training varies between wineries. Some places are very good. They give their new employees a written manual with all sorts of information about making wine and lots of verbal instruction. This includes spending time with the winemaker and then, every six weeks or so, with the viticulturalist, who will come in to explain what's going on in the vineyards or actually take them out in the vineyards. But at a lot of wineries it's mostly shadow training: "George has been here five years, so follow George around for a while." Or they'll walk people around the winery and introduce them to the staff: the winemaker, the manager, and maybe the GM. And they'll give them a bit of wine to sample and the winemaker's notes to memorize—pretty minimal. But the places where I consult—if they listen to me—generally have good training, which is important because it not only provides staff with the necessary information but it sets the right psychological tone. Good training says, "This place is serious about me and this job." When I started in 1978, there was hardly any real training at any winery in the valley. It was mostly shadow training—follow a senior staff person around and learn as you go—which is terribly inadequate.

There are many important elements in tasting room design: lighting, counter design, crowd flow, cash register placement, and much more. Two of the most overlooked aspects are flooring and acoustics. Architects often want to use tile, which is all wrong. I suspect they've never had to work on tile themselves. It is just brutal on your feet. Mats on the floor behind the counter help, but the staff aren't behind the counter all the time. I have a saying, "Tired feet don't sell well," which means your staff won't sell as much wine or merchandise if they are in pain. Carpet or wood on the tasting room floor is much better. The other critical thing is the acoustics. I don't know about you, but when I'm out to dinner with my wife and I can't hear her, I don't think very positively about that restaurant. It's the same with tasting rooms. And for the staff, having to shout all the time wears them out.

You also want to design a tasting room so that you seldom have second rows, that is, visitors standing two deep at the tasting bar. You don't want people having to lean over the shoulder of the person in front of them to taste. They are not going to have a great experience, and you're not going to sell much wine to them. One way to minimize this is to use a 360-degree counter. Think of the bar in the old sitcom *Cheers* with the staff inside and counters all around them. Of course you need more staff, but it eliminates second rows. Or you could have a second counter which is opened up when the room gets busy. Staff refer to these busy times as "being slammed"; I prefer to think of them as waves of opportunity. If you don't have the right counter design or enough staff, you lose out on a great opportunity to increase sales and wine club sign-ups. Another aspect of tasting room design that I think is important is to make your room look like a wine shop, not a gift shop. There are four main categories of stuff sold in tasting rooms: wine-related accessories like glasses and wine openers, books, food, and apparel. The focus should be on the wine.

Next to wine quality, the most critical part of a successful tasting room is staff, staff, staff. Good staff can overcome bad architecture. Good architecture can't overcome bad staff. I've been in multimillion-dollar tasting rooms and had the gal not greet me at all, and then pour me the first wine and then sit down on a stool and read the newspaper—totally ignoring me. Not much chance I'm going to buy any wine in there. And then I've been in a winery where the guy is so charming and friendly and engaging that I have no choice but to buy wine from him. In fact, that happened to me a few years ago at Dutch Henry Winery, where the tasting counter was just two barrels with a plank of wood across them.

Is there much of a difference between family-owned and corporate wineries?

There's a lot of variation. It's not like the corporations only own big wineries and the families only own small ones. Some family places are relatively large, like Beringer, which is a very big facility, and some corporations like Diageo own really tiny places like Acacia. In my experience there are positives and negatives with both from the point of view of working there. With corporations the paychecks are good and they're on time and the benefits are good—all the bells and whistles are there. But it can be a little less personal. With family operations, the positive for visitors is that they may be able to meet a member of the family, which is really important to them. The downside for employees is that you can have conflict. Mom comes down in the morning and tells you one thing to do in the tasting room. Dad comes in the afternoon and says, "Why did you do that? Move it back." The son or daughter comes in the next day and says, "I don't like either one of those. Put it over there." It can be frustrating and unpleasant.

There are about four hundred wineries in the valley now. Out of those, probably half have tasting rooms, and far fewer have tours. The wineries that don't have tasting rooms are either too small, don't have the right licensing, or just aren't interested. Maybe they produce a cult wine and already sell everything they can make. Some just think it's too much work. And some just aren't aware of how profitable a tasting room can be. To me, it just doesn't make sense not to have a tasting room. If you don't have one, you are going to be much more dependent on distributors for your sales, and cultivating distributors can be very time-consuming. God bless distributors, they sell a lot of wine, but a tasting room gives you a lot of bang for your buck. Plus, you are getting retail prices by selling directly to the consumer versus FOB [free on board] prices from a distributor. Plus, in the tasting room you get publicity. When visitors have a good time in a tasting room, they remember it for months and years. When I was at BV, I remember people coming back years after their first visit and asking for their former server by name. They'd say, "This is where we discovered BV wines and we've been drinking them ever since." The tasting room has incredible public relations value, and this is especially so if you have a wine club. Wine clubs have only become popular in the last fifteen years or so. It's a winner for the people who sign up because they can quit any time they want and in the meantime they're having a good time trying different wines. When they come to the valley, they get free tastings and feel like they are part of the winery family because of the special attention they receive. Wine clubs also offer incentives for the staff, who get $10 to $20 for everyone they sign up.

For years the tasting room was taken for granted. This really turned around after 9/11, when there was a slump in the wine business and people were really scrambling for money. I noticed then that a lot more respect was paid to tasting rooms. I used to feel like the lone voice in the wilderness in favor of tasting rooms. People would respond, "Yeah, yeah, yeah." Tasting rooms today are bigger and better than ever, and there are many more of them.

Nearly every winery in the valley now charges a tasting fee. I still have to explain why to some people because there are wine regions where wineries still do not charge. The main reason is to recoup the cost of the wine and tasting room labor. A lot of wineries take the sting out of the fee by refunding it when you purchase a bottle of wine. Sometimes the fee is used as leverage to get visitors to join a wine club. For example, I was just doing a reserve tasting at Hess. The tasting fee for reserve wines is twenty bucks. The tasting is held in a special barrel room and is really nice. When we finished the tasting, I said to the group's host, "Now I have to charge you the $80 for the tasting; however, if you join our wine club the tasting is complimentary. There are lots of nice features and you save $80 right off the bat." He said, "That's a no-brainer" and signed up. But not everyone understands what a wine club is.

Some people think that tasting fees are charged to get rid of freeloaders. A lot of people in the wine business can remember when they were at college at UC Berkeley or Davis and came up to the valley with their buddies to get a free buzz—to taste all those wines for free without buying a bottle. Some people think charging a fee is a way to reduce the number of drunk drivers. Well, not really. The local highway patrol will tell you that the fatality rate around here isn't because people are driving drunk, it's because people are driving too fast for a two-lane road lined with oak trees. Oak trees are like concrete pillars with no protection around them. I knew a manager who died even though she was wearing a seat belt because she took her eyes off the road for a minute and ran into an oak tree. You run into one of those and that's the end for you.

There was a letter in "Dear Abby" some years ago in which a tasting room server complained about co-workers drinking and driving. A local person from Napa wrote in saying that it was the ugly secret of the wine business. So I wrote a letter. I wrote that I had seen no more or less drinking than in any other business. There are always a few people who push the envelope, but overall most people who work in tasting rooms are pretty cognizant of the effects of drinking and what the penalties are for DUI. When I was a bartender when I was much younger, I had every imaginable liquor and high-end drink available to me. The first two weeks I was like "Yee haw!" But you soon realize that you can't drink and do your job. I drink at home and that's it. I don't drink at work. Sure, when we open a fresh bottle [in the tasting room] we are responsible for tasting it to make sure it's not corked. But you can taste just half a teaspoon and get a sense of whether the wine's good or not.

What changes have you seen in recent years?

There are more wine regions today. Back in the '70s and '80s, if you wanted to go wine tasting, it was Napa or Sonoma. Now Paso Robles has forty or fifty wineries and probably as many tasting rooms. Lodi has twenty or thirty really nice tasting rooms, especially the Lodi-Woodbridge grape center, which has interactive computers and is a really nice place. You can also go to Gold County and find wineries there. Customers are also more sophisticated. People are more food and wine savvy than they were in the past, especially here in the

Bay Area. But people in any metropolitan area—New York, LA, Atlanta—and around those areas have become a lot more knowledgeable. More tasting rooms are offering small appetizers to go with the wines. The biggest trend I am seeing now is that more customers are looking for an intimate experience; a good example of that would be the Swanson [Vineyards] tasting room.

What do you think the main appeal of wine tasting in the Napa Valley is?

People go out wine tasting not just for the wine. I think people come to Napa because they are also looking for a nature feel. Take all Napa's tasting rooms and put them on Market Street in San Francisco and see how well you do. To people living in urban and suburban environments, wine country is really bucolic and pretty. The vines are manicured and they turn wonderful colors depending upon the time of year. I think people are also looking for a kind of Norman Rockwell feeling. That's what I love about some of the smaller wineries that have a winery dog or cat. I was told that when people pull into the parking lot of one winery, the dog walks over to greet them at their car door and then walks them over to the front door. You can't bottle a memory like that. I think society is very fragmented now and the sense of family and connectedness is much more tenuous, so this kind of thing—which harkens back to another time—appeals to many people.

Tasting Room Server / Jim McCullough

"Good wine sells itself, but it's how you treat people that matters."

Jim McCullough has a long and rich history of work in the wine industry. We met him at Saddleback Cellars' rustic tasting bar where our son—who valued Jim's Irish-American wit, knowledge, and sales acumen—then worked. Jim is tall and has a deep melodious voice and southern-style charm which he uses to good effect with visitors, especially attractive women. He began his career in wine as a tour guide and tasting bar server in Calistoga in the early 1970s and returned to the tasting bar thirty years later. In between, he held several regional and national marketing and sales positions in the wine industry. His story reveals the diversity of experience and depth of wine knowledge many people bring to their work in Napa's tasting rooms.

——

I grew up in Philadelphia but left in 1962 when I enlisted in the service. My first duty station was Bolling Air Force Base in Washington, D.C. I spent a year as a member of the USAF Presidential Honor Guard before I was reassigned to Armed Forces Radio and Television. My second duty station was Lajes Field on the island of Terceira in the Azores. I spent nineteen months in that Atlantean paradise before I was transferred to Lowry Air Force Base in Denver, and that's where my broadcasting career began after I was honorably discharged. I worked for several years in radio broadcasting. Then in 1973 a friend of mine was moving to San Francisco and wanted company. I said, "Sure, why not? Let's go to San Francisco."

When we landed, we decided to live in Vallejo, which at that point was attractive and still had some of its old character. We rented a beautiful Victorian home for $185 a month. He was in the men's wholesale clothing business and traveled to little towns in California and commuted into San Francisco. But the commute from Vallejo to the city finally drove him nuts, and he decided that he'd made the wrong decision and moved back to Colorado. I didn't go with him because by then I had started to make my way into the California wine business. I was hired by Hanns Kornell to work as a tour guide at his wine facility in Calistoga. Tourists would come in and we would take them into the champagne cellars and introduce them to the idea of sparkling wine and how it was created. Then I would lead them across to the office and they would taste. It was a modest beginning for me. I think I was paid $2.85 an hour, maybe

$3, enough to afford a cabin in Calistoga for $50 a month. I also had begun to talk to Harvey Posert, who was then the public relations arm of Napa's wine industry; he later became Mondavi's PR man. Harvey gave me reason to believe that I was exactly who he was looking for. At that time my hair was long and I had a full beard—I looked like the '60s generation. His idea was to get funding from the state to hire younger people like me to send out to lecture on wine around the country. I loved this idea; it would have been a job I couldn't make up in a dream. But in the end, he didn't get the funding he needed.

In the meantime, Hanns Kornell had hired an overseer just out of military service, a lifer in the service, and we did not get along. I was looking for a way to escape this guy when some of my buddies arrived from Denver and wanted me to join them on a tour to British Columbia. Gas at the time was 20 cents a gallon—this was just before the first oil crisis—so we were able to do it with little money. We had a wonderful trip through Oregon, Washington, then over to Victoria and Vancouver. Then we headed home to Colorado. I later toured more of Canada with my Canadian girlfriend. I don't know how we did it. We drove a '66 Buick with three cats on board. We camped, of course. Sometimes we gave ourselves a break and stayed somewhere for a shower. The best part of the trip was the beach in Nova Scotia. We met some very nice people. During the trip, I'd go into the Canadian state [liquor] stores and look for a wine we could afford and we got lucky. The Canadian state store system had bought some Mommessin; they were producing a *rouge* that was for sale all across Canada. That's what we enjoyed all summer, good burgundy from France for $2 a bottle.

Before I returned to Colorado, I wrote a letter to the manager of Liquor Mart, Phil Reich. Liquor Mart was the major store in Boulder, Colorado. I said I was coming back from Canada and would like to apply for a position at Liquor Mart and here are my credentials. When I got back, I called him and I was hired. I started making $3.70 an hour and spent most of it at Liquor Mart every weekend. This is when I learned everything I needed to know about wine. The store sold everything. The wholesalers wanted to make sure this new idea of a big box store with extensive wine section worked; the store was the size of a supermarket and had room for all their brands.

At Liquor Mart there was a group of men who in many ways later became the prime men in the sales of fine wines throughout the United States, and I happened to be lucky to have been one among them. One guy in our circle, his name was Jack Vesey, had a cellar. He was younger than all of us, but he had an uncle who turned him on to the joys of wine when he was seventeen. What he had in his cellar blew the rest of our minds; we couldn't even afford one bottle. They ranged all the way back into the nineteenth century. He spent all of his money from whatever source to buy wine. And he'd have us over to his house on Sunday and serve us in crystal wine-tasting glasses. Sometime in the preceding week, he'd set up the wines so they would settle out [the sediment would settle]. He opened with Bordeaux, never less than ten to twenty years old, and later moved on to Burgundy. There would be ten to twenty of us on a Sunday and we would go through ten bottles in a tasting, each getting an ounce or so of each wine. We'd each chip in $10 to $15 to cover the cost, but I'm sure in many cases it didn't cover the cost. We would talk about the wines. It was a great experience, the kind you really learn from. At the end of the tasting he would bring out the *bouche,* the good mouth. This would be a dessert wine of great age which would blow our minds. Without those tastings, none of us would have had the grounding for our own wine businesses later on. I thank Jack Vesey. He trained a lot of us in the business and made us more knowledgeable and marketable. One of us, Rene, went on to become the American representative for Château la Mission Haut-Brion. He had an office in San Francisco. Something nearly as grand and all-American happened to me, but that was ten years later.

I worked at Liquor Mart on and off for two more years while I was taking courses at the University of Colorado. In 1976 I was told by the university that I needed to graduate to make room for returning Vietnam vets, that I couldn't be a special student the rest of my life. So I graduated in theater and communications. After I graduated, I thought to myself, "Let's go get a good job." Unfortunately, for a lot of jobs you had to have an MA, not just a BA, but I was tired of school and didn't want to go back. So I called up a friend in the wine business whose name was Pat Fraser. He had started as the wine buyer at Liquor Mart in Boulder and put it on the path to becoming the great wine store of Colorado. I also credit Pat with helping all American retailers figure out how they could become big box wine stores. At the time Pat was the sole wine buyer for a major wholesaler. I called, and he said he might have something. After I passed through several interviews, I became his wholesaler's wine man for Aspen and Vail. This was August 1976 and I was thirty-five. It turned out to be an awful snowless winter, but at least it gave me plenty of time to learn my territory, learn my book [inventory], and learn the two hundred different licenses [retailers] available in that area.

My goal—like any earnest wholesaler representative—was to sell something to each account in my territory. If you achieve 50 percent coverage with two hundred accounts, you're known in the industry as a "worker." I came closer to 70 percent by 1978. In the meantime the company had decided why not give their wine guy water too? So they added Perrier and guess what? Aspen and Vail loved it. I sold tremendous quantities of French-bottled water there, along with truckloads of wine and beer. I didn't do liquor. They kept that separate. Their Denver liquor man, however, didn't want to make the two-hundred-mile journey up to Vail and Aspen and then travel another hundred miles going around to accounts. I knew a guy who wanted a new job, so I arranged an interview for him and he got it, and we became a team. To make a long story short, by the end of the third year we were doing $2.5 million in business. This was 1979 when the annual gross for this major wholesaler was $36 million, so this was exciting. They liked to brag about us—their "mountain men"—up there selling liquor, wine, beer, and water at the best accounts.

We were doing very well, but at a certain point I grew tried of the requirements. In the liquor business you have to attend a meeting every week. Regardless of wind, rain, blizzard, sleet, hail, snow, you had to be there for the most hideously boring meetings constructed by man, seemingly with the sole purpose of stupefying each other. So down we went [to Denver] every week, and at a certain point I looked at what we were billing [selling] and I looked at what I was being paid, which hadn't gone up at all—it was as little as 2 percent a month—and decided something needed to change. So I went to them and said, "On the merits of what I'm selling up there, you need to raise me." They said, "We can't do that, Jim, we'd have to raise everyone." There was no such thing as merit pay or advancement. So I said, "Fine. You get to keep the job because I'm prepared to leave." And so I did.

I was lonely up there. I was a bachelor living with the bears in a tiny cabin way up the Crystal River in the middle of an apple orchard. And what did I do all week? Drive between Aspen and Vail, Vail and Aspen, Aspen and Vail, and then down to Denver—forget that. I thought, "I can do without this." Plus, I had money then. So I said to myself, "Let's go back to Philadelphia and see where it was that you came from and left in 1962." My mother was a little put off by this because she expected me to keep the job I had and stay with it, but she trusted me to do better and I did.

Even before I got back to Philadelphia, the phone's ringing with a job offer. Marimar Torres, who was the only daughter of the Torres wine dynasty in Spain, calls to offer me the job as the East Coast representative, based in New York, for her family's wine. This is how I entered the national scene. But first I spent the summer with my family on the Jersey shore like every other self-respecting Philadelphian. In September I went to work for Marimar Torres.

The first thing that happens is that she takes me to Spain in December. I am on my first overseas trip besides my service years. I'm in a suburb of Barcelona in the area of great sparkling wine. Freixenet is one those. The winery opened up later in Sonoma under the name Gloria Ferrer. So I am in Spain meeting Marimar's two brothers and eventually her father and mother. The two sons were approachable and the daughter was the most approachable of all. On my first day there they have me over for lunch at a tavern right by their winery. We had a nice time together. Then the father wants to meet me and he takes me out to an up-scale restaurant where extraordinary shows of presentation are performed in his honor, a cadre of waiters moving like dancers in a well-produced choreography. There were six or seven waiters helping us. I had picked up the flu and begged to be excused, but no one says no to the father so I had to go. He asked what my symptoms were and then he wrote me a prescription as if he *was* a doctor—actually he was a doctor of pharmacy— and then sent his driver out to a pharmacy to get it. Anyway, I lived through the night. His wife and I took a great fancy to each other and remained close until she passed. Marimar and I always got along except in business meetings where we tended to go at it. She had moved to America, had a failed marriage, but brought her family business up to forty-five thousand cases [annual sales]. That doesn't sound like much until you realize that at that time we sold Torres wine by the container, not by the case. The smallest container held eight hundred cases. So if you got a wholesaler in Minnesota to buy, he had to buy eight hundred cases, which was a whole lot of Torres wine to sell. But the price was so little at first, $13 a case, that it didn't really amount to fabulous money. Later, costs increased.

By 1984 we had built sales to 105,000 cases. I had been given the Midwest and West to look after and moved back to Denver. Gloria Call took over for me in the East; she was very good. One day in 1984 Gloria calls and says, "Guess what? Marimar is putting Torres, our Torres, into Chateau and Estates." This was a division of Seagram's. My response was, "Great. Now we don't need to bicker with her [Marimar] anymore." Terrible response on my part and an even worse decision on hers because the line [brand] died. It died a terrible death. Everything we had done over the years to build it up eventually came to a close. In those days, and it's probably still true, the new company coming in assures the employees who are working there that they'll be fine: "We'll bring you in. We want to know where the business is and how to maintain it." But this stage never lasts long.

Seagram's gave me a special assignment. Their Chateau and Estates division had one California winery named Gundlach Bundschu. It had been started by the last of the true California wine pioneers, two Bavarians who had bought land in Sonoma in 1855 and opened a winery in 1858. It suffered a disaster in the 1906 earthquake and then closed with Prohibition but continued farming grapes for other wineries, especially Sebastiani. A member of the fifth generation, Jim Bundschu, still owned the estate and vineyards called Rhinefarm. In 1970 Jim and his brothers-in-law decided to resurrect the old stone winery and again make wine. I had first heard the melodious name Gundlach Bundschu back in 1977 when I was working in Colorado. Pat Fraser called me up from Denver to tally that we'd added "this great old winery" to our portfolio. He had bought fifty cases of their very old vine Zinfandel and wanted to know if I could sell it up in the mountains. I said, "Certainly," and did. It was a superior wine. In 1984 I'm asked by Chateau and Estates, which now owned Torres, to shepherd Gundlach Bundschu's winemaker around southern California to meet major accounts. So I fly into Burbank and Lance Cutter flies down from San Francisco. We spent two days together in LA—a book and a movie in itself—and when Lance returns to Sonoma, he crows to Jim Bundschu, "I think we've found our man." I didn't know it, but Lance had more or less been interviewing me, thinking I might be the person—the magician—who could make the fifty thousand cases of wine they had stored in their warehouses in Sonoma disappear. Lance had built Gundlach Bundschu's production to fifty thousand cases a year and needed to sell it in quantity. He was near desperation. He didn't think the mighty Seagram's could sell that much wine. They were at heart a French importer. He desperately wanted to believe that I could and tried to convince Jim Bundschu. On Lance's recommendation, Jim called me to out to California for an interview.

Jim Bundschu is a true prince of the realm. He had blond curly hair and is still a laid-back Californian of the Alfred E. Neuman "What, me worry?" school. I don't think he broke a sweat except when he was digging postholes. But his brow did furrow when I told him what it would take to sell his mountains of wine. He's a smart guy and sought a second opinion. I never learned who he consulted, but whoever it was advised him unequivocally not to leave Seagram's: "Leave Seagram's? You'll die! It won't be pretty. Don't do it." But Jim and his father had sold their grapes to August Sebastiani and had watched August build his winery into a million-case brand. Jim remembered August's dictum to never let anyone else do your marketing and sales for you: "Do it yourself. Make it personal."

So he decided to leave Seagram's and managed to reach an amicable agreement with them. He then offered me the job of being the winery's sole sales representative. I moved to Sonoma in the spring of 1985, and as soon as I got there, Lance showed me his warehouse. There was barely room to sidle sideways between the walls and the towers of pallets loaded with cases waiting to be sold. "Dear Jesus, Mary and Joseph," I thought. "What have I gotten myself into this time?" But I put my nose to the grindstone and didn't look up until the end of 1986. I did nothing but think about how to make those cases go away. We managed to sell 48,858 cases in our first full year in just three-quarters of the country [part of the agreement with Seagrams], the three of us—Lance,

Jim, and me. And that's the story of how I became the national sales and marketing manager for Gundlach Bundschu and stayed there for thirteen years and did very well for myself and for the family, which is the oldest extant wine family of California.

But change is inevitable. Just as Jim's father took him into the business, so Jim looked to his son Jeff, who was coming out of the University of Southern California to come into the business and eventually take it over. I decided to step down and let Jeff hire his own age group and chose his own lieutenant. I made up a list of twelve candidates. He interviewed one and hired him. They paid him $20,000 a year more than I ever was paid because Jeff was tuned into the way things were done. They got along very well, but the new chief left after eighteen months when he got an offer from someone in Napa that made him an equity owner with 10 percent or something like that. So the winery's marketing and management has since changed hands many times.

I had moved to Albuquerque, New Mexico, then and tried out semi-retirement. I bought an adobe with huge cottonwoods in a section of town with a park. I was happy there, but I was still only in my fifties and wanted to work. One wholesaling venture fell through because the people who hired me almost immediately sold their business to a group in southern Florida. Then came 9/11. After that it became nearly impossible to get a hearing from anybody because wholesalers were overloaded with lines and were starting to downsize. So I decided to sell my house and at the age of sixty return to a vagabond life. In 2003 I went to Oregon and got a great job as assistant wine steward at a fabulous Fred Meyers supermarket which had great credibility in wine. Then someone made me an attractive offer at a smaller outfit in Jacksonville, Oregon. I didn't realize then, however, how seasonal the business was there—it was a summer destination. So I returned to California in 2004, where I had originally started my wine career, and began to work in tasting rooms again. I've worked at several—Hartford Court, La Crema, Ledson, Flora Springs, Saddleback. I have to admit that I prefer being the main mogul in sales and marketing, but I'm not that now. So it has been a test to work in tasting rooms again. I enjoy dealing with the people who come in. The big test for me is, "Does he play well with others [co-workers]?" And I admit, I'm not a high scorer. I have always had difficulties dealing with authority, dealing with the way things are done when I can see better ways. So here I am with forty years' experience and a mind still full of good ideas and strategies for marketing and so on, and I am not listened to even for a split second.

When it comes to the public, I enjoy the job. When people come in the door I say, "Now, how did you get here?"

"Well, our driver recommended it."

"Well, welcome," I say. "Is there any special reason why you're in California?"

"It's our honeymoon," they say.

I ask about what they're going to do with their evening and their next day. I make recommendations. In the end, they're going to have a better honeymoon if they follow the advice. It might have been an accident that they ended up here [in this tasting room], but they are going to have a better time because they found someone who took the time to talk to them. I take joy in their happiness. I feel it. I feel their pride and their excitement to be in Napa Valley. "Yes, it's nice here, isn't it. That's why we work two jobs to stay here—it's gorgeous," I say. I try to wrap them up in a genuine welcome. When I have only two people in front of me, I have all the time in the world to talk to them. I tell them a bit about the winery. I tell them about the wines and ask them what they think. "I have one more wine for you," I say. They absolutely love it. "Yes, it's nice, isn't it." At that point, they are writing out their application for the wine club.

Good wine sells itself, but it's how you treat people that matters. You find a way to speak to them person-to-person, real-to-real. You get involved with them, you're happy for them. Too many couples tell me how disappointed they were at another winery, one of the more beautiful ones. They say it was a cold and expensive experience for them. The couple that was just here said the same thing and told me how much they enjoyed talking to me. They didn't buy much wine, but they filled out an application for the wine club. Even when I don't get a wine club sign-up, I can usually encourage people to buy a few bottles and then I've done my part for the winery. My contention is that without someone like me to make that happen, wineries cannot exist. There's something in the character of Californians which makes them never want to be seen as a person who sells. Selling is boldly done in the East as opposed to the West. My feeling is that the social contract in our world is "I sell, you buy" or "You sell, I buy." It's an understood thing in many cultures. I'm Irish, and the Irish are known for their ability to speak, their wit and their directness. I don't pressure people, but I don't mind asking them if they want to buy. Some people need to be asked or want help selecting wines, whether it's only one bottle to make a memory or several that they'll enjoy drinking with friends back home. If you serve wine and never ask for the sale, you're just serving and not selling, and I don't think that's the purpose of tasting rooms. Tasting room sales and wine clubs allow people to bond with the winery and vineyards they visit. Jim Bundschu had a back label that said something like, "By uncorking this bottle, you are joining us in a celebration of life and our vineyards." A bond *is* created when you buy a wine and enjoy the fruit of a vineyard's labor.

I've often met people in tasting rooms that I would love to know better. The very first time this happened to me was at Hanns Kornell Winery many years ago. In walks an absolutely stunning couple; he was white and blond and she was very pale cocoa. I was almost aghast at how beautiful they were. I found out that they were in Calistoga on a photo shoot. Often people come in who are just so enthusiastic or interesting that you'd like to know them. Sometimes you do make a connection, but it seldom lasts. I continue to know some people I've met this way but mostly through Christmas cards and even that drifts. Sometimes people e-mail and I script handwritten notes in reply, but do I get answers? I do not. And I just go "Damn." One of the sorrowful parts of the job is that you seldom maintain relationships with the people you meet for very long.

The job is also very tiring. At the end of the day, I'm whipped. In my diary I've put a few lines into it after every session. I often write, "Whipped." After dealing with people all day, I need time to myself when I get home. The last thing I'd do is run off to a bar to say hello to people. I unwind by having two cold beers. If I have a film of interest that I want to watch or a big book of interest, that's how I relax. Right now I am reading a biography of Thomas Hardy. I also tend to worry about transactions that didn't work out. If something went wrong with the register or I made a mistake, it makes me nuts. I go home and stress about it, even wake up in the middle of the night with angst dreams. Fortunately our accountant, Noreen, saves me. She looks at my mistake in the morning and says, "It's all right. Don't worry. It's gone."

Salonnier / *Shawn Larue*

"We want our guests to leave feeling like they just attended a small party in their honor."

A few Napa Valley wineries have established their own private tasting salons. The best-known, and perhaps the first luxury wine-tasting salon in the United States, is at Swanson Vineyards. It offers only three seatings a day, each accommodating eight people. Shawn Larue is the salonnier, a sort of master wine educator. He is a former social worker and PhD candidate in psychology who left the academic world to follow his passion for wine. Middle-aged, lithe, and goateed, Shawn is an engaging and erudite wine scholar, with a talent for teaching.

My interest in wine goes back to 1990 when I was a grad student in psychology in San Francisco [at the California Institute of Integral Studies]. I was paying my way through school by driving a limousine for a hotel in San Francisco. I did that for five years; it was one of those things you do as a student. Incidentally, I have never made more money than when I was a limousine driver. Part of the job involved taking clients to posh restaurants and wine bars, and in doing so I got to know people in the food and wine industry. I got invites to a lot of places and gradually acquired a sense of wine. In fact, I loved it. Before then, my entire experience with wine was limited to White Zinfandel, which was the only thing my palate could tolerate at that time. I am "bitter sensitive," which means that the tannin in red wine is difficult for me, so Cabernets were out of the question. So I came at wine very slowly. First the White Zinfandel then maybe Chardonnay and maybe a Riesling, which is a little sweeter, and so on before my palate finally progressed.

After my gig was up with the PhD—I had finished my course work and entered that strange world called ABD [all but dissertation] when I finally decided psychology wasn't for me. I got a job as the academic administrator in the mathematics department at Stanford. While working there, I found myself fleeing north on the weekends, usually to Sonoma, rarely to Napa. Sonoma for me was real country and bucolic in a way that Napa wasn't, although now that I live in Napa I see it differently. I found myself having these great experiences visiting different wineries, especially the small wineries in the Dry Creek Valley region. These experiences weren't just with winery staff, but with the tourists

Salonnier
Shawn Larue.

as well. I was having all these impressionable conversations with people who were perfectly at ease talking about the magic of wine and conversant with all those delicious terms associated with wine—"bottled poetry" and such. These were not drunken conversations.

This was 1996, when I was thirty-two years old. I'd return to Stanford from these great weekends and be back on campus dealing with graduate students and staff and faculty from around the globe who sometimes had difficulty relating socially with one another outside the classroom. And I thought, hey, on Fridays I could create a social and bring together students and faculty in a more relaxed setting. I would get the faculty to bring wine and the students to bring cheese or bread. So we started doing these little wine social things, and they were a hit. I was starting to get the wine bug.

In 1996 I was on a date and we were at a restaurant in San Francisco, and I vividly remember feeling mesmerized by the color of the wine as it was being decanted. I'm sure that sounds strange, but I remember it as if it were yesterday. It was a Domaine Drouhin "Laurene" Pinot Noir from Oregon and I remember thinking—before I'd had anything to drink—that I had never seen anything so intoxicating. Ever since then, the color of wine has always been something I'm really tuned in to. Color is part of the sensory picture of wine, not something to overlook or take for granted. In fact, it's always something I try to impress upon the people who visit our winery. Anyway, it was at that moment that I realized I was in the wrong line of work. Around that time I had a back injury and had a disk removed, and while I was recuperating I decided to take a little trip to Europe. I was on a high cliff rising from the Mediterranean Sea, overlooking the city of Antalya in southern Turkey. It was my first sight of the Mediterranean, and something just clicked in me. I decided right there that I wanted to be involved with wine. I submitted my resignation [to Stanford] the next day. I was that convinced.

I was willing to go to Sonoma or Napa and do anything to be in wine. I sent out over forty résumés. I applied for jobs in tasting rooms; I applied for cellar rat positions. I was willing to do anything, but most wineries weren't interested. I had fairly good credentials but no experience in the wine industry. Then I caught the attention of someone at Niebaum-Coppola who thought I had "admirable enthusiasm," which he said was a major requirement for the job. I had a master's degree in social work and of course I'd had a job at Stanford, but really nothing relevant to wine other than my enthusiasm. Knowing the industry now from the inside, it is surprising that nobody responded, particularly considering how we go about hiring people here at Swanson. More often than not, we hire people from completely different industries, everything from high-tech to brilliant fashion designers to pastry chefs. We like refugees from other walks of life. In fact, that is what we look for. Sure, it's nice to have people with wine backgrounds, but we'd rather bring in a wider breadth of experience and enthusiasm like I had. But I guess most wineries aren't like us. The culture of hospitality here in Napa can be very one-dimensional.

So, I started in the tasting room at Niebaum-Coppola. I wasn't there long when my enthusiasm caught the attention of management. I think they saw that I clearly liked what I was doing and wasn't doing it just for a paycheck. So within a few months, I was given more responsibility dealing with trade. I managed to get some good notice from people who wrote letters back to the winery. Niebaum-Coppola Winery had opened a café in San Francisco and had ambitious plans to create another restaurant–wine bar in Palo Alto. I was asked to be the regional manager and help in the top-to-bottom development of "Café Niebaum-Coppola in Palo Alto." Ironically, this meant commuting back and forth from St. Helena to San Francisco and Palo Alto every day for months—the very thing I had sought to escape. I became totally involved in building the café and wine bar, but the whole experience was drawing me further and further away from wine. It was clear to me, and probably to them as well, that I was not a restaurant person. All I wanted was to do wine. So I left that position a month after the café opened, having had the life sucked out of me.

I felt I needed to reconnect to what brought me to the wine world in the first place, and to do that I decided to go to Burgundy [France]. It was the middle of winter, not the correct time to go in terms of doing tastings and meeting people. In fact, I tasted very little; rather, I simply went out each day walking and observing. It was their pruning season, so I was able to walk around and see all these families out pruning. I remember the air quality was horrible because everyone was doing controlled burns. Here in California we have regulations about how and when you can burn, but there was less of that in France.

Being in Burgundy reminded me of what I had been missing, and that was my passion and excitement for wine. During my time at Niebaum-Coppola I hadn't had time to walk in the vineyards because there was a restaurant to open, people to hire and, in some cases, people to fire—business to be done. Yet vineyards and wine were the things that grounded me. It's both the feeling of being connected to something that's growing and the visual symmetry of it all. The agricultural cycle of these grapevines connects me to the seasonal cycles of growth and rebirth. You might find it odd, but I think about that a lot. To me, that was always missing in my city life. In the city there is little sense of the change of seasons, other than it's raining or it's cold, and particularly so in San Francisco where the climate is so skewed, with summer being cooler than the fall. In the countryside each season brings different, predictable things. At some psychological level, you know when the harvest is over and winter is on the way. And you see the change much more clearly in the landscape. The grapevines become barren, the river rises, and there is frost on the ground. Because the changes are visual they connect with me and I'm able to make sense of them. One of my co-workers feels the same way, and we talk about it.

I have real personal difficulties when the weather starts to get colder, and there is no growth on the vines. My mood just goes into the tank and my melancholy goes up. Equally I am aware that when the fava beans, legumes, and mustard—cover crops—bloom and the cherry blossoms emerge that we are close to spring and my mood goes dramatically up. I think my mood improves naturally as it gets lighter and the days get longer. I've probably always been like that, but I didn't always understand it. Living in the city I just knew "I feel really depressed in winter." But I didn't really understand its causes. Up here in Napa I have connected the dots.

Anyway, back in Burgundy I decided that when I returned to California I would absolutely not go back to a big winery. I needed to be in a place where I felt a kinship with the culture and very close to what we were doing—making fine wines. I applied for a few jobs, and Duckhorn, a wonderful winery, offered me a position in their tasting room. The pay rate was a little bit alarming, a lot less than I had been making. It was going to be hard to come down, but then I reminded myself that two years ago I was willing to work for any pay just to be in wine. Still, it was difficult to put my money where my mouth was. While I was considering the Duckhorn job, I saw this little job ad in the newspaper. It was Swanson Winery and their idea was to create a tasting room in the tradition of an eighteenth-century Parisian-style salon. It would be a place where people with a serious interest in something, whether it be philosophy, literature, fashion, or fine wines and food, would gather under one roof and at the direction of an inspiring hostess or host indulge their interest and increase their knowledge. To me the concept was fascinating, but the job ad didn't give any details.

I called, and fortunately they invited me in for an interview. I was just on the verge of saying yes to Duckhorn when I walked into Swanson's salon. As you walk through those doors, you are surrounded by the most exquisite accoutrements and artifacts and whimsy and a burst of pink coral. The very first thing I saw, no kidding, was these old Burgundian wine vessels that said Clos de Vougeot, Gevrey-Chambertin, and other names of historic wine districts in Burgundy. I mentioned to the person that I literally had just been there, in those very villages in Burgundy, just last week. It turns out they had been interviewing for quite some time and hadn't found the right person.

Later I learned that they saw in me someone who understood the salon concept. I'm sure it showed that I was clearly in awe of this beautiful room and its splendid furnishings and décor. My interview with Alexis Swanson had little to do with whether I knew how to conduct a wine tasting. We talked for nearly two hours about all manner of things, and just a little bit about wine. She asked me questions like, "Where do you eat?" "Where do you go?" "Who do you give your loyalties to?" Looking back, I now understand that these are the important things to her. It wasn't what wine industry experience I'd had but rather did I have familiarity with Cipriani, Hermès, Chanel, and other luxury brands that were innovators in their industries for generations. Alexis was looking for a certain level of sophistication because what we do here at Swanson is not just about the wine. The wine speaks for itself. It's beautiful wine, all of it, and I don't need to spend time talking about how it shows bright cherry and has the nose of fig and melon, or that it is rated such-and-such by Robert Parker. I'll certainly discuss that at the salon if it comes up, but more important is being able to entertain eight strangers around a table for an hour, some of whom aren't quite sure how to pronounce "Merlot," or are wondering what I think of Two-Buck Chuck, and next to them might be others who want to talk about how spectacular the 2000 Bordeaux vintage was, and want to discuss trellising techniques and biodynamic viticulture. It is not unusual to have all of those things come up at the same table. Alexis Swanson's interest was in finding someone who could make that whole complicated group dynamic work, and do it so that nobody felt left out.

Do you give visitors a tour?

We don't offer a tour. Our view is that by the time people come to us, they've seen their share of catwalks and steel fermentation tanks. And if they haven't, and they want to know about the wine-making process, I'm happy to talk about it. But mostly we feel that the people coming here, and paying $55 per head for the experience, are looking for more than the usual tour and tasting. Personally, I have no interest in going on a tour for the umpteenth time. Swanson is very much an experience. This will sound like I am boasting for us as a winery, but I do believe that we offer the finest, most personable experience in the Napa Valley. The paradigm that we have set is to take exquisite care of everybody who walks through our front door. That's our principal priority. Yes, we are going to be showing our wine, but most important, we want our guests to leave feeling like they just attended a small party in their honor. If we do that, the wine will sell itself.

I greet every guest out front with a glass of rosé. My first technique is to look at each person: "How do you do, my name is Shawn."

"Hi, I'm Jim."

"Hi, I'm Dorothy."

"Jim and Dorothy, it's so nice to meet you." I'll just say it once, solidly in my mind so that I can remember the names. With a group of eight, it's easier to remember their names if you have couples rather than singles. And it's a little easier if they arrive a few at a time. Then after everyone has assembled, I take them inside and have them sign our guest cards, and introduce them to my colleagues, Hilary and Holly. I want to include everybody. I want them to feel like they are coming in to meet all of our family; I even want them to meet all of the dogs. The dogs are part of the scene, and on any given day there could be several canine co-hosts. "Here's Tallulah. Here's Lita, and this is Jean Laffite. This old man is Harvey."

As soon as I can, I go back into the kitchen and quickly write down their names and where they are from as a way to remember. So midway through the tasting I can say, "Dorothy, you're from Des Moines; what are your feelings about this style of Chardonnay?" People always want to feel they are heard and that they genuinely matter. So Dorothy may be charmed that I remembered her name and that she's from Des Moines. I'm *not* always successful with this;

and I'm always disturbed when I've failed to do it. But I can tell you, to get it right is beyond meaningful.

We get a spectrum of visitors, including some who are on their first trip to wine country, and even a few who are only here because their wives dragged them along—they'd rather be out drinking beer or playing golf. I try to get a quick gauge of the level of experience of the group. You get little clues, like what they say or where they've been. If their itinerary for the day includes a private tasting with Rick Forman or Nils Venge or a visit to the Brown Estate, you know they've got some wine background. Versus somebody who is up here for the first time and they've been on a standard tour at Mondavi and then went to Niebaum-Coppola. There is absolutely nothing about the experiences at Niebaum-Coppola and Mondavi that is substandard, nothing at all. It simply gives me some general clues as to this guest's familiarity with wines from our region.

If they're not wine savvy, I know that I can't be slinging jargon around. I'm not going to talk about malolactic fermentation as though everybody knows what I'm talking about. Instead, I might say, "One of the interesting things about our Chardonnay which makes it so appealing is that it doesn't go through malolactic fermentation." Then I'll stop and say, "By the way, is everybody clear about what malolactic fermentation is?" And interestingly, even those who might know may say, "Yes, but I would love to hear it explained again." And there are many, of course, that have no idea what it means. This allows me to explain not only a concept that guests can actually taste during their visits to various wineries, but also why our wine is unique. I feel most fulfilled when guests have "Ah-hah!" moments, where some mystery has been unraveled for them. As I see it, my role is as ambassador for our brand, salesperson, but most importantly as a provider of education.

I'll try to use and explain terms that they may come across in their own reading, in wine journals or in the wine section of the *San Francisco Chronicle* or *Wall Street Journal*. Terms like "New World Chardonnay," "Old World Style," and *"terroir"*—a term you hear all the time now. There's always an opportunity to educate. I'll try to ensure that everybody, no matter their background, gets it. Usually if someone asks a question like "What's *terroir*?" I'll first ask if anyone at the table can explain it. If somebody offers, I say, "Great, Sam, please have a crack at it." It's not unusual for me to hear new and insightful explanations, and honestly confess: "Sam, that is so much better than I could have explained it." And I might just then say, "And there's another part to it also, and that includes this." The more I talk to them, the more likely they are to ask me why I'm no longer doing social work. I jokingly say I still am. I'm working socially, I'm just not taking my clients' problems home with me at night and suffering over them. My job requires a lot of active listening, and that gives visitors a more complete experience—a human experience. We provide a wonderful little place to sit for an hour with great wine. It's much more an experience than anything else. It can be magical where there is a lot of social exchange and mixing, sometimes even hooking up later for dinner. That's wonderful, I love to see that.

What are your visitors like?

I can easily tell if I've got a table of southerners—like people from New Orleans, Savannah, or Charleston—as there is a certain style and display of social grace. And I don't mean this to apply only to the upper-crust society, but it's an observation generally of salon visitors from the South. You hear a lot of "Ma'am" and "Yes, sir." It's also been fascinating to see tourists with new wealth, and I've seen that a lot in Texans.

We see a disproportionate number of visitors from places like Plano, Texas, and even more from Houston. There seem to be great concentrations of wealth in these places, and also a great interest in wine. When they come into *our* territory [Swanson], there's an interesting dynamic. In Napa, Cabernet Sauvignon is for better or worse the reigning king of grapes, and the conventional wisdom is that Napa Cabs are the most exquisite wines. Napa boutique and so-called "cult wines" are principally Cabernet Sauvignon. Well, some of these monied guests that I'm talking about, whether they're from Plano or wherever, are coming into wine as a new thing in their lives, a new avocation, and in coming to the Napa Valley they are expecting to explore a world populated exclusively by Cabernet Sauvignon because that's all they've heard about. Well, they arrive at our salon and the first thing that they get is me, a guy dressed equal parts Paris and San Francisco with splashes of wine stains, with a very friendly dachshund, presenting them with a chilly pink wine (Rosato or Sirah). You can see the raised eyebrows, and I can hear what they're thinking: "Oh, it's one of *those* wineries." Then they come inside and there are the pink coral walls. They're in our pink, decadent, but whimsical kingdom. It's especially interesting to see how someone who wants to present himself as the expert in his group sizes all this up. I am saying "he" because this applies almost entirely to men. In his mind, what he knows is that Cabernet is king, yet he is being served the redheaded stepchildren that get kicked around in popular culture: Pinot Grigio, Rosato, Merlot, Petite Sirah, Sangiovese, and a host of critically acclaimed dessert wines. Of course, we also have the elegant and beautifully complex Cabernet Sauvignon; ours is called Alexis. It's wonderful to see the transformation taking place in minds conditioned to exalt Cab and only Cab. At the salon, they've enjoyed Pinot Grigio with caviar on a potato chip, rich Cab-like Merlot paired with Mimolette Vieux cheese, and others before their lips ever get to our Cabernet. Seeing a closed wine mind open is a frequent Swanson salon outcome.

I see that raised eyebrow, too, when out front I'm presenting that chilly pink wine in a stemless Riedel glass, which is very casual, like a tumbler. If it's not the raised eyebrow, I can sense the energy. If I'm on, I am happy for that because that's my challenge. I can almost directly translate that raised eyebrow into what's going to happen at the table. Usually he'll have the social grace not to say it directly, but what he is thinking or would like to say is, "You're not really a serious winery. It's all very nice, but there's really not serious wine here." I take that on directly as an enthusiastic challenge. My job is not to confront, obviously, but to try to draw him out of his comfort zone, to sort of seduce his palate with seriously delicious wine that is not only Cabernet. I ask, "What is it about Cabernets that you really enjoy? Is it the forceful tannin? Is it the taste of the grape? How about ratings?" Let's talk about ratings. Sometimes, somebody like this will talk for fifteen minutes about how Robert Parker or the *Wine Spectator* rated this and that. He will try to enlist other people at the table into his view, and the particularly frustrating part for me is when he starts saying to the table, "Well, you need to go over to this or that winery. If you can get your hands on their wine, you're golden." Now, I'm thinking to myself—as I curse under my breath—"We've got to bring this back to Swanson. We are *here*. People are paying for this, and people want to know about us. They're *here* for a reason." But how to tell this person to stop being an imbecile, and please recognize that you're in a social situation. That's my challenge. That type of individual can come from a lot of different corners, but at the risk of overgeneralizing, our great friends from Texas and other bastions of new wealth have their fair share.

At the table, I want people to ask questions. I tell them right away to liberate those questions. I say there is so much mythology and downright fiction about wine that "I can promise you the unasked question is the one everybody wants to have asked and answered." Interestingly, people will almost always say, "I know this is a naïve question, but do you add stuff like cherries or currants to get these flavors into wine? Do you put oak chips in the barrel? Do you use some kind of butter extract or some sort of oil that gives the impression of butter in a Chardonnay?" Or they'll say, "I know this is a really naïve question, but what is the difference between Merlot and Cabernet? Can you tell by putting a grape into your mouth what the wine is going to taste like?" Those questions come up over and over and over again. And they're all wonderful and important questions, and they are all opportunities for education and opening people's minds. Of course, you also get questions from people who are simply asking not because they earnestly want an answer, but because they want to be heard and to display their erudition.

Overall, it's only a small percentage of our guests that grasp everything we are trying to do. We'd love to see that number grow. I've noticed that our European visitors tend to really get what we're doing because it is not such a big cultural jump for them—and many, for instance, are familiar with the French Champagne salons.

At Swanson, we believe that winery hospitality has been missing the mark, that as American wine consumers have become more sophisticated and travel to visit wineries—some coming every year—they are tired of merely showing up at a winery, bellying up to the tasting bar three sweaty people deep, and having three wines poured for them with very little discussion. "Here is our Chardonnay. Here's our Zinfandel. Here's our Cabernet . . ." You know the model. I remember this myself when I was coming up every weekend. Geez, I would jump at any opportunity to get in front of the winemaker. "Can I do a barrel sample? Wow." Getting a little bit behind the scenes was what I wanted. Wine tourists *crave* that. Today most tourists want a piece of what is beyond the bar, and they will pay for it. Frankly, that has been a part of our thinking here—introducing not just the many ways people relate to wine, but also how luxurious experiences are accessible in our world.

The Swanson family has given me a lot of latitude with hosting our visitors. I'll sometimes take them out and we'll pick a cluster of grapes to sample. During the crush I have them observe the fresh fruit coming in from the vineyard and being pressed. I'll have them put their glasses right under the tank, to get free-run juice. Sometimes I'll take them into the tank room and ask, "Who wants to taste the fermenting juice?" We'll taste and compare it to the final product. It's all very spontaneous; I don't necessarily have a plan to do that all the time.

In pursuing the goal of providing a better experience, we bring out some heavy hitters. We serve delicate wild American caviar. We serve exquisite cheeses and proprietary curried-chocolate bonbons, we open six or seven bottles of wine for each tasting, and we serve them in Riedel crystal. It's not cheap; in the end we break pretty much even on tasting fees covering the cost of producing our tasting experience. However, the salon model has been successful for us because it is engaging, educational, fun, intimate, and it connects our guests with several common denominators, notably wine as integral to the dining table. It is effective because it embraces the high with the low, and speaks to those travelers seeking the hidden gems in Napa's big jewel box. Equally important, our visitors have a chance to be heard, to be listened to. Just having somebody like me say to them, "Karen, that is a really wonderful question. It's something I've been thinking about myself"—I think people just love to feel heard and acknowledged. This is what we do here, and it's something that I really enjoy being a part of. I don't want to be behind a bar serving a mass of people. In what little wine tasting I do on my days off, I get antsy and nervous when I'm at a tasting bar and I'm trying to get the eye of the person behind the counter and there are glasses everywhere and there are drunk people. I now see a bar as a barrier. We could no sooner have a bar in our winery than we could allow someone to come into our tasting room without us first proactively going out and greeting them at their car—with a chilly pink wine.

I try to relate everything back to a lifestyle, meaning that wine is not just an accoutrement to a lifestyle, it is integral to it. Wine is a social lubricant around a table, not in the sense of getting drunk, but integral to a meal. I point out the contrasts in culture between European societies and ours, and where wine fits in. There's a stark difference, and I try to talk about that. I also try to get people to understand texture, the way the wine feels on the palate, rather than their getting frustrated trying to detect the flavor of fig or clove or cassis. When someone expresses frustration when they can't identify all these exotic fruit components and bizarre descriptions noted on a wine list, I'll say, "Me too! They say I should be detecting 'tobacco leaf, leather, and fresh highway tar amplified by toasty hazelnut and spicy clove,' and I'm happy to confess that all I 'get' is some cherry and a whole boatload of alcohol." I offer the theory that much of the palate's education comes only after tasting thousands of wines, which takes a lot of practice, a lot of tasting to get there. So I'll try to take the frustration away and emphasize instead what is more accessible. "How does this wine literally feel on your tongue? How aggressively does it grip your palate? Does it have good weight? Do you sense the acid? Is there a parting of the Red Sea in your mouth—'the tannic evacuation'—or are your gleakers ignited instead, as in the presence of acid? If you can sense the acid, then you're halfway home when it comes to thinking about pairing wine with food."

I think being a good wine educator goes back to my social work experience, and essentially that's the person I am. Alexis Swanson has been superb at reminding me that this job has been the perfect platform for me to be able to do what I am inherently good at. And she's been equally adept and generous at stripping away from me the things that I'm not good at, of which there are countless examples. Like I can be somewhat "time challenged" in the mornings and show up to work a bit or a great bit past the appointed time. And my patient colleagues will articulate, when coaxed cleverly, my numerous irresponsibilities and limitations. I also do particularly poorly dealing with intoxicated people. Now that might seem strange, and maybe I'm in the wrong line of work, but this is behavior that makes me deeply uncomfortable and even vulnerable. For one, I have to make a decision whether they are too drunk for me to pour for them. Actually that rarely happens. But when it does, you have to deal with the attitude—"What do you mean you're not going to pour for me?"—that sort of thing. And if I do pour, their behavior can be very unpleasant and spoil the experience for everyone at the table. Keep in mind, our table is a little community. So this one person's behavior dominates the table. When people have had too much to drink, they frequently ramble and aren't sensitive to the dynamics of the table or to their effect on everyone's experience. This, in my mind, is the toughest situation. Dealing with it diplomatically is where the rubber hits the road, where you really earn your money and retain your dignity and that of the Swanson family.

What is your daily work routine like?

The workday has seasonal fluctuations just as the vineyards and winery do. But taking a typical summer day, I usually arrive, shamefully, a few minutes late, around ten o'clock, even though I only live three minutes away. Our first tasting is at eleven o'clock, so for that first hour I am preparing the table— setting out glasses for six or seven wines with six different stems, lighting the candles, putting out the fine chocolates, cutting the artisanal cheeses that we put out with the wines. Then there is putting out the individual tasting card that shows the wines we are pouring that day. All of that takes us a full forty-five minutes. I try to be ready by a quarter till eleven, when people begin to arrive. We are pretty clear in our confirmation letter about being on time. I'll conduct the first tasting from eleven until noon or so. As I wrap up the tasting, I'll talk a bit about any special things we have going on in terms of wine selections, library, older wines, and finally our wine club. Our wine club, Le Club des Bons Vivants, is fundamentally important because it's the way people stay intimately connected to us, and frankly it's an important part of our direct-to-consumer business. So I'll spend the last five minutes just talking about the value and benefits to joining our wine club.

Once everyone leaves, we've got to prepare for the next tasting at one thirty. I've got my iPod or the stereo blasting, playing very inappropriate music loudly to get myself clear and ready to go for the next one. The third and final tasting of the day is at four o'clock. It is a step down in terms of the amount of wine we pour, and we don't serve all the cheeses, and there is no caviar. It's primarily about our core wines. By five fifteen all the visitors are gone and we're busy cleaning up, and with any luck we are out by six.

I'm always better at the first tasting. I'm a morning person and that is when I am most fresh. My most difficult is the middle tasting. Many people have just eaten lunch and sometimes have already had a lot to drink. They are just a little bit lethargic, and that must have an influence on me. I think you always pick up on the energy of the guests. We often talk about this work as a performance. It is like doing a play three times a day or teaching the same class three times a day. If you've ever done that, you know it's exhausting. But I also think being here at a family-owned winery makes it easier than being at a corporate winery where I would be just one of many servers behind the tasting bar.

Still, the work greatly impacts my energy by the end of the day. It's so intense—three groups and three hours of interacting and orchestrating every-thing—that by the end of it I feel like crispy charred toast. After work, I often don't have the energy to be social. It's not just an hour or two, it is sometimes the entire night. I am always in the process of evaluating whether I'm in balance or out. A really good thing for me after work is to take my dog, Tallulah, and walk in the vineyards. I used to have a motorcycle, and that was tremen-dous release for me. I don't participate socially much here in the valley. Every weekend and many weeknights people in the industry get together at social things—a winery doing an open house, a hospitality event, or just sitting at the bar at Bouchon. But the energy is often just not there for me to do it after a long day or weekend at the salon, which can feel as if I've just concluded a forty-eight-hour tequila bender through Tijuana.

Let me close by saying that what we do at Swanson is still quite fresh and original. There are now seated, private tastings at a few other wineries, and several whose hospitality model is eerily close to that which we created a decade ago. Still, there is simply no wine experience in Napa or Sonoma as kooky, crazy, exquisitely charming and which celebrates the marriage of high and low by making a luxury lifestyle easy and accessible to anyone. Swanson has raised the bar, no pun intended. In fact, we often host representatives from other wineries who come here because they have heard that what we do is the best of the best. Sometimes they're starting something new themselves and want to do a little market research. Already, there are several wineries that have created a Swansonesque kind of "salon" experience. We discovered one winery, locally, that had some representatives visit us and then opened up shortly after, and I'm not kidding you, a similar setup, right down to the eight-sided table, the wine-filled chocolates, the exquisite cheeses, and the same starting times. I know about imitation and flattery, but absconding with another member of the industry's cultural paradigm is personally troubling to me. Every winery has its story, and every winery thrives to the extent that they celebrate and articulate their unique story through their wines and presentation experience. For me it's been a great honor to be part of Swanson's still-magnetic ten-year-old salon experience.

Wine Tour Guide / *Don Partier*

"You've never worked a day in your life."

Touring the wine country in a limousine with an experienced tour guide has become a popular way for visitors to see the Napa Valley. A dozen companies and twenty small independent operators now offer limousine and bus tours. "Sit back and enjoy the most customized and safest method to tour and taste at multiple wineries," claims the website of Beau Wine Tours, one of Napa's largest operators.

We were cycling when we came across Don Partier sitting in a long black limo near Silver Oak Winery in Oakville, waiting for his clients to return from a tasting. We had already done several short interviews with different limo drivers and were seeking a good subject for an in-depth narrative. So, we stopped and asked the driver if he could recommend someone. He said, "You're looking at him. I am the dean of wine limousine drivers." We thought his claim a bit boastful, but as we began to talk, it became evident that Don Partier would make an excellent subject.

———

To understand how I became involved in wine country, you need to know first that I was raised in San Francisco in a French and Spanish family; one grandfather arrived from Strasbourg in 1907 and my mother's parents came from Córdoba, Spain. So wine was part of my childhood, diluted with water, of course. Many families in San Francisco, especially the Italians, made wine in their basements and sold it by the jug. I had a few relatives doing this. There were never cars in their garages, just barrels. It was pretty bad stuff.

After graduating from the University of San Francisco in 1966, I went to Washington, D.C., to work for the government as an intelligence analyst. I think some of my peers were impressed by my ability to pick out good wines and to organize wine-tasting parties. I certainly never thought of a career in the wine industry, but that would change upon my return to California. I suppose wine was in my blood. In 1970 I had one of those "eureka" moments. I knew America would someday become a wine-drinking nation—at the time the wine business was mostly confined to ethnic communities—and I apprenticed myself to a prestigious importer named Julius Wile who sold high-end quality wines and spirits in the New York area. I spent five years with Julius Wile and was exposed to the great wines of Europe. I visited vintners in France, Germany, and Italy, and I wrote a few articles about what I had seen and learned.

Don Partier.

One day I read in the *Wall Street Journal* that Nestlé, the chocolate people, had bought Beringer's winery in St. Helena. That was 1975, and they bought the whole package for just $3 million. I contacted them and they hired me as assistant marketing manager at Beringer. I have been involved in the wine business ever since. After ten years with Beringer, I joined Fetzer Vineyards to help grow that brand. In 1997 I went to work for a financial magazine called *Research*. It was different and stimulating, but after the dot-com bubble burst and the market took a tumble in 2002, the magazine hit hard times and I was looking for work.

I was wondering what to do with myself, when I saw—almost by accident —an ad on Craigslist for Beau Wine Tours. I signed on part-time and helped them with marketing, and taught their limo drivers about the wine industry. I even gave the drivers quizzes and exams. At that time Beau had five stretch limousines; they now have twenty-five stretch limos, four sedans, two stretch Hummers, and two thirty-four-passenger buses. For the five years I was there, their business grew between 40 and 60 percent each year because of the booming interest in wine and wine touring. I decided to get my own town car, so I am now working as a tour guide and traveling wine educator.

As I predicted years ago, the golden age of wine has arrived. Wealthy people who've made money in other endeavors have gotten into the business. They spare no expense to see their name on a wine label, buying the best French oak [barrels], the best centrifuges and presses from Switzerland, and doing whatever is necessary to make superior wines. People come from all over the world to visit northern California's wine country.

What kinds of people take limousine tours?

They are mostly middle to upper-middle class and mostly middle-aged. They have been to college, have some interest in wine, and are interested in seeing wine country. There's been an increase in the numbers of millennials [those born between 1977 and 1994] touring wine country. They have an interest in the lifestyle which some describe as "affordable extravagance." My thirty-year-old son, Jordan, recently bought a home and his first appliance purchase was a wine storage unit. We seldom get children on tours; maybe one in five hundred trips includes a child. Wine country is an adult playground. It's no fun for kids to watch people drink wine, and wineries don't do much to entertain them. A few provide crayons and coloring books to keep them busy, but that's about it. Some people return every few years and will request a specific tour guide. One couple from Arizona rents a home every June in Bodega Bay and hires me every year to take them on a wine tour. They usually invite a group of friends and relatives to come along.

Can you describe your routine?

My routine begins the day before a scheduled tour when I call my clients to find out what their interests are. Then I decide on an itinerary. All of my tours are customized. Some people only like drinking big bold red wines or what I call "fruit bombs." For them I will be sure to plan stops at Stag's Leap [Wine Cellars] and Joseph Phelps [Winery]. I get a few customers who know exactly where they want to go, so I don't have to plan an itinerary for them. They read wine publications like the *Wine Spectator* or one of the many books about the valley's wines or wineries and have already made a list of where they want to go. I make the winery appointments for them. These are usually people who want to add to their wine cellar and know exactly what they want. In this case, I act more as a driver, getting them from A to B with interesting anecdotes along the way.

For most clients, the day begins when I pick them up at their hotel or bed-and-breakfast and lay out the tour I have planned for them and explain why I think they will enjoy it. I always wear black shoes, a suit, and a tie. If it's really hot, I'll wear a vest instead of a jacket. And I always wear a pocket watch. My dress identifies me as a professional. Of course, when I'm in the car and talking, people know I'm more than just a driver, that I'm the pilot and will be taking charge of their day. I tell them that we are not going to visit large corporate wineries because they are often crowded and it will waste a lot of our time. I suggest instead that they discover some unique wines at smaller wineries they can tell their friends at home about. I often choose where they'll have lunch—often a picnic or a special panini salad luncheon at the cantina behind Tra Vigne [St. Helena restaurant].

On a fairly typical day, I leave my houseboat in Sausalito at about seven thirty in the morning to drive to Napa to pick up one or two couples at the Marriott Hotel. I take them first to Trefethen Vineyards. The vineyards come right up to the buildings so I'm able to take them outside and give my little wine seminar next to the vineyard, which I call "The Three Lives of a Vine." I talk about the planting of rootstock, grafting, and training and pruning the vines. At Trefethen the wine selections are excellent, and I recommend that they try a dry Riesling to start with. It's the only dry Riesling made in the valley, and it sort of invigorates the palate and allows people to get in the mood for larger more weighty wines. From Trefethen we go to Yountville, and I show them one of the most famous restaurants in the world—the French Laundry. I describe the food there, show them the garden across the street, and then take them to Jessup Cellars' tasting room one block away. Their winery is located on Mount Veeder. We don't go to the winery itself because that would mean thirty-five minutes traveling up curvy roads and then thirty-five minutes to come back down. At Jessup they taste ten mountain-grown wines which are very distinctive because they are dry-farmed, which means no irrigation. Without irrigation, vines are stressed, which produces some rich character. I brought an Englishman here once who said he was a blood relative of Queen Elizabeth. It was his favorite winery, and before I drove him back to the San Francisco airport we stopped at Jessup and he bought $1,700 worth of wine.

From Jessup, I take them to Cakebread Winery, where the wines are famous but a little bit pricey. If I have people from Florida, I take them to Sawyer Winery instead because Mr. Sawyer is from Florida. I sometimes take my guests to Elizabeth Spencer, a unique winery that buys small lots of grapes from different areas. For example, their Pinot Noir comes from Sonoma, the Sirah from Mendocino, and so on. You can taste all these different wines under one roof, which amplifies the experience and provides a good opportunity for me to discuss the elements of *terroir.*

At each winery, I take my clients into the tasting room and introduce them to the proprietor: "This is Mr. and Mrs. So-and-So from New Jersey or

Minnesota or wherever." Then I'll say to my clients something like, "These people make a really great Pinot Noir" or "You must try their Merlot." It's just a little introduction to the wines and the winery. I think it's distasteful and unprofessional when drivers just pull in and tell their clients, "The winery's over there. I'll be in the parking lot waiting for you." You should be more engaged with your clients. Once my clients are settled in the tasting room, I go back to the car, maybe take a short nap, or read *The Economist* or *Newsweek*. This is my downtime. But I also use it to get on the phone and make appointments. I'll call the next winery we're going to and let them know how many people I have in order to make sure that they have room for us. Sometimes I make reservations for lunch. I usually don't eat with my clients, but I often sit with them for a while and keep the palaver going. I've learned from years of doing this that good talk makes the day more enjoyable. Later, I'll have my own lunch while they are tasting.

After lunch I may take them to Beringer because at one thirty they have a cave tour. For $10 they can taste five wines and get to see the caves. I also give them a personal tour of Beringer and show them where my office used to be in the Shakespeare Room of the "castle" [Rhine House]. After Beringer we go to see Napa's new castle—Castello di Amorosa—a full-scale replica of a medieval Italian castle. It took Daryl Sattui fourteen years and $40 million to build it. He owns a popular winery in the valley which I don't visit because it's always so crowded. The castle puts me near Calistoga, and at this point we turn around and head south on the Silverado Trail, on the other side of the valley. The next stop is Silverado Winery, the winery that Mickey Mouse built—well, the Disney family was involved in building it. My last stop will be Stag's Leap or sometimes, depending on the clients, Regusci or Black Stallion.

With most tourism there are definite seasons. My business is at its height during the crush or harvest—mid-September to mid-October. Over the Thanksgiving and Christmas holidays it tapers off and it's very quiet in January, which is when I take off to Hawaii or Mexico for my own vacation. In February we get "snowbirds," people from Minnesota and Michigan who have not seen their mailboxes since November. They come to California despite it being the rainy season because to them a typical Napa winter with 55-degree days is absolutely balmy, and everything is so green here at that time of the year whereas back home everything is brown and gray and covered in snow. The real numbers of visitors begin to arrive in mid-May and then it's busy all summer long, reaching its peak during the crush.

During harvest the traffic can be really intense, so it's my mission to try to keep out of the traffic as best I can. I try to do that by heading north up Highway 29 in the morning and then crossing over and driving south down the quieter Silverado Trail in the late afternoon. It's no surprise that people don't like the crowds on the roads or in the tasting rooms. I've had people go into a tasting room, see too many people, and turn around and come out. That's why the trend for tour guides—unless it is a large group—is to take people to smaller, family-owned wineries where they can sit down and have a conversation, and maybe even meet the winemaker. That's the ultimate experience.

After the last winery, we continue down the Silverado Trail, take a right turn on Trancas Street and back to the Marriott Hotel, where we started. We've spent about six hours, visited six wineries, and have driven sixty miles—thirty up the west side of the valley and thirty back down the trail on the east side. I think most people come away having learned a lot, and they've also had lots of photo opportunities as well as lunch in a beautiful spot. Usually I've had a great day, too. I've met some nice people, I'm able to give them a little education about wine, and I've had a drive through one of the most beautiful spots in America.

Some of the most enjoyable experiences for me are taking around young couples where the gentleman has planned to propose to his lady in the vineyards or in a wine cave. One September I helped arrange a special lunch at O'Brien Estate. They produce wines named Attraction, Flirtation, and Seduction and often do special events for couples. My client and his lady friend enjoyed tasting the wines and reading the back labels. Then they had this gourmet picnic that included, of course, a bottle of wine. My client had sent me a poem he had written, and I had had a friend design a back label with it written in calligraphy ending with "Miriam, will you marry me?" You can imagine her surprise when she picked up the bottle.

I also enjoy taking young couples around who are on their honeymoons. For most people, a honeymoon in the Napa Valley is an unforgettable, lifelong memory. I also arrange wedding packages. Since Napa doesn't allow wineries to have weddings, I take people just over the county line into Sonoma, marry them there, and then bring them back to Napa. I've also had couples schedule their entire wedding, honeymoon, and everything around a reservation at the French Laundry, which is the only three-star Michelin restaurant in California. Most of the groups I take out are couples.

A fairly new development has been the high rollers who arrive on a private plane and have a limo waiting for them to take them to dinner with a winery owner or winemaker. They are planning to buy thousands of dollars' worth of wine and are typically just here for a day. I also do large corporate groups and wedding or bachelor parties. In this case, there is a bus driver and I'm the host, guide, and wine educator—the guy on the microphone doing a rap about the vines and barrels and vintages. Large groups can be difficult; people are sometimes abusive. For some reason, when people are in a large group they're less interested in tasting wine and more interested in having a lot to drink, in get-

Stone fence and vineyards.

Mumm Winery.

The Oakville Grocery has become one of the Napa Valley's tourism icons.

The French Laundry in Yountville.

Jean Dubuffet sculpture "Faribolous" at Clos Pegase Winery.

The interior of Caldwell Gallery on St. Helena's Main Street.

Ballooning over the Napa Valley.

Winning bidder during Saturday night's live auction, Auction Napa Valley
2009. Photograph by Jason Tinacci.
Courtesy of Napa Valley Vintners.

The valley and vineyards in autumn. *Photos by Vi Bottaro Photography.*

ting drunk—at least some of them are. They don't ask many questions either. Basically, you're just transporting them from tasting room to tasting room. My job on these trips often involves crowd control, making sure nobody gets too inebriated.

Bachelor parties can be hell. Tour companies have rules about the use of their limos and buses. Any client who vomits, for example, is obliged to pay a $500 charge to have it cleaned up. Clients know this in advance. Fortunately, it doesn't happen often. But when clients do get out of control—the moment someone vomits or there is a fight or they get thrown out of a winery—the limo or bus driver calls in and reports it to the office. He is then told to turn right around, and take them back to their hotel. That's it, trip over. It happens, but it's very rare. Most visitors are upstanding people with a genuine interest in tasting good wines and enjoying the beauty of wine country.

Most wineries don't like having big groups and some prohibit them. You've seen the signs outside saying "No buses." Nobody wants their tasting room suddenly inundated with thirty-five people or even sixteen people from a stretch Hummer. It changes the whole feeling in the tasting room. Suddenly there's a lot of noise, and many people thrusting their glasses at the wine hostess at the same time. I once saw two sixteen-passenger buses drive into the Frank Family Winery at the same time. The guys from the tasting room came out and said, "We can't handle this. One of you will have to go." The two drivers flipped a coin, and the loser left. The guys who only drive the buses with big groups get exhausted and can't work as many days a week as limo drivers do.

Most limo drivers are sixty-something and at the end of their regular careers, but like me they're not the retiring type. Beau Wine Tours has a driver who used to play bass guitar with Merle Haggard; he has a place in Sonoma and drives for them three days a week, and he's very content. Then there is a guy who worked for the *Wall Street Journal.* There's a schoolteacher who works part-time during the school year, but full-time during the summer. You can earn a decent living being a tour guide for a company, but younger drivers don't usually last long. Most of them want to move on to something bigger and better or else they want their own limo and to go out on their own.

As you drive tourists around the valley, what do they comment on most often?

The beauty of the valley and its intimacy, particularly up-valley where it's only a mile wide. You can stand on the parapets of Castello di Amorosa and look right across the valley to the hillside on the far side. It's really intimate. When I take people to choice spots, like Sterling, where they take the gondola up to the winery, they say the valley looks like a landscape painting. Of course, the visual experience is enhanced by the wine and glorified by the food. It all works together. Most people ask questions like, "What are those propellers out there in the fields?" [wind machines used to stir up air when there is frost] and "Why do the vines look different?" [styles of trellising and spacing]. I get lots of questions about the grapes and wines, such as why a wine tastes a certain way. I remind people that nothing is added to wine; it's simply grape juice but with complex flavors and aromas that suggest things like black cherry, chocolate, anise, and even weird things, like pencil lead, barnyard, and saddle. Actually, winemakers do sometimes add a bit of ascorbic acid, but nothing else.

A lot of Europeans say they feel like they are in the Land of Oz with all these wineries packed into such a small valley, each one offering an array of goods for sale in their tasting rooms. There's nothing quite like this in Europe. The valley is a lot more beautiful than many of them expect. But because it's difficult to ship wines home to Europe, they are not usually interested in buying; rather they just taste and try to absorb the whole experience of California wine country. Some are surprised by wine clubs, which are a new facet of wine distribution in America.

The people behind the tasting bar sometimes get a commission on what they sell, so there's an incentive to sell, which most are very subtle about, but not all. That's one reason why when I walk into the tasting rooms I just introduce my clients and then leave. I don't want to be involved. In many countries, drivers and tour guides get a commission for taking people into a retail establishment. There is not much of that in the Napa Valley, other than an occasional bottle of wine. Out of every hundred stops I make, maybe one proprietor will give me a bottle of wine and say, "Thank you for bringing these people in. Here's a bottle of my best red for you to enjoy." There's never an exchange of cash. Absolutely not.

Do many people buy wine during their tour?

I'd say about half the people buy wine. A few buy large quantities, not just two or three bottles but several cases. The average middle-aged couple probably buys about a case [twelve bottles] during the course of the day. A lot of them also buy some other merchandise from a tasting room or gift shop, like a poster of winery doors, a wine tool of some sort, or a book. It's usually something they can't get at home that will remind them of their trip. Sometimes I'm surprised at what people bring back to the limo, like a T-shirt with mock stains on it that says "This is my wine tasting shirt."

Do you find any differences between the men and women on your tours?

I don't see much of a difference in their knowledge of wine, and both ask intelligent questions. One difference is that most women have a smaller capacity and will often share a tasting. More women also have favorite labels of wine that they want to see and taste: wines that people have told them about or that they've read about. These days every newspaper seems to have a midweek food or wine section and there are wine columns in many magazines. Even *Newsweek* now makes wine recommendations in every issue. There is a trend toward what I call "girls' day out." These are groups of mostly middle-aged women who are celebrating a birthday or else reuniting ten or twenty years after graduating from college. They lease a limo and celebrate their friendship with some fine wine and food and a spa session. There was a feature on television on *Good Morning America* a couple of years ago about groups of women going out on a wine tour followed by a mud bath and massage. The program claimed this was the number one best outing for women who wanted to spend time or celebrate together. I offer a specialized tour called "Women and Wine." I take my clients to wineries that have women winemakers or that are owned by women. I also offer a "Ghost Winery Tour" which visits wineries that were abandoned during Prohibition and later resurrected. Most are impressive, century-old stone structures. But my most popular specialized tour is "Hollywood in the Napa Valley," which visits places and wineries associated with films like *Walk in the Clouds* and *Pollyanna* or with filmmakers like Francis Ford Coppola's Rubicon Winery and the Frank Family Winery.

How much longer do you plan to work in tourism?

I am in my mid-sixties now but I hope to do this job for at least another ten years. I love what I do. I can't see completely retiring while I'm having so much fun showing interesting people around the Napa Valley. I took Jack LaLanne around and he's in his nineties. I take all sorts of interesting people around—doctors, hedge fund managers, celebrities, the full gamut. I took Jessica Simpson and her then husband around for three days while they filmed the last of an MTV series called *The Newlyweds*. Later, I got a call from the singer Luis Miguel, who wanted to take the same tour; he brought Melka, a television personality from Ecuador. I like interacting with people and I can tell stories and anecdotes all day long. It's always satisfying when people enjoy hearing your stories. The only complaints I've ever gotten about my tours came from two groups of younger clients who thought I talked too much. I was just trying to be professional, to give them a lot of information as I always do, to keep the time flowing, keep them entertained, but they thought it was too much. I have two younger brothers and they're both retired, although one—a retired high school principal—is now working as a wine steward in a specialty shop in Reno. He's discovered that everybody loves to talk about wine and he's gotten immersed in it himself. His last comment to me was "How long have you been doing this wine stuff?" I said, "Over forty years." Whereupon he replied, "Then you've never worked a day in your life."

6 / *Food and Fine Dining*

The French Laundry / *Chef Thomas Keller*

"This is where I want to be."

Thomas Keller is the only American chef to have two Michelin-ranked three-star restaurants: the French Laundry in Yountville and Per Se in New York. His restaurant career began humbly as a dishwasher at the Palm Beach Yacht Club, where his mother managed the restaurant. During the summers he worked at several restaurants in Rhode Island and met Chef Roland Henin, who hired him to cook the staff meal at the Dunes Club hotel. It was in this difficult position—"low man in the kitchen hierarchy"—that Keller discovered his real desire to cook and began learning the fundamentals of classic French cuisine. Several years later he went to Paris on a self-designed apprenticeship in several Michelin-starred restaurants.[1] In 1984, at the age of twenty-nine, he returned to New York where he worked for several years before moving to Los Angeles in 1990, where he became executive chef at the Checkers Hotel.[2] It was on a visit to the Napa Valley in 1992 that he discovered the French Laundry.

Today Thomas Keller is the epitome of the "modern chef" that he discusses in his narrative: entrepreneur, author, and celebrity—the latter a characterization which makes him a bit uncomfortable. He has received many accolades, including Best California Chef in 1996 and Best Chef in America in 1997. In 2007 Keller was appointed president of the American Bocuse d'Or team: "When Chef [Paul] Bocuse calls you on the phone and says he'd like you to be president of the American team, you say, 'Oui, chef.'" Taking on this task is also in keeping with Keller's commitment not only to fine cuisine, but also to mentoring the next generation of chefs.[3]

—————

It all started in 1992 after losing my job in Los Angeles. I was on a trip to the valley with my then girlfriend, who was a wine distributor. We were driving by what was then Table 29 and the chef there, Jonathan Waxman, was a friend from New York. It seemed like many chefs from New York were then migrating west; there were a couple in LA, including myself, and of course Jonathan in Napa. So I stopped by to see him. Jonathan knew of my situation and said, "Thomas, there's this great restaurant for sale up in Yountville called the French Laundry. It would be perfect for you." I thought, "That's interesting," and decided to drive by. It was closed that day, so the restaurant was dark but I walked around the property and just fell in love with it. The building and grounds resonated with me. It was magical. I felt an emotional connection to it right away. From that point on I said, "This is where I want to be." I wasn't thinking about the Napa Valley, about what it represents in California or in the States or in the world—about its wine-producing reputation. I was just thinking about the French Laundry: this little stone building on the corner of Creek and Washington streets. I called Don and Sally Schmitt [the owners] and said, "I am really interested in buying your restaurant." I came back up the following week, and we talked and negotiated on the price for about five minutes. I don't know how many people they had spoken to about purchasing the restaurant or if they had spoken to anybody, but they had a price in their heads and to me the amount they were asking seemed reasonable.

They were also looking for the right person to buy and they took a leap of faith with me. I was unemployed, not the first time. I had been fired from my job, not the first time. I didn't have any money, not the first time. I was considered to be a chef who was, to put it mildly, emotional in the kitchen. People who know the restaurant industry are familiar with the emotional outbursts that happen in restaurants, especially in kitchens. I was also known for not being able to control costs, whether in labor or food. But I was also a chef known for being able to cook really wonderful food, for being dynamic, and for being—pardon me for using the word "creative" loosely—for being creative. I did have that going for me. I'd had great reviews by the press and wonderful reviews by my employers and my partners. Nevertheless I thought, "This is my last opportunity." I was thirty-seven years old at the time and I felt that if this didn't work out, I'd have to move somewhere and just lie on the beach for the rest of my life.

So I put together a small package about the restaurant: my vision, my goals, what it meant to me. Bob Long [friend and vintner] invited me on a trip to Italy with a friend of his, and I took two copies of my proposal with me. I gave one to Bob and one to the other gentleman, and said, "Please read this. This is really what I want to do. You are both living in the valley and know the valley, and you can give me some advice about whether you think this is a good idea or not." The other gentleman said, "You know, this is the worst idea I have ever heard. Terrible! The restaurant costs way too much money. You'll never

THE FRENCH LAUNDRY

"OYSTERS AND PEARLS"
"Sabayon" of Pearl Tapioca with Island Creek Oysters
and White Sturgeon Caviar

SALAD OF ROASTED CAULIFLOWER
Sultana Raisins, Brussels Sprouts,
Almonds and Madras Curry

MOULARD DUCK "FOIE GRAS AU TORCHON"
Asian Pear Relish, K&J Orchard Chestnuts, Black Truffle
and Red Ribbon Sorrel
(30.00 supplement)

SAUTÉED FILLET OF JAPANESE MEDAI
Broccolini, Lily Bulbs, Niçoise Olive,
Pine Nuts and Navel Orange

"BOUDIN DE CUISSE DE GRENOUILLE"
Piperade, Country Bread, Meyer Lemon,
Fennel and Pernod Emulsion

"BEETS AND LEEKS"
Maine Lobster Tail "Pochée au Beurre Doux," King Richard Leeks,
"Pommes Maxim's" and Red Beet Essence

FOUR STORY HILL FARM "POULARDE KIEV"
"Lentils du Puy," Sugar Pie Pumpkin and Swiss Chard

MARCHO FARMS NATURE-FED VEAL
"Cœur de Veau," Tokyo Turnips, Chanterelle Mushrooms,
Nantes Carrots, Watercress and "Sauce Blanquette"

BEECHER'S "FLAGSHIP RESERVE"
Hobbs' Bacon, Romaine Lettuce "en Feuille de Bric"
and San Marzano Tomato Compote

PHILO GOLD APPLE SORBET
Poached Prunes, Apple "Croquette"
and Spiced Cider

"PEANUT BUTTER AND CHOCOLATE"
Maple Toffee, Chocolate Ganache
and Gros Michel Banana Sorbet

STRAUS CREAM "GÉNOISE"
Jacobsen's Farm Figs, Lemon Curd, Yogurt Streusel
and Fig Leaf Ice Cream

MIGNARDISES

PRIX FIXE 250.00 | SERVICE INCLUDED

6640 WASHINGTON STREET, YOUNTVILLE CA 94599 707.944.2380

French Laundry menu.

THE FRENCH LAUNDRY

SOY MILK SHERBET
*Tomburi, Navel Orange, Scallions
and Ginger "Nuage"*

"DÉGUSTATION" OF FUYU PERSIMMON
*Young Fennel Bulb, Pine Nuts,
and Aged Balsamic Vinegar*

MARINATED MATSUTAKE MUSHROOMS
*Rice Porridge, Edamame, Mizuna, Yuzu
and "Sauce Japonaise"*

JIDORI HEN EGG OMELETTE
*Eggplant "en Feuille de Bric," Garlic Confit,
Jingle Bell Peppers and Mint Pesto*

ROASTED SUNCHOKE ROYALE
Lobster "Knuckles" and Romaine Lettuce

YUKON GOLD POTATO "MILLE-FEUILLE"
*Petite Onions, Brussels Sprouts
and Caraway-Mustard Emulsion*

HAND-ROLLED CHESTNUT "AGNOLOTTI"
Celery Branch, Burgundy Truffle and Celeriac "Velouté"

"ROBIOLA TRE LATTI"
*Globe Artichoke, Broccolini, Olive Lavosh
and Petite Lettuce*

"QUICHE"
*Bleu de Laqueuille, Oregon Huckleberries,
Pickled Cauliflower and Port Wine Reduction*

WHITE VERJUS SORBET
*Brown Butter "Financier," Spanish Peanut,
and Concord Grape*

COCONUT "MARJOLAINE"
*Maralumi Chocolate Mousse, Almond Meringue
and Coconut Milk Sorbet*

"POIRE BRIOCHÉE AU GUÉRIDON"
*Dried Fruit Chutney, French Laundry Honey
and Rum Raisin Ice Cream*

MIGNARDISES

PRIX FIXE 250.00 | SERVICE INCLUDED

be able to do what you want to do. You'll never be able to be successful in the valley." And Bob said, "I think this is a great idea." And of course I listened to Bob. From that point on it was determination and my strong desire that kept me motivated every day. Every day I woke up with this knot of anxiety in my stomach, wondering how I was going to raise the money to buy the French Laundry. My biggest asset during this whole period was my ignorance. Had I known in the beginning what I was getting into—all of the hurdles, all of the challenges, all of the frustrations, all the anxiety, all of the failures that would come with it—I would have said to myself, "This is impossible. I'll never be able to do this."

Then I was on a quest for the next eighteen months to put together enough financing to buy the restaurant. For eighteen months I got up every morning, filled out applications, wrote letters, did whatever I had to do to make sure that I was going to be able to buy the French Laundry. I certainly felt miserable at times: when you are standing at the end of an aisle in a grocery store trying to peddle olive oil to people who don't understand why they should spend $20 for olive oil just so you can make $20 for that day;[4] when you are going to an ATM machine every night and borrowing money just to pay your attorney. I made a lot of cold calls trying to find possible investors. Some days I woke up with a list of ten names: "Do you want to invest? Do you know somebody who would?" Every day I just tried to do a little bit better than I had the day before. As it turned out, we obtained a real estate loan from the Bank of America in St. Helena. I also found forty-eight people who signed checks to become private investors in the restaurant. With so many investors, no one would lose a lot of money if we failed and no one could tell me what to do. When I remember it now, it was really a wonderful experience because it set the stage for who I am today and how I run my business. When I was living it, it was something else.

The French Laundry opened in July 1994 and lost money the first six months. Our first full year, I think we made $6—we broke even. But since then we have been on sound footing. The past fifteen years seem like a blur, as something that passed just like that. On the other hand, if I look back on individual events or the experiences I've had with certain staff members, it seems like it's been a lifetime. It's certainly been rewarding, and it's because of the people: not only the individuals who were involved in helping me acquire the restaurant, but also those who supported the philosophy behind it, which still is to do a little bit better than we did the day before. Seven or eight years ago I was sitting with a chef friend from New York who had just finished his dinner. I don't sit very often in the dining room, but it was the end of the night and I sat with him for a few minutes. Then I said, "Excuse me, I have to go back into the kitchen." "It's one o'clock in the morning," he said. "Aren't you done?" I said, "No, we have to write the menu for tomorrow." He looked at me, kind of puzzled: "What was wrong with the menu you had tonight?" That kind of stopped me in my tracks. "I don't know, there was really nothing wrong with it," I said. "We had a really great menu tonight. But that's not what we do. We challenge ourselves every day and rewrite our menus, rewrite our scripts. We always want to improve." At the end of each night, the chefs sit down together and talk about the menu for the next day. From the beginning there has been a real sense of collaboration and a commitment to evolution.[5]

There is no such thing as perfect food, only the idea of it. The real purpose of striving for perfection when you cook, besides taking pleasure yourself, is to make people happy—to make a difference for the people who come to our restaurant. Food is very important to people. Traditional foods stir memories. A food like a roast chicken or even mashed potatoes has reference points to moments in your life that have touched you inside. But there is also intellectual cuisine: cuisine that you may not have reference points to, food that you may never have tasted before. If you taste a strawberry dipped in some strange spice and hold it in your mouth for ten seconds and drink a liquid for fifteen seconds and then ask yourself, "Do I like it?" You may or you may not, but you can't say that it's "good" or "bad" because you don't know. You've never tasted it before. This kind of food stimulates thought, a process in your head. At the end of a meal at the French Laundry your hunger is completely satisfied and so is your intellect.

Every new generation—whether it's in art, music, fashion—every generation has new ideas and this is what is going on with food today. My approach is to give the diner many different experiences but to focus on specific flavors or combinations. I want people to experience surprise with each bite and to pique their curiosity. So I serve nine to twelve small courses. I want them to taste just enough to say, "That was so good; I wish I had one more bite." Each plate is a different experience, a different flavor and feel. I isolate flavors and enhance them, either by making them more intense than the foods they come from, or by varying the preparation technique. When I make liver and onions, I might roast a whole foie gras and serve it with four different onion preparations—confit, roasted, glazed red, and glazed white. To achieve the effects I want, I serve courses that are small relative to most restaurant portions but perfect quantities. Some courses must be small because of what they are: a quail egg is small and one bite is enough.[6] With foie gras, truffles, and caviar, however, I serve slightly too much because I want people to know what these foods are all about.[7] People may only have eaten them in stingy amounts before. I want them to be able to taste them and think, "Oh, now I understand."

I came to the French Laundry from an urban environment: New York and then Los Angeles. So had a lot of the other people who worked here in the early days, and we were used to having somewhere to go to eat after service. It was really a shock to us that when we finished service at the French Laundry at eleven o'clock, everything was closed. There was nowhere to go. Everything closed at nine o'clock. So we thought, "We need to open another restaurant so we have somewhere to go after work!" There are so many people in the hospitality industry in this valley. Whether it's the wine industry, the hotel industry, or the restaurant industry, there are just so many people, and I knew they were clamoring for places to go after work. So lo and behold, a little restaurant down the street from the French Laundry called the Fisherman came up for sale, and we leased it and opened Bouchon, a French bistro based on an urban design.

I went back to my memories of France and the small, family-run restaurants I had visited during my travels. When you go there, they'll put pâté on your table. You take a slice, and then they put it on the table next to you. There's a feeling of community; a place to gather socially. We opened Bouchon in 1998, and Jeffrey Cerciello and Joshua Schwartz, who worked for me at the French Laundry, became the chefs. For both our team and the Yountville community, Bouchon became exactly what we had hoped—a place for people to come together well into the evening to enjoy great food and one another's company. Now Bouchon has become my signature bistro, with outposts in other cities like Las Vegas and Beverly Hills.

We opened the Bouchon Bakery five years later, also because of a need. There are some wonderful artisan bread makers in northern California, but unfortunately none of them wants to make a piece of bread smaller than three kilos. We needed rolls for the French Laundry, multiple rolls, different varieties, and having them fresh—baked twice during services. The only way to accomplish this and control the quality of the bread we were serving was to open our own bakery. A benefit of opening the bakery was the retail store. Now when I go there, I see young children in the bakery and friends in the courtyard. It's become a gathering place—a communal environment—and it's a wonderful thing. I am so proud to walk by there in the morning and see people out enjoying themselves, reading the newspaper, chatting, talking. It has become a wonderful place for neighbors and for guests to come and have coffee in the morning, a sandwich in the afternoon, or a cookie in the evening. But it began in order to fulfill a need for the restaurant.

Chefs are control freaks. They need to be able to control everything that has to do with their restaurants. Cooking, no matter what level, is about two things: ingredients and execution. That's it. No matter what you are doing, it's always about the ingredients and the execution. If you can get a better ingredient than I can, even if you execute a little less well than I can execute, you'll probably be a better chef because of the ingredient. At the French Laundry we have worked very hard to acquire the best ingredients. We work closely with farmers. They are so important to what we do, and to the quality of what we do. Without them, chefs would be hard-pressed to have the stature they have now. I hope that the whole farm-to-table, farm-to-plate movement is really happening. My first concern is quality. We have our own orchards and our own garden. We have almost three acres planted today. The garden has evolved every year we have been growing it. What we grow is based on what the chefs are looking for. Tomatoes, of course, are always in abundance. Artichokes. We planted asparagus two years ago. We don't really need to grow it because the asparagus from the Sacramento delta is amazing and close by, but we do it because we like the interaction [with growing] and we like the knowledge that it brings. Our garden is not only about the vegetables and fruits that it brings our kitchen or about the food costs that it offsets—it is actually more expensive—it is education. It gives young cooks the opportunity to learn about asparagus and other foods.

I use local suppliers if the quality is there. If there's a local supplier of butter but it's not good butter, then I am not going to buy it regardless of its being local. It has to be superior. I don't define "local" as geographic distance. To me, the issue is quality. Geographically local food was more important before World War II than it is today because we have learned so much about the transportation of food and we are able to do it quickly and at a very, very high success rate. If I can get great lobsters from Maine every day at my back door, then for me that is a local product. Of course, there are a lot of implications in redefining *local* this way, especially today when we're talking about sustainability and carbon footprints.[8] These things weren't really buzzwords or concerns even ten years ago. But my definition of local is quality. When I support people like Diane St. Clair in Vermont whose butter is amazing, and buy Keith Martin's lamb and Ingrid Bengis's lobsters, I am helping give them a market. These are knowledgeable people, and if they don't have a market-place for their products then they are going to go out of business. Certainly Keith Martin in Waynesburg, Pennsylvania, doesn't have a geographically local marketplace for his product. I support him because of the high quality of his lamb but also because I think someone like Keith, who is farming sustainably, has a great opportunity to impact how we raise livestock in our country—the same thing with Ingrid and Diane. That's more of a concern for me, and I think it helps offset the carbon footprint I am leaving now. These people are really concerned about sustainability and quality and need to be supported.

We have to have respect for our food. When I worked in the kitchen of a small restaurant near Catskill, New York, I asked my rabbit purveyor to show me how to kill, skin, and eviscerate a rabbit. I figured if I was going to cook rabbit, I should know it from its live state through slaughtering, skinning, and butchering. He showed up with a dozen rabbits, hit one over the head, knocked it out, slit its throat, pinned it to a board, and skinned it in about five minutes. Then he left me there with eleven others. I had a hard time killing my first rabbit. It screamed loudly and broke its leg struggling to get away. It was terrible. The experience taught me a lot about respect for life and the sacrifice animals make for our benefit. Killing those rabbits was such an awful experience, I would never squander them. And I decided to use all my powers as a chef to ensure that those rabbits were prepared beautifully.

Is there anything that you would characterize as Napa Valley cuisine?

Where you have wine, you are going to have great food; there is just a synergy between the two. The Napa Valley is also the only place in our country that's really all about food and wine. That's why people come here. They are either sophisticated and already know about food and wine or they come because they want to learn about it. Either way, I think that the Napa Valley offers a unique experience for people who want to experience food and wine. At the French Laundry we're trying to establish the notion of a world wine list, representing all the great wines from different regions and countries around the world. Of course we sell more California wines because people come to the Napa Valley for California wines. We are in California; certainly that is something very special—an artichoke is much fresher in California than it is going to be in New York or Memphis. But there are other agricultural areas around the world that have wonderful climates for growing and the same opportunities we do to get quality products. It is really about quality. One thing that may be unique about our community is the percentage of really good restaurants we have. Everyone who lives in the valley should be really grateful that we have such high-quality restaurants. No matter what the format they're in—even the Mexican taco trucks—we don't really have bad restaurants. Wherever you eat, I think you'll eat well. You may not eat great, but I think you'll eat well.

You are wearing your chef's jacket; are you going to be in the kitchen today?

Every day. I don't take a day off. But I don't do what I did twenty-five years ago or even ten years ago. The whole point is being responsible to your restaurant, and part of that responsibility is understanding that you are not going to be able to keep doing what you have been doing all your life and that you need to find the people who will replace you. You need to challenge them and give them opportunities to learn and to take over. I was in the mix for thirty years. Then your knees start to go and you can't be on your feet for sixteen hours a day. So you pull away a little bit and you start to mentor. You give back to that young team so they can go on and do what you have done. This is what affords you a legacy. If you continue to do work beyond your [physical] capabilities, quality is going to diminish, and by the time you're done, you are going to be physically drained and the restaurant's reputation is going to be diminished. Why would you want to do that?

The one thing that bothers me the most about the growth that has taken place with my business and with my new roles is that you start to lose a personal connection with people. Even here at the French Laundry, I walk in and I am not really sure who everyone is because things evolve when I'm not here, things move on. We have a hundred people on staff. All of a sudden I am faced with "Who is this person?" And that bothers me because there was a time when I was as close-knit with them as they are [with each other] today. And the older I have become, the younger my staff has become. But I try to look at it from a big picture point of view. The fact that they are still as close-knit—regardless of my involvement—is really a great success for me. It brings me great gratification that our culture [at the restaurant] continues to place enormous value on community spirit and we take care of each other. Our chefs [at the French Laundry; Ad Hoc, Keller's third restaurant in Yountville; and Bouchon] also have a sense of community—we are all in the same area so that makes sense. But we don't seem to have the same degree of community among chefs in the valley as I experienced in New York. I am not saying that it is purposely not done here. I just think we are all really busy, and maybe it's because we are spread out more.

What is your relationship to the Yountville community, which, as you know, is sometimes referred to as Kellerville?

I think the community has mixed views of me. Some people love me and some people really don't like me. It's like anything or anybody who becomes a personality. I don't really consider myself a celebrity, but there are always people who resent what you've done and who don't want to support you. Fortunately, there are also people who are very thankful for what you've done and who do want to support you. When I first moved here and took over the restaurant, I had some real conflicts with my next-door neighbor across the street, but over the years we have become friends. Some people you can win over, some you can't. I think it is important to do community-minded things. I pulled together people from as far away as Quebec to donate materials and equipment to rebuild the Little League concession stand because the town wasn't willing to fund it. We have an open house for the community at Christmas here [at the French Laundry] and we do Bastille Day at Bouchon. But it's like life, you can't win over everybody. And if you try, you're just going to be spinning round and chasing your own tail. You really have to establish your values and your goals and go after them. The people who share them will support you and the people who don't, won't. When my friends say "Kellerville" to me, it's with humor—it's a joke. But other people say it with a degree of malice, like "Keller! He thinks it's Kellerville." It's really irrelevant to me. George Yount, our founder, is buried in our local cemetery, and it couldn't and shouldn't be anything else but Yountville.

My career is my life, so living in the Napa Valley brings me satisfaction personally as well as professionally. I spend two-thirds of my time here. The valley has changed extraordinarily in the sixteen years since I have been here, but we still are an agricultural preserve—therein lies our salvation. We have areas of commercial development, and I think that's fine. Some of the resorts—the Calistoga Ranch, Solage, or Bardessono here in Yountville, even the expansion of the Vintage Inn—are all in response to demand. I don't like everything I see in terms of design or architectural elements, but that is personal preference and I'm not a deciding factor in what aesthetics should be allowed in our communities. There has been so much prosperity in the valley which everybody benefits from, but you have people who are naysayers—"We like it the way it was before." There is this whole sense of nostalgia. But my house was a crack house at one point. Do people really want to go back thirty years to when there were crack houses and vacant buildings and the place was a mess? Do people want unpaved streets? Is that what we really want? Are we really against the prosperity that we have experienced because of development and demand, because people are excited to come and see us? The whole nostalgia idea and resistance to change—of having this the way it used to be—is an interesting phenomenon. We always seem to be against what is happening, and I think that is an inherent problem in a lot of communities in the Napa Valley.

A woman called me years ago and said, "I am really upset." She was writing for the *St. Helena Star,* and she said, "I don't understand why we can't get into your restaurant! I am writing an article about accessibility, and reservations at your restaurant are full. We can't get in." I said, "Well, you have a choice. You can't get into my restaurant because people think we are doing a good job and they want to come, or I can start doing a bad job tomorrow so people won't come and then you can come any time you want." We're trying to establish an experience, and we're basing it on what we know we can do best, which relates to the number of customers we can serve. Some of our guests can get rude when the restaurant is full and they want a reservation. If there's a Broadway play you want to see, and you call up for tickets and they're sold out, I don't think you scream and yell or say, "You need to put another seat in there for me. Do you know who I am?" As much as we don't want to say no to anybody, sometimes our reservation book is complete.

One serious issue that tourism and development in Napa have created is the high cost of living that pushes a lot of workers out.

I understand it completely. It is a difficult problem that we face all the time. Between all of my restaurants, we have over three hundred people that work for us, and where do they live? Probably the furthest our employees live is American Canyon [about sixteen miles away]. About 15 to 20 percent, maybe more, of our staff live in Napa [city] and a large majority live between here [Yountville] and Napa or here and St. Helena. We supply as much housing as we can for our staff. Our chef lives next door. We have two houses across the street where we do affordable rents. We have three other houses in town where our staff lives. So we do what we can, but it is an inherent problem. Once again, everybody voices the need for affordable housing, but nobody wants it in their backyard. So at the end of the day, we are total hypocrites. The people that are yelling about it the most are probably the most hypocritical.

I opened Ad Hoc in 2007 largely because of this need. I had been trying to build an inn right across the street from the French Laundry, and one of the county's requirements for approval was to provide low-cost housing or employee housing. We didn't have a place to build it until the Wine Garden, a local restaurant, became available. We bought it right away because it gave us the space we needed to build low-cost housing, which then theoretically gave us the entitlement to our inn.[9] We ended up opening Ad Hoc there. It all happened in four weeks. The idea came up when I was sitting with my chefs at the end of service on March 31. After we had talked about our menu for the next day, I said, "Guys, we now have this restaurant down the street. What should we do with it?" So we talked and we all decided that a family-style restaurant would be a wonderful idea. I sent out an e-mail on April 1, 2006. I was just finishing work, it was two o'clock in the morning, and I sent an e-mail out to the upper management in our group [Thomas Keller Restaurant Group]. It said, "Let's open a restaurant here. We have this property. It can be a simple restaurant, four courses, no choice, simple wines, five days a week. Let's all have fun." Nobody responded. They all thought it was an April Fool's joke.

Ad Hoc was supposed to be temporary, because for the last fifteen or sixteen years I've wanted to do a hamburger restaurant. I was introduced to In-N-Out [West Coast hamburger franchise] down in LA, and I just loved that business model, but so far it had eluded me. I've never really had the opportunity, the time, or the focus to open my hamburger restaurant, and with the Wine Garden location I thought I now had the perfect place. But Ad Hoc became so popular that people were writing me letters, calling me on the phone, leaving me death threats, saying, "Don't ever change the restaurant." Some people said to me, "Thomas, you're such a genius. How come no one has ever thought about this kind of restaurant before?" And I thought, "Wow, that's interesting. What a selective memory people have." Because when I bought the French Laundry, that's what it had been. It had a four-course menu that cost $49.

Chefs today often have multiple restaurants. A lot of my colleagues do. I have nine, which just boggles my mind because I'm not the kind of person that really needs to have multiple restaurants. I like to do one thing, and I have already done it with the French Laundry. I still have the first car I ever bought. I have many things that I've had for a long time. But chefs today have the ability to go worldwide. All our developments in Yountville have happened for a reason: Bouchon because we wanted somewhere to eat; the bakery because we wanted to control our bread production; Ad Hoc because we needed a place to build low-cost housing and because I wanted a place to someday put my hamburger restaurant. I don't really think of anything that we've done in Yountville as expansion because it's right down the street.

The last generation of chefs had one menu, one restaurant, and one kitchen. For their entire lives they were dedicated to one menu. They didn't change their menu every day, they changed it seasonally. They might work on specific items for months, for years, for decades to perfect them. Their restaurant was their home. The modern chef is somebody who has enormous opportunities because consumers or guests are that much more sophisticated, that much more knowledgeable, that much more demanding. So we continue to become better cooks. We continue to develop better products. And we continue to have more opportunities to bring these experiences to our guests. The last generation of chefs seldom did the things we do today. The modern chef thinks about different things, like writing cookbooks, designing china, working on Hollywood films, being on TV.[10] I wrote *The French Laundry Cookbook* in the summer of 1997 with the help of Michael Ruhlman, who put my words on the page. It was an amazing experience—so many people worked on it. But I feel it is my book: it has my stories in it, my emotions in it, my recipes in it.

It has now sold over 450,000 copies. When you have a success like that, the publisher, the writers, the photographers, everybody says, "Let's write another book!" But I was afraid and apprehensive. I worried that the feelings and memories I had about that summer would be diminished. You know how it is to have a great experience, then you do it again and it's not quite the same. Plus I felt that I had said everything that I wanted to say when I wrote *The French Laundry Cookbook,* and it was finished, over. I couldn't say anything else. So for two years I really resisted pressure to write another book. Then one day I thought, "This is really stupid. Maybe it's kind of selfish." We have an opportunity to write a second book. I have a publisher and an editor, but more importantly talented individuals who are more than willing to write the book. My name is on the cover [of *The Bouchon Cookbook*] because the publisher needs to have that, but it's really chef Jeffrey Cerciello's book. There are stories in there from me and my voice in there, but it is really about Jeffrey and his work. And now we have another book out [*Under Pressure: Cooking Sous Vide*]. Again, it's not my book. It's Jonathan Benno's, the chef at Per Se [in New York], Corey Lee's, and Sebastien Rouxel's.

Jonathan came to me one day and yelled, "Chef!" He does this all the time when he wants to get your attention. "Chef! We have to be the first to write a book about *sous vide* ['under vacuum'] cooking," he said. This time I said, "Okay, have at it. We'll get Corey [Corey Lee, then executive chef of the French Laundry] involved." So Jonathan, Corey, and I sat in a hotel in Berlin while we were on a trip and mapped out the entire book. We got Sebastien [Sebastien Rouxel, then head pastry chef at Per Se and Bouchon Bakery in New York] involved a couple of months later. The book is really Sebastian, Corey, and Jonathan's cookbook. I feel immense pride when I look at it. It is written for professional chefs about a new technique that's taken hold in our kitchens called *sous vide* cooking.[11] The basic technique was actually developed in the 1930s by Hills Brothers here in San Francisco to keep their coffee fresh, and in the 1960s a company named Cryovac began processing turkeys and freezing them. Before this technique became available, you didn't have turkeys in grocery stores year-round. What Cryovacing does is extend shelf life and the freshness of products by eliminating oxygen and the potential for bacteria growth. Remember "boil in the bag"? It was introduced in the late 1960s and early 1970s, but it didn't become popular because chefs weren't doing it. There was nobody leading a movement.

Today, *sous vide* technology and cooking is becoming extraordinarily popular with chefs because of the control it gives them and the intensity of flavors it produces. We know that vegetables cooked *sous vide* are more flavorful because the flavor doesn't leach into the water, and we know also that all vegetables need to be cooked at 83 degrees Celsius. If it's 82.9 degrees and you put a carrot in a *sous vide* bag and put it in the water bath, it's not going to cook. It could be in there for days, for weeks, and it's still going to be crunchy. But at 83 degrees it cooks. For chefs, it's all about control. We cook a rack of lamb at very specific temperatures, for very specific amounts of time, which allows us to be consistent and that's very important for us. With *sous vide* we can put a rack of lamb in a 58.5-degree water bath for 30 minutes and it's going to come out medium rare every time. This could create problems because as chefs we "cook" and if we are not cooking but using this technology, then are we losing our ability to be cooks? Here lies some danger. So when we think about using *sous vide* technology in our restaurants, we are trying to use it in ways that still allow us to be responsible to the craft of cooking.

Today's chefs are not just chefs, we are business people, entrepreneurs. We are here not only to give our guests a great experience, which is important, but to have great experiences ourselves and to give those experiences to our staff. If we are happy, if we are in an environment that is productive, if we are in an environment that is challenging, if we are in an environment of encouragement—one that continues to afford opportunities to the next generation of restaurant and food people—we are in a position to leave a legacy. At the end of the day what you want to try to establish is a legacy that lasts beyond you. I think about Don and Sally Schmitt and what they started at the French Laundry that I am so fortunate to have today, and I know, one day, that I'll pass that restaurant on to somebody else and the legacy will continue, and therein lies the true meaning of success.

The Front of the House / *Salvador Aguilara and Josefina Gonzales*

"This is fine dining, so you need knowledge about food and wine."

Salvador Aguilara was twenty-two when he arrived in Napa in 1992 from the small city of Valle de Santiago in Guanajuato, Mexico. He moved into his aunt and uncle's home, where one of his brothers was already living, enrolled in the English as a Second Language (ESL) program at Napa Valley College, and began working in the first of several restaurants. Like so many other recent immigrants who enter the restaurant trade, Salvador began as a dishwasher, working in two restaurants—the Red Hen Cantina and Ruffino's—while perfecting his language skills. He moved up to become a "busser" and later was promoted to waiter. He then worked at three other restaurants before starting at Étoile, Domaine Chandon's restaurant in Yountville.

Salvador's partner, Josefina Gonzales, left Mexico City a decade later, moving with her parents and brother to tiny Angwin (population 3,148) in the hills above St. Helena. She had been studying English in Mexico and resumed her studies at Napa Valley College. A neighbor introduced her to Salvador and through him she obtained her first restaurant job. She is just one of several friends and relatives he has helped to find restaurant work. They both starting working at Étoile in 2005 as back waiters (assistants to the wait staff) before becoming waiters.

———

Josefina. This is fine dining, so you need knowledge about food and wine. They trained us very well here; we had courses and tests. We have a meeting every day before shifts start so we can talk about food and wine. Usually it is about the new dishes we have on the menu. Or if something changed on the menu, like seasonal fruits and vegetables, we'll have a discussion about that. Whenever there is a new dish, they cook it up for us so we can try it and we know what to expect with it. I think we have tried all the dishes on the menu. If we need to refresh something in our memory, they will go over that. In other places I worked, it is more like you just take orders, but here you are required to be knowledgeable about food and wine and how they interact.

Salvador. Luckily, the chef and the winemakers suggest a wine to go with every single dish. That makes it a little easier for the guests and for us too. But

Server Salvador Aguilara inside Étoile's dining room.
Courtesy of Domaine Chandon Winery.

people definitely do ask for our recommendations, about 90 percent, because here we have mostly tourists. Tourists usually ask about the food, and about the wine, especially the women and the older people. If they ask me something, I just go, "Okay, what kind of food do you like? What kind of wine do you like?" Then I go in that direction. We are trained to always try to not recommend only one dish. It is all about reading the guest to see what they like. Sometimes they have already chosen two dishes, and they just ask us which we think is better, but by that time we already know what they want. People don't come here just to have a hamburger and head out to the wineries; they come here for the whole experience of fine dining. People spend two and a half to three hours at dinner. Even for lunch, an hour and a half would be average. When they come to wine country, they want to see what it's all about. They want to learn about the wine, about the food. And they are willing to learn from us. Even something as little as how to open a bottle of sparkling wine, they are like, "Wow. We are learning something new here."

Josefina. Some foods people have never tried before. When foam started, they were like, "Oh, my God, there is soap on my food." I would say, "It is not soap, it is just foam." That and the caviar that Poncho [pastry chef Francisco Enriquez] makes. He makes fruit caviar—it's the texture of caviar—and they go, "Caviar on my dessert?" It is like tapioca all made out of fruit, and they go, "Wow!"

Salvador. The guests ask about wineries. Most of them don't really want to hear about the big wineries like Mondavi. They want to hear about local wineries, family-owned wineries that they can go see and taste good wine. Tourists want to get to the heart of the Napa Valley. For locals, we are a special place for birthdays, and anniversaries. For special occasions this is the place.

Josefina. We get people from all over. Lately we have had a lot of tourists that are not from the United States: South Americans, Brazilians, a lot of Asians—Japanese, Chinese especially. Asian people are very, very polite. They are the easiest people to serve for sure. They never complain. Even if they don't like something, they are polite. Tourists from South America, they are so grateful to see us: "Oh, finally someone who can explain it to me." That is where it comes in handy to speak their language. Even when Brazilians are here speaking Portuguese, we can still communicate and they are grateful for that. One couple invited me to come to Brazil for Carnival. They gave me their card, telephone number, and everything and said, "Just come and visit." I have had people hugging and kissing me and I have had people who have sent me thank-you notes and bottles of wine: "Thank you so much for your service, here's a bottle . . ." You can actually make friends with some guests that come here. Sal [Salvador], remember the guy and his friends that come in all the time for lunch and buy all this very expensive wine and they spend like thousands of dollars? I was serving them one time, and they opened a bottle of Bryant Family Cabernet. I don't remember what year it was, '96 I believe. Well, this bottle was nice. So I opened it and I was pouring the wine for them. They are all guys, eight or nine of them. They were having fun, and they always talk dirty. And I was pouring the wine, and one guy said a dirty word and then he started to get all red in the face and he said, "I am so sorry Josefina. Here, have a glass." So he poured me a big glass of the Bryant Family and said, "Here. I am so sorry. Just accept my apology and walk away because we are going to keep talking about this." I said, "Okay, bye." So I got a great glass of wine by just hearing a dirty word. It was actually very funny. They were just having fun, talking among themselves and then I get a big fat glass of Bryant Family '96, which is very expensive. We all tasted it in the back [the kitchen].

In this place we work as a team. We divide the restaurant by sections, but we help each other all the time. It doesn't matter whose table it is; if they need something you provide it for them. We have a system for taking orders. We are required to write it down for the kitchen and there is always a copy posted on the board in our waiter's station, so you can reference that if you forget. You can't go to a table and say, "Who has the salmon?" You are supposed to go there quietly, place the food down, and leave. We always start with whoever is in seat 1. The person with their back to the kitchen will pretty much be number one on every table. So when we take the orders we count clockwise, one, two, three, and if we put a little circle on number two it means there is a lady sitting in this position. This is so we can get the food to the ladies first. We have to follow this system because the kitchen doesn't know which order is for a lady or a gentleman. They just see the seat numbers. If they see a circle, they say, "Oh, okay. The first dish goes there." We note it in the computer too: seat 1, lady seat 2. It doesn't always work, especially on big parties. Some food is going to be ready before others, so you can't let it sit there and get cold. If it is a big party, we just start going in order around the table so we don't mess it up. You can't stand there thinking, "I've got 1 and 17," and trying to count chairs in your head because it doesn't look nice.

If a guest asks for a server in particular, he will be seated in that person's section. People love him [Salvador]. They do, even though he has an accent and sometimes people will not understand him, they love him. He has charm or something, I don't know [*smiles*].

Salvador. People say, "Where did you get that accent from?" "I was born with it," I tell them. Most people guess Italy or the Middle East, but not Mexico. I tell them Mexico, and they go, "No. You really are?" It's funny how people request me or her [Josefina]. They just kind of do. But again, we like people. Even if I am upset at the kitchen or at my co-workers or at my friend or whatever, people don't ever see it. I can be so upset because I just had a fight with someone or even with a table—you can get upset with one table—but at another table I will have a big smile. People like to see smiles. At many restaurants waiters think, "They are older people, they don't know how to tip," or "Oh, they are Chinese, they are only going to give a 10 percent tip." Many people just think about the money and do not give the service guests deserve. Then the guests do not tip well. When you serve people well, you will be surprised. All you have to do is be nice to them.

Yesterday I had a table and it was dessert time, so I take them the menus. They are looking at the menus, and I am back in the kitchen getting coffee and she [Josefina] comes to get me. "I tried to take the order from table 15 but they really want to talk to you."

Josefina. Yes, I went to the table, but whatever I would have told them, they wouldn't have cared because as soon as I said, "Can I help you with anything?" they said, "We have made our decision, but we want to talk to Salvador because he needs to recommend some wine." I am like, "Well, what are you looking for? A dessert wine?" I mean, it is not that I don't know my desserts or my wines. She says, "I really don't want to be mean, but I want to talk to him." I was like, "Sure, I will send him your way."

There is one person who comes in every month with a friend, and she always drinks a bottle of reserve wine. So whenever I see that she has a reservation, I have her bottle ready and she is so grateful for that. I also have her table ready. People appreciate those things even if you don't remember their name. You go to the table and say, "Welcome back. I remember you were here before." They say, "Yes. You were our server last time." And if you remember any little detail they will be grateful forever. She always has dessert first and then they go from there, have lunch or whatever. They love the things our pastry chef makes; Poncho is the best at desserts. I have a couple of ladies, they request me. It was one of their birthdays. They always come for their birthdays, and I always bring them a candle. They always have the tomato salad so I always tell the chef in advance. And they are super happy: "Oh, you remembered!"

When you have a guest that comes back and requests you, then you know you have done your job. That is always nice, but you have bad experiences too. For example, today I got to the table and asked if they had any questions and the guy was just a total mean person. He was saying to his wife, "Let's just order." And she goes, "Well, what are you having? The scallops?" And he said, "Don't order for me! Just order [for yourself]." And he started to be mean. I was like, "If he wants to talk to her like that and she loves him, then it's not my place. But he's not talking like that to me." I walked straight to my manager and I said, "I do not want to deal with that table. The guy is being mean and I am not putting up with it." He said, "Say no more. That's all I need to know." And he took care of it. But that is very, very rare.

Salvador. This is when experience comes in handy because when you have been doing this for a long time, you know how to stop people without being rude. But with some people you have to step up and be rude back to them. Then they mellow down and will leave you alone. I am not sure why. Maybe they are used to going places and getting away with it—you know, "The customer is always right." So when somebody says, "No, you won't do that to me," they stop. They do not want to play the game anymore because they know they are not going to win. But in order to do that [stand up to a customer], you have to be professional all the time and always do your best. If you have proven yourself to be a good employee—a good waiter, the type to do your best all the time—then the manager is going to back you up when you meet the one person who acts like that.

I really enjoy working here. I like interacting with people. This is actually one of the best places I have worked. It is a big company, and if you are full-time, they have good health benefits. They give you all the benefits. Also we have a break room downstairs with a refrigerator and couches and tables so you can really enjoy your break. Right before service, they feed us lunch or dinner. We even have showers in the bathrooms if you want to take a shower. We have locker rooms. So many restaurants have just a dining room, and the kitchen is so small you're always saying "Excuse me." Here the kitchen is really big. I would say twelve people work in the kitchen at the same time.

Josefina. When we get off work, we go straight home to see our kitty and do chores—laundry, dishes, clean the house. We watch TV together. Sometimes we go and visit his sister or we go and visit my mom. But we do not go out to drink. We just go home, relax. In the restaurant industry a lot of people know each other and when they get off work, they go straight to the bar to have something to drink, then they go home. We don't. We go straight home. By the end of the week, you are really tired because it is physical work but it is also mental. You get stressed with all of this and that you have to do. This for this table, the other table needs water, the other table needs wine, this table needs silverware, and that table needs soup or dessert menus. Your mind is always busy and running, running, running. The restaurant and the kitchen here are very big and far away. Just to get some butter—even though the kitchen is behind this wall [where we were interviewing]—you need to go over there and then through the dining room and then more stairs, more stairs, and then into the kitchen and then back. So it is a lot of work, but I get more tired mentally than physically because every table needs something different and you must remember everything.

Salvador. Today we had nine people sitting right here and everybody wants something different. Many times it is hard to serve big parties because there is always someone who is going to be ready to order and other people who just want to relax. Then you are in the middle. But the funniest part is when you bring the check to someone, they fight for it and you are in the middle again. Sometimes they just grab it from you and fight over it. You see that a lot. It's just like, "Can't you make up your mind before, make an agreement about who is going to pay and not make these scenes here?"

Josefina. You learn a lot working here. You start to like food and wine, and you get to know people. It is good money too. I can't complain. People easily spend $160 per person on dinner before tip, and for lunch my average last year was $70 before tip. People spend about 50-50 on wine and food. Actually many people spend more on wine than they do on food. Food is the same price, but wines vary a lot. You find bottles for $100, $300, $400, $600. We even have wines for $4,000. It is not very often that we sell those, but we have them on the menu. We had a party last week of twenty-seven people and the bill was almost $11,000. The tip was $1,800. We all share the tips equally. Many people who finished college end up working somewhere and making less money. Some go back to the restaurant business because they can make more money here. But you have to like it to make good money. If you don't like it, you won't make good money at it.

Salvador. When I came here I had never drunk wine in my life. I knew tequila, beer, the stuff they usually drink in Mexico. Well, not everybody. Obviously, they also drink wine but most people just do tequila, beer. Once I started working here and going to wineries, I started to learn about wine. You get into it. You start liking it. You start with the Domaine Chandon wines and all these white wines, and then you move into the big red wines. At first you don't like them, but then you start playing with the food and the wine. It is interesting how food can change with wine and wine can change with food.

Josefina. We have included more things in our diet, that's for sure. Also the way we cook things. My grandmother was visiting recently and she was like, "Oh, I really like the way you cook the fish now." I grill the fish for her, so it is really different.

Salvador. We try to take family to different places to eat. I mean if they come from Mexico, we are not going to take them to a Mexican restaurant here. Because they are going to say, "This is Mexican?" Not really. The food is different, so we try to take them to other places—Mediterranean, French, Italian—so they can appreciate that food also. I go to places where I used to work because I know people there and I know they [my family] will like the food, rather than go on an adventure to some place we've never been before.

Josefina. The economy and culture in Mexico are different. In Sal's case, if you have twelve children, the family is not going to go out to a fancy restaurant so they will not be introduced to new things like sweetbreads. They will not get the taste of fine dining. Here it is totally different because you have the resources to go out and say, "Let's go out and have an adventure." Now I eat foie gras. Now I eat sweetbreads. Now I eat my beef rare to medium rare; before it had to be medium to well, cooked all the way through for sure.

Salvador. It is interesting. We have had bad service at restaurants many times. When we go out, they don't know that we work in the industry and that we know what to expect. Our perception is different now; we notice things. We expect the things that we would do for people and when we don't get them—well. You can go to the best restaurants and notice things that many people don't notice.

Josefina. We were at the French Laundry in February [2008] and we noticed a couple things. [*Laughs.*] Our waitress was the biggest thing that we noticed. Our water glasses were empty like two, three times before somebody filled them. We got a bottle of wine and we finished it before the entrées and we were never offered another bottle. We got the food and we were debating with each other whether they were microgreens. He was saying, "It's micro . . ." I don't remember what I said. My friend Maria was saying, "No, no, no, I think it's . . . but I'm not sure." So we asked the waitress, "What is this?" She says, "Oh, that's got to be mint." We are like, "Okay, thank you." We know what mint is and it was definitely not mint. And this is the French Laundry.

Salvador. What made it worse is that she wasn't confident. I'm not saying I'm that good, but it's important to be confident. I may have an accent, but I am confident about what I say. Even if you don't know much about that wine or something, if you talk about it with sincerity and confidence, people are like, "Oh wow, you're right." But if you are not confident, people will not believe you. And you have to be able to read your guests. Here in the valley you either have guests with good knowledge or they don't know anything, so whatever you say to them, you have to be very careful. You have to read them.

Josefina. I like living here. It is very nice, really quiet. For me it was a shock at the beginning because I grew up in a big city. Imagine, Mexico City is five times New York. It is really busy, there are a lot of things to do, and it is very fast-paced living. When I got here, I lived in Angwin, so you can imagine—it was pretty boring. Now we live in Napa [city] and I like it. I like it a lot because we are really close to San Francisco city, so if you want to go dancing it is really close.

Salvador. I've never lived in a really big city. So this is pretty nice, quiet. But it keeps growing. There are more restaurants and more opportunities for work; that is one of the pluses. I just like to live day by day and see where it takes me. Sometimes I feel like if you plan something and if you don't get it, then it's frustrating. But if you don't plan, you just kind of get there. I definitely live a much better life now than when I first moved here. When I first moved here, I was working eighty hours a week and I wasn't making that much money. I'm not saying I'm making a lot of money now, but I'm definitely not working as much or as hard as I used to. I want to stay in the valley for a long time. Maybe when I retire I will go back to Guanajuato, but I am not planning on it. [Five of Salvador's siblings live in Napa; four work in restaurants. His mother spends half of every year in Napa and the remainder in Mexico with her other six children.]

Josefina. In Mexico the families are very close together. You never actually leave your family, and my family is here. And if I ever go back, I wouldn't go to Mexico City to live because I am not used to it anymore. Every time we visit, it's scary. I have a good life here—my job, my house, my family, everything, my partner. I am pretty happy here.

Napa Valley Cooking School / *Chef Barbara Alexander*

*"You can't **not** enjoy yourself here."*

Barbara Alexander is executive chef and director at the Napa Valley Cooking School in St. Helena. A native of Vancouver, British Columbia, Barbara's cooking career took her to England and Australia before she moved to the Napa Valley in 2000 with her husband, Master Chef Adam Busby, now director of education at the Culinary Institute of America. We met Barbara while attending one of her evening cooking classes and decided then to try to interview her. She is entertaining and refreshingly down-to-earth. Her classroom that evening was filled with laughter as well as fine food and wine.

———

I grew up being interested in food. My dad's extreme working-class Australian, but for some reason he has always been fascinated by food and culture. He left Australia in the 1950s and after circulating all through the United States, he went to Canada. That's where I grew up—in Vancouver. But we also had a summer cabin, and as a kid we went clamming and fishing and collected mussels. I took a mussel shell to kindergarten once and proudly told them that I'd been eating mussels on the weekend. I was ostracized at the lunch table after that. My parents weren't rich, so we never ate out at extravagant restaurants, but we did eat at ethnic restaurants when no one else did. We were the only family that I knew of who ate at a Japanese restaurant. We'd walk in, and they knew us by name. This is back in the mid-'60s in Vancouver.

My dad was a bit of a maniac when it came to food. On Sundays he'd move the table into the living room and we'd have what he called "fireside dining." We'd sit around the table, and everyone would get to drink wine or beer, and water when we were too young. Other kids were like, "What?" Cooking and eating were just a really big deal in our house. My mom would watch Julia Child—probably inspired by my father—and write down recipes. Kids would come by for dinner, and instead of spaghetti and meatballs, she would have concocted something extravagant. Of course it was embarrassing, especially as a teenager. At birthday parties, she'd make fancy food when most kids would rather have hot dogs. My parents were kind of ahead of their times; we didn't have any soda in the house, either.

My parents were always taking cooking classes, and they used to drive down to the Napa Valley on wine-tasting trips. When I was ten, we traveled through Europe for a whole year, which was great and very stimulating. My parents were huge Francophiles. That's where my first big food memories

Chef Barbara
Alexander.

come from. I remember tasting cultured butter and eating fresh croissants and
great French food. They were both schoolteachers so we had to kind of nickel-
and-dime it, but still food was a huge part of our lives. If I introduced my family
to somebody who didn't like food, they'd be appalled. In my relationships, if a
guy wasn't interested in food right at the beginning, it was pretty much over:
"What do you mean, he doesn't eat oysters? Get rid of him!" It was nothing
for my family to drive across Vancouver to buy a loaf of bread and then drive
all the way to the other side of town to get some special handmade sausage. I
grew up like that. I have a five-year-old now and she's already going down that
road. The other day in Safeway she said to me, "Why are you buying that here?
I thought you didn't buy meat here?"

I did a degree in English literature at the University of British Columbia
and was planning to go to law school. Then one day I was on a bus and I met
a guy who was in cooking school and the light just came on. I couldn't believe
that I had never heard of anyone going to a full-time cooking school. It was a

small school in Vancouver owned by a Frenchman named Dubrulle who ran it like an old-style French cooking school. I loved it from the second I went. My parents thought I was completely crazy, even though they loved food. They thought I'd end up having a career flipping burgers. But they became supportive almost immediately because they could see that I was more interested in cooking than in anything I'd done in school so far.

I apprenticed at the Pan Pacific Hotel in Vancouver. While I was there we participated in a big culinary Olympics—a big competition and food show sort of thing. I was standing in front of my food; I had won a little gold medal and I was pretty proud of it. There was a man standing beside me who was obviously French. He started speaking to my French chef and said, "Whose plates are these?" And my French chef said, "Oh, this little girl here." And so I was introduced to this man who turned out to be Philippe Jeanty. He was young—he's not that much older than me—but he was the chef at Domaine Chandon. I started talking to him and got really excited. And he said, "Why don't you think about coming to do your externship at Domaine Chandon?" I couldn't believe this. I think I was twenty-two or twenty-three. He invited me to come down and see the kitchens, so I came down to Napa with a girlfriend. We did some wine tasting. We went to Mustard's and Cindy Pawlcyn was the chef. I was just blown away that a woman could be at that level. Then we went to Domaine Chandon and it was a great experience. We had never really been to a fine dining restaurant on our own before; we were only in our twenties, so we had no idea. We'd been tasting wine for free in the valley, and we were offered a couple of glasses of Champagne. So of course we said, "We'll have one of those. We'll have one of these." We ended up with a huge bill; we didn't realize they were charging us. But it was really fun. I checked out the kitchen, and Philippe offered me an apprenticeship. I was so thrilled. That was my first introduction to the Napa Valley, and of course I totally fell in love with it. I just really wanted to be there, but those plans changed. I went back to Canada and I did all the legwork and paperwork that needed to be done, but no visa comes. That was around 1985, and I wasn't exactly necessary to the American economy. They said, "No. You don't have enough experience. If you were at a certain level as a chef, we would think about it. Blah, blah, blah."

I finished my apprenticeship [at the Pan Pacific] and went to work for Hervé Martin, who had been the executive chef at the hotel and opened his own little restaurant in Vancouver called the Hermitage. Later I became the sous chef at a restaurant called the Rain Tree which was in the forefront of Pacific Northwest cuisine. We didn't use any produce or anything that came from more than five hundred miles away. We didn't get strawberries from Mexico. We didn't get passion fruit, papayas, or pineapple. We used only local ingredients and had some local growers who grew things for us. This was about the time that Chez Panisse was getting really popular, and people were on to this idea of having things grown for them. It was a real eye-opener for me and really interesting, especially in the winter months in Vancouver. That's not exactly a great time of year for produce. I worked there for a little while, then I went to London and worked in various restaurants for a couple years. But I was really on a path to Australia, which is my dad's homeland. After England, I traveled through Europe doing the backpacking experience with a couple girlfriends and then I headed down to Australia.

I lived with my aunt and uncle in Sydney. By this time I had some pretty good qualifications under my belt, and I got hired as a sous chef in the Hotel New Hampshire, which almost immediately became a chef position because they fired the guy who had been in charge. That was my first chef job, in about 1991. I ran the kitchen of a hotel that was in the entertainment industry, which was fun. Lots of Aussie actors, musicians, and bands came through: Joe Jackson, Tom Cruise and Nicole Kidman, Michael Hutchence from INXS, Oasis, Tina Turner's backup band and dancers—wow, can they eat! It was great timing for me to be young and meeting all these people. What I realized very quickly, however, is that people in rock bands don't necessarily like good food. What they were thrilled about—and I guess the owners had known this—was that I could cook American cuisine. They wanted burgers and ribs. I served Kurt Cobain from Nirvana a hamburger every night for five nights; he just couldn't get the burger that he wanted in Australia and loved the "American" burger I made. I also served Keith Richards but only half a meal as the owner kicked him out halfway through his meal for smoking at the table. Those Aussies are not starstruck like us!

In the meantime, I had been following a woman named Christine Manfield who had her own restaurant called the Paramount. She had started cooking in her forties after a teaching career and become very well known. She'd had two restaurants before that—the Paragon and the Phoenix—and now she has a new restaurant called the Universal. She is a unique individual and a really talented chef—a visionary as far as food goes. She was cooking pan-Asian cuisine with a sort of a modern Australian influence. I found her intriguing, so I applied for a job and she accepted me but I had to start at the bottom. I went from making great money and being the executive chef at this hotel to barely surviving. I had to get rid of my car, my apartment, and all of those things, but I really wanted to work with her and learn. This is not uncommon in high-end restaurants. They had no idea what my skills were going to be, so they said they'd start me as an apprentice, which is why I got such a ridiculous salary. But that's the "in," and where you go is up to you. Within three months I was their sous chef and then went on to become their chef de cuisine, which is pretty much the executive chef of the restaurant. And then we opened a store together—Paramount Stores. I wasn't financially invested in it, but it was almost like our project. The shop sold all kinds of pre-prepared items—very high-end. All the movie stars like Nicole Kidman ate there. It was very chic and a fun environment. I worked with Christine and her partner for nine years and can really put most of my education down to those nine years. I loved it. We remain close friends.

I left Australia for a bunch of reasons, mostly breaking up a relationship, and came back to Canada and began working with some old colleagues. There was this restaurant called Lola's that everyone referred to as the "refugee camp" because of all the displaced chefs who ended up there. Adam worked there as well, but I didn't meet him because he worked a different shift. Then the cooking school I had attended, the Dubrulle Culinary Institute, asked me to come back and create a bread-making program for them. So I went down to the Napa Valley and took a course at the CIA. I also worked at Steve Sullivan's bakery, Acme Breads [in Berkeley], and a couple other bakeries. Then I went back to Canada and wrote a bread-making program and started teaching bread making and culinary as well. This was in 1996. Then Adam was hired by Dubrulle. This is a remotely funny story. When I was still in Australia, my mom sent me a newspaper article about this hot young chef in Vancouver. I thought he was really cute, so I put him up on my bulletin board and every day when I'd do my orders I would look at him. When I came back to Vancouver I thought I'd just get some advice from him—like where he thought I should go. So I got him on the phone, but you know how you can tell when someone isn't really listening to you, isn't reading you. He said, "Listen, if you're trying to apply for a job, just drop your résumé off with my maitre d'." I was furious. I hung up and said to my mom, "What an asshole! I'll never work for that guy." Then one day my boss told me, "This great young guy is coming. You'll love him." And I said, "Who is it?" And she said, "Adam Busby." "Oh, God," I said, "I don't even *like* him." Of course, that changed immediately and now we're married.

In 2000 we came down to Napa and applied at the CIA and both of us started working there. I worked there for a year when this job came up. This job is much more my scene. The CIA at the time had a lot of corporate business like teaching company employees to work with stock bases. The people at the CIA were great, and I got a lot of inspiration from them, but when this job was coming up, I came over and took one look at the campus [the up-valley campus of Napa Valley College] and said, "Wow. This could be so unbelievable." The cooking school had a fairly low profile back then, but I knew it could really be something. Over the years it has become more prominent with the different chefs who have come and worked here. They bring their own energy, and the cooking school is in a continual state of change. We are becoming more sustainable. That's my personal interest, but the college is also very supportive. You may know that the main campus [in Napa city] is the largest solar campus in California. We're going to do that up here [in St. Helena], too—we're going to be solar. We're very opposed to the egg industry in the United States, and we've been supporting organic farmers. But if we have the ability to do so, we would rather support ourselves. Tomorrow we're getting a flock of twenty-five chickens. It's going to be this really neat cycle; we'll use the vegetables from our garden at the school, then we'll feed the scraps to the chickens, and then the chicken poop will become compost. I've purchased chickens for their temperament as well as egg laying. We can't have birds attacking people because our students are going to want to go into the coop. We're getting a large coop built by a local guy. He charges twice as much as other coop businesses, but I want to keep it local. People are going to ask where we got the coop, and I can't say "China!"

Farm-to-table is the new catchphrase. Two years ago people were talking about slow food. But now we're talking about the farm-to-table idea. The Napa Valley is a breadbasket. It was strictly agriculture before the growth of the wine industry. Then a lot of the other agriculture filtered away. But if it weren't for the growth of the wine industry, there wouldn't be the growth we've seen in tourism, and we wouldn't be where we are today, which is looking at other agriculture again. Alice Waters started this forty years ago. But it has taken people this long to go, "Okay, maybe it is wrong to get Mexican strawberries." It should have been a no-brainer. Now, people are using more local produce. If you go to Martini House, if you go to Cook [both restaurants in St. Helena], you're going to see right on the menu where they are getting their vegetables from or who is developing their meat. I think it's great. It's not always easy in a restaurant because you have to look at cost as well. And especially in these economic times when people are tightening their own purse strings, it's getting a little difficult. But we are trying to do it [at the school]. We don't order any farmed fish anymore; we only use line-caught fish. If it wasn't available in the old days, we'd have said, "Whatever. We'll use frozen Scottish salmon instead." And the students would have been okay with that. But everything has changed now, especially here in the valley. Most of our students are from the valley or the surrounding area and are pretty educated about food and don't want to use farmed salmon. They would take us to task for it if we did. We really try hard to make sure everything fits with this philosophy and with Napa Valley's image. This is an agricultural center. We need to grow as much as we can of our own product. That is the way things are going. I notice it with our night-class customers who are very educated about food. When I mention books like *The Omnivore's Dilemma,* half the class has read it. Two or three years ago, not a soul would have read it or even heard about it. Since I've been here [since 2002], it has swung around 180 degrees.

I have so many people today asking me about raising chickens, about growing vegetables. Of course it really isn't cheaper to grow your own vegetables or eggs, but I think we are on the brink of something. People still want to get their food cheaply. They want to be able to afford it and they *sort* of care if it's organic and grown locally, but I think the scale is about to tip. And when it completely tips, I think people will not mind paying more. Food prices are going up anyway.

How would you characterize Napa's food identity or cuisine?

That's kind of tricky. I don't think it has found its identity yet. I think the growth in the wine industry happened much faster than the growth of the food industry. And maybe because the wine industry started out largely as this French and Italian thing, these are the dominant food influences. It's taken a really long time to get away from French and Italian restaurants. I think it is hard for the valley to break away from that Tuscan-Italian flavor thing. Americans love Italian food, and so I think when you open a restaurant, especially in a tourist area, what are you going to choose for your cuisine? Italian is a safe bet. When we first moved here in 2000, it seemed like almost all the restaurants were Italian in one way or another, definitely a Mediterranean influence. The climate is Mediterranean and the wine is Mediterranean, so it makes sense. But I think we're just starting to see people break away from this with the farm-to-table movement—cooking with local produce and turning it into a modern California thing. That's probably the future. Todd Humphries at the Martini House is doing his own kind of modern California cuisine, once again using local products. I think when Terra opened, it was so unique to have this Japanese-French fusion cuisine. And of course Thomas Keller does some pretty unique things, but it is French-based. Cindy Pawlcyn has always done her own thing—comfort foods grown in her own garden. She would be more what I call California cuisine. There seem to be three factions: Italian, French, and Californian. Maybe we are going to see more of a blending with that.

It's fashionable to be a foodie these days. I was just talking to a girlfriend of mine the other day. She's never really liked food. She's thin. She doesn't eat much. She's one of those people who would take a pill instead if she could and that would be fine. She said to me, "You know, I wish I was more of a foodie because it is so chic to be a foodie." Isn't that funny? It's like what you were talking about—cultural capital. If you know what foie gras is, it gives you just a little score up from the other guy. Fennel pollen is pretty chic right now. It grows on the side of the road here; you could harvest it yourself. It's really nice on fish. It has a nice light fennel flavor. Twenty years ago, people didn't even know what fennel was, let alone fennel pollen. If you know the names of two or three wild mushrooms, that's pretty chic. Nobody ate pork belly five years ago. If you said "pork belly," people went "Eewh." Now if you say "pork belly," even if they're thinking "Eewh," they'll say, "Oh yeah, that's good." It started with basic stuff like balsamic vinegar and truffle oil. But even people who don't eat out have heard of truffle oil these days.

People are always in search of new ingredients. The very hip thing today is cooking things in plastic bags—*sous vide.* "Under vacuum" is what it means. They're been doing it in France for fifty years; Thomas Keller wrote a book on it. If you toss the term *"sous vide"* around at a cocktail party, it's chic, I guess. There are probably new trends out there moving forward that I'm not even aware of. With wine, we take it for granted that everyone knows what a Sauvignon Blanc is, but if you go to a different part of the country it gives a person some sort of credential or kudos to know a varietal like that.

What part does wine play in your thinking when you design or create dishes at the school?

It plays a big part, especially here in the valley. We have access to such great product. It's kind of like putting the icing on the cake. You create this beautiful dish and you want to make sure the wine goes with whatever you are serving, so you either choose wine that it tastes really good with or you adjust your dish to go with the wine. I think this is a big part of a chef's role here. I don't think you could be a chef in the Napa Valley without knowledge of wine. It's impossible. I get vintners and vineyard managers who are food enthusiasts coming to my classes who know a lot about food and wine pairing, and we can't be serving the wrong wine! So it becomes a big part of what we do.

How many tourists take your classes?

We get quite a few what I'd call "recidivist tourists"—people who come back to the valley time and time again. They'll call and ask what classes we're offering during the time they will be here. A lot of hotels know about us, and their concierges suggest us. And let's say you're a local who is entertaining someone from out of town and you're wondering what you can do with your friends that would be a unique experience for them in the valley. We get some tourists this way. We have a much bigger local following, but when I say "local" I mean as far away as San Francisco and Sacramento. People will drive up for cooking classes. We do get a number of private groups like corporate groups that come up here to play golf and their partners take cooking classes. Or the classes might be part of a team-building exercise. And we get people who are changing careers, who want to try something new. A couple of years ago we had a lawyer from San Francisco who used to come up for classes, and she loved them. She started coming with her husband, then she ended up coming up on her own, then she ended up taking the full-time culinary program, and now she's doing catering. She still does law on the side, but she was tired of just the law.

What is it like to be a woman chef?

It has changed over the years. In my early years, it was really bizarre. It was highly unusual to be a woman chef, and there was a lot of prejudice against it: "Women shouldn't be in the kitchen" and "Women should only be serving" attitudes. It has completely changed, although it's a little hard for me to judge because I have achieved a position where I am not being questioned by people anymore. You still run into the old sexist attitudes sometimes. Laura [Chef Laura Lee] and I took a class recently, and there was an old French chef there who was not really treating me like I was at the same level as the male chefs. Sometimes when I am cooking with Adam, people will ask a cooking question completely looking at Adam like I have nothing to do with it. So there is a bit of that, but it's nothing like it was twenty years ago. When we teach cooking school students, we see a pretty even gender split. I sometimes wonder if the male students are thinking, "Oh God, do I really want to be taught by two women chefs?" But I've never gotten that feeling from any male student; I'm talking about people in their twenties.

The image of all chefs has changed. When I first started cooking, I was enrolled in law school and so were a lot of my friends. We'd go to cocktail parties, and people would be going around the room with introductions—so and so works at Perkins & Willis and so on. Then they'd come to me: "What do you do?" And I'd say, "I'm a chef." And people would just go, "Oh, really?" and move right on. Now it's different. I was just with a girlfriend in Vegas. She has her PhD from Cambridge, which is a really big deal. But when we'd meet people and I said, "I'm a chef," they'd go, "Wow! That's really great!" My girlfriend was joking with me later: "Jesus, I spent all this money and time getting my PhD at Cambridge and no one wants to hear my story. Maybe it's my thesis?" She's in economics and wrote something like *NGO Spending and Its Relevancy in Africa*.

The image of the chef has gone full circle. It used to be when I wore my chef's jacket out on the street, people weren't interested. Now if you wear your chef's jacket over to the farmers' market, you're practically attacked. People whisper, "Oh, who's that chef? Who's that chef?" Chefs are laborers. There are a few famous chefs—like the Thomas Kellers of the restaurant world—but for everybody else, it's a really hard job without much glory. I mean, it's artistic and there are great things about it, but really it's no different than other laboring crafts—like being a welder. Well, maybe it's a little more chic than being a welder, but it's not really that different than being a draftsman or in construction. What makes us different is the creativity. But people watch the food network and think they might go to cooking school because it looks like so much fun. But this is a bit of a disservice to us because it's really hard work.

Still, I always tell people, "If you work in the Napa Valley, it's not going to hurt you. Everywhere, all over the world, they've heard of the Napa Valley." The name has a lot of clout behind it—justly or unjustly. People think the Napa Valley is trendy and full of wealthy people, winemakers, vintners, chefs. And it's true. In some ways, I think chefs have a bigger profile than winemakers. If you take your average person and ask if they can name three chefs in the Napa Valley, they can do it. I'm not sure they'd be able to if they were asked to name three winemakers. They do know the names of wines and wineries, though. People know Harlan Estates, but I don't know if anybody could name its winemaker. Maybe they think Harlan himself is crushing up the grapes. So it's almost like chefs leapfrogged over the winemakers. And now quite a few wineries have chefs. Many people can tell you who the chef is at Beringer [Winery], but can they tell you who the winemaker is? I doubt it. Of course, I suspect that winemakers might have something else to say about this.

Is there much of a community among chefs in the valley?
The cooking school and restaurants are very different from one another. It's definitely not a close-knit community here, but it is very respectful. We have a lot of work-related dealings with chefs in restaurants, but socially we don't hang out together because they work until eleven or twelve at night. The restaurant business is so busy, and you're so tired. It's so grueling that a lot of people don't have room for socializing. You get two factions: people who are married to somebody in the business or else got married so early in life that their partner has learned to accept their lifestyle, and then you have single chefs who don't really have any time to date. Being a chef definitely appeals to a certain personality [*laughing*]. Almost every chef I know is pretty intense in one way or another; sometimes they drown themselves in that intensity. The restaurant industry is a lot like the fashion industry or the art industry or the music industry. There is a very small percentage of people who are fabulously successful, then there is a very broad middle class, and then there is a pretty decent-sized lower class—the people who work prep day in and day out for eight bucks an hour. The thing about the Napa Valley is that the lower echelon

is almost all Hispanic. What's unfortunate is that many of them don't have the time, the money, or maybe the language to go on to cooking school which would bump them to the next level. We're always very interested in getting more Hispanic students.

What are your general impressions of the impact tourism has on the valley?

It's a love-hate relationship. Let's start with the things I don't like. I really hate the traffic, and I worry about what happens when people are tasting and then getting into their cars and driving. We have such a poor system of transit and taxis here that people are kind of driven to drive. Having said that, without tourists we wouldn't have jobs. So for that reason tourism is great. What I really like is that when tourists come to the valley, they really enjoy themselves. You can't *not* enjoy yourself here. It is unbelievably beautiful; we forget how beautiful it really is. The food is great and in most restaurants you're going to get a great meal with good service. The service aspect here is really great because people want tourists. People just seem to really enjoy themselves here. They're eating. They're drinking. And they're outside in the beautiful sunny environment. When my brother comes, he'll go out and buy ten loaves of bread. It's so insanely good here. We pretty much have it all. There isn't really much to complain about.

But it is expensive here. The taxes are high. I also think that the people behind the scenes are paid shockingly less than what tourists would expect—the winemakers, the chefs, the vineyard workers, the gardeners. They are just toiling away. I really don't think tourists see that side of the Napa Valley. I keep thinking about the vineyard workers and how hard they work with two or three jobs. We've got a guy who works in the vineyards during the day and comes in here and cleans the campus at night, every day of the week. Yet you have people who can easily drop $150 on a bottle of Cab. There is this weird dichotomy. It is a very strange area to live in, but I love the valley. When I come back after being away and I'm driving up the valley—it is unbelievable. People are friendly. It's not too right-wing [*laughing*]. That is weird as well; there's all this wealth in the valley and yet it still is this outpost of "limousine liberals" or whatever they're called. People are interested in food and wine.

From Back to Front of the House / *Edgar Bonilla*

"If you have money you can live very well, but money is not happiness."

Since moving to the United States from Guatemala fourteen years ago, Edgar Bonilla has worked at various jobs in wine tourism. Like so many recent immigrants and second-generation Latinos in the valley, he has worked hard to support his family and to learn English. Unlike many others who have had to find homes in less expensive areas outside the valley and must commute to work, Edgar feels fortunate to live in St. Helena near his job and quality schools. Although he never expected to be involved in tourism, he likes many aspects of his work at the Culinary Institute of America in St. Helena and has learned much about wine and food over the years. Edgar is married to Yendy Perez, also from Guatemala, whom he describes as "a very special lady." They have an eight-year-old son and an eleven-year-old daughter.

I came here in December 1996 when I was twenty. We were from Guatemala City. After the civil war, all the guerrillas came into town. There was no work and a lot of violence. I graduated from school as an automobile mechanic and I had my own car. My mom had her own house, and we didn't worry about money. My stepdad was doing well buying used cars in the United States and bringing them back to Guatemala. That was a good business, so we were living well. We were, I would say, in the middle class. But that was a problem, you know. People see you with a lot of money, and my stepdad got killed. My mom had an American friend who lived in the house right next to us when she visited Guatemala. She used to say, "Hey guys, if you ever go to the U.S. and you want to stay there for a little while, talk to me. I live in a very nice place." So the first thing my mom said after my stepdad got killed was, "Let's go to the United States and try to get a better life. We'll go to where my friend lives." We got visas—my mom, my little sister, and me—and came straight to the Napa Valley.

The first thing we did was start working. I was looking for any kind of job to survive. My mom was working a little, but my sister was too young to work. So I figured that I was the guy and I needed to come up with the cash. A friend of mine said, "They're looking for a dishwasher at this restaurant." It was about six blocks from where I lived. I thought, "I don't think I'm going

Edgar Bonilla.

to need that much of a language if all I need to do is wash dishes." So I went there and they hired me right away. Most of us were Latinos, a lot of Mexicans, a few Guatemalans, a couple from El Salvador and Honduras. I worked very, very hard, I guess because it was my first job and because I didn't know the language. If you don't speak the language then they think you are uneducated or that you don't realize things. So the first thing, I wanted to learn what they were saying. I wanted to learn to communicate. I like talking to people, so I took English classes at the Napa College in St. Helena. I was going two days a week and working two jobs, washing dishes at Tra Vigne [St. Helena restaurant] and at the Culinary Institute [CIA].

At the CIA, back then, I think I was the only Latino washing dishes. The rest of them were Americans. It was hard for me to get that job. I went there, and they were like, "You know Edgar, I don't know if I should give you the job—you can't speak English." So I said, "You know, I am really willing to work and I learn things pretty quickly. Let me show you how I can do this." I don't know how they understood me back then, but they knew I wanted to work and gave me the job. I mean, here I was with my mom and my sister. I needed to pay rent. I made minimum wage at both places, about $5.75. As a dishwasher you don't get a share of the tips and no health benefits, either. I worked sixteen hours a day. I worked at Tra Vigne from 5 PM to 1 AM, very late. Then they asked me at the CIA to come in at 6 AM. I did it for about two years. It was too much. And sometimes my hands, because you're going from cold to hot water, the next day you cannot move your hands. People say, "Oh, that's not good for you."

When you first come, you don't mind what you do; you just want to make money. But after being here for one or two years and you learn the language, you say, "It's time to step up and do something else or ask for more money." I wanted to work in the front of the house [restaurant] like some of my friends, bussing tables. I said to myself, "I don't know if I'm going to like it but it's more money and I'll practice my language at the same time." So that's what I did. I stopped working at the CIA then and started bussing at Tra Vigne. That was like having the same two jobs. Instead of making $5.75 here and $6.00 over there, I was making the same money at one job because the bussers made $100 a night in tips. Back then I wanted to go to college and do something different, but I guess you get addicted to the tips and you stay there. Then you become a father and you can't go to college, so you stay and do what you have to do.

Tra Vigne was a very nice restaurant, but the management was really tough then. I remember one day the front manager—he used to own part of the restaurant but he's not there anymore—and the chef were yelling at each other over something. At the time I didn't understand. Latino men don't yell at each other. We say, "Let's go outside and do some boxing." Anyway, I saw them and I thought they were going to start fighting. They went outside yelling at each other, but nothing happened. And that's how they treated everybody, even the servers. This manager was angry all the time. He'd tell everyone, "Bring me a double espresso." All I am thinking is that this guy is going to die from having too many espressos each day. The chef was Italian-American and he'd be in the restaurant for twelve hours, working hard, and he had a family and kids at home. They would do three hundred or four hundred dinners a night, so there were all these trays. Sometimes the servers would make a mistake, mess up the order. And they would go back to the chef and say, "You know, I'm sorry but I messed up on table 32." And the chef would go, "What! What were you thinking?" And he'd get a pan and slam it and make a big deal about it. All the servers wanted to quit and get new jobs, but they were all making such good money, from the tips primarily, they would never quit.

A lot of food got wasted at Tra Vigne. I don't know why, maybe people weren't hungry, and the dishes were big. I remember this dish, it was a big piece of roasted chicken. People would only eat half of it, and I would have to throw the other half away. The ribs, same thing. I threw them away. At the CIA, the same thing. The students were making all this food, cooking and baking. I would think, "Who's going to eat all that food?" All that food that no one eats gets thrown in the garbage. I would think, "How do you do that here in America? You could send that to Guatemala or some country that is dying for food." I never said anything; it's kind of like something you don't talk about. You get used to it when you see that every day. And what are you going to do?

I liked talking to the customers at Tra Vigne. You'd see locals in there, especially the winemakers. You could tell the tourists. They come in and want to enjoy themselves, so they order a lot of wine and ask you questions: "What's your favorite plate on the menu? What's your favorite salad?" I started learning about the food and the wine little by little. Then I started to enjoy new food: Caesar salads and Italian food, all those pastas. I didn't like garlic then. I love garlic now. I have great memories of Tra Vigne, of meeting people all the time, of drinking great wine. I bussed there for five years, and then I started at Auberge du Soleil, the very nice hotel [resort]. A friend of mine who worked at Tra Vigne got a job there, so I went there to be a room service server. I had a great experience over there. I mean, you get to meet these movie stars, football players, very wealthy people. There are people there from all over the world, from Europe, from India. I got tired of two jobs, so I decided I would just stay at Auberge working daytime. I work there in room service for five years.

I can see that for a lot of people here in the U.S. money is not a problem. People will do whatever they want. When I worked over there, there were two rooms that were over $3,500 a night and I saw one couple staying there for a month. I was like, "Wow." Back in Guatemala if someone has money it means you've got your own house and you have your own cars. Here I see really big money. I've seen amazing things here. I remember this old couple. From what I hear, he was a famous architect. They were some of the people who stayed for a month in the $3,500-a-night rooms. They come every year to stay at Auberge and stay in the same room for a month. They made us paint the room. They will call the desk and say they don't like the color of the room and tell us they want it painted a different color. They wanted us to put different tables in the room and stuff like that. And we did. Even when you brought salt and pepper to the room, you had to double-check the salt and pepper and clean it up very nice. The monitor would remind us to double-check. And every day at seven you'd have to bring a cappuccino extremely hot. And if you didn't bring it extremely hot, they'd give it back to you and make a big deal about it. Then your monitor will come to you and say, "These people are VIP and you have to be on top of it." My experience is that every time I go to the room, they are never sitting down together. They were doing their own things. They were both in their own thoughts. They would go to the pool and she would be sitting there and he would be sitting here. It seemed like a pretty sad life. What I thought was, "If you have money you can live very well, but money is not happiness."

At Auberge, they put a service charge on the bottom of the ticket [the bill].
A lot of people saw that and thought it was for the server, but it wasn't for us.
It was for the hotel. I didn't like that very much because after people see the
service charge, they're not tipping you. So I didn't get a lot of tips. I wouldn't
say "never." There was one day that a guy ordered caviar from me, so I went
down and delivered it and he comes out with the chunk of money and he says,
"How much is this?" I say, "It is $180, sir." He gave me $200. Then later he called
me back and said, "You know what? That ounce of caviar wasn't enough. Bring
me three more ounces." And there was something else. When I came back
down, he said, "You know what, Edgar, I didn't realize that I gave you $20. So,
here." All of a sudden, he gave me $180 in tip. That was one of the only times
that happened. If that had been every day, I would still be working there.

I used to go to this gym a lot and a friend of mine said they were looking for a forklift driver at this wine warehouse. It was the Napa Valley Wine
Warehouse. It was something different, and he told me I'd get $16 an hour
and good benefits. But the office manager, this American lady, decided to start
me at $12. She said, "We'll keep you here a few months and see how you do."
Which I didn't like, but I said okay because I wanted to do something different.
I learned the job like this [snaps fingers]. Even the other workers there saw I was
good. There were only three workers in the warehouse; they were all white,
and then the other two ladies were Americans.

After three months I knew the job and I said to the manager, "I've been
thinking about it and I know the job now. Do you think I can start making
more money? Because $12 is not enough." She said she'd think about it and the
next day she offered me $13 or $14. I was very upset. There were other people
there who didn't even know the job and they were getting $16. Much later she
offered me the $16 an hour, but she said, "For your full benefits, you'll have to
wait some more." So there was a lot of waiting. Finally, I'd had it up to here and
wanted to leave. She never appreciated what I did. I just wanted to make what
everyone was making because I was in the same job. I told her I wanted to go
back to the restaurant business, and I gave her my two weeks' notice. And she
was like, "Oh Edgar, are you sure you want to leave?" She said we could talk
about money, but by then it was too late for me. So I left.

One thing I liked about the wine warehouse is that you get to meet these
great winemakers that come to pick up their wine and they say, "Oh, here's a
bottle of wine." So pretty much you get a bottle of wine every day, which is
great. And Christmas we got $3,000 from the owner because he owns Flora
Springs Winery. So that was great. I don't want to make you tired only talking
about money, but that's why I moved from job to job.

Then I started working as a limo driver. That was great because I met a
lot of tourists, drove them around, and did some wine tours with them. It was

a fun and easy job. And good money. It was me, the owner, and his wife, just the three of us. He knew that I was always willing to work. So if there was a weekend and he and his wife didn't want to work, he would call me at seven or eight and say, "Okay, Edgar. I have a wine tour for you in Calistoga. I want you to be here at ten or eleven; the people will be ready at eleven thirty at Brannan's [Brannan's Grill]. Just clean the inside of the limo. You might want to get a few beers, put them in the ice bucket and get them ready." So I pick them up, greet them. They would say, "This is the plan. This is what we want to do." Most people would bring me a list of wineries. Some had maps and everything. We would do four or five. A lot wanted to go to Sterling [winery] because of the cable car or Schramsberg because of the tour and the caves. Quintessa, too. And Robert Mondavi because they've got a great tour. Some people didn't really want to be where all the traffic is on [Highway] 29. They wanted to go on the Silverado Trail, where it is more relaxed. On that side of the valley, people liked ZD Winery and the one that looks like it's from the Middle East [Dariosh].

Once people drink, things change. I got these two couples once and they were Canadian. I tried to be nice: "How are you today?" I was trying to talk to them, but they were quiet. We went to the first winery, and they were still quiet. At the second winery, they started to talk. By the fourth winery, they were joking and throwing things at me, having a good time. Most of the people that come to the Napa Valley want to have a good time. They forget about what's going on at home. I would usually take them to four or five wineries. About half the people ask me questions like, "What is your favorite winery, your favorite restaurant, or your favorite hotel?" Some people ask me about my accent: "Oh, are you from Mexico?" "No, I'm from Guatemala." A lot of people think that all Latinos are Mexicans. A lot of my friends are Mexicans; we all hang together—Mexicans, Colombians, Salvadorans, Guatemalans. Most people treat me well.

Once people drink, they always ask if I can drive them one more hour. I say, "Sure," and call my boss and he says, "Tell them it is $60 more." They say, "Okay. Fine." Then they say, "We have dinner tonight, can you drop us off at the hotel and pick us up at eight and then drop us off and pick us up after?" The Napa Valley is well known for good food. In Yountville you have the French Laundry. People tell me, they do that once in life. Bouchon is good. In St. Helena there's Martini House and Terra. People are always very happy about those two places. While I am waiting, I would taxi people to places close by. My boss would call me and say, "People are waiting at Auberge and they want to go to Martini House." Things like that. A normal day sometimes goes from eleven thirty in the morning until eleven at night.

My boss only had two cars and they were getting pretty beat-up. He wanted to get new, better limousines, but they are expensive. He said, "You know, Edgar, I'm done with this business. I'm going to try to get some new cars, but who knows when. So I guess this is it for now." So, I moved to the CIA in 2006 and started working in the restaurant again as a back waiter. Then I took some wine classes at the college and after that I moved to the front of the house as a server, and now here I am. As you can see I've pretty much done it all in the Napa Valley.

Someday I'd like to open my own business, maybe a wine tour guide. I also like sports. I coach little kids' soccer. So I might keep doing that. Or maybe I'll go to school and do something I really like. I'm not saying I don't like what I do right now, but you know. We [immigrants] all want to become citizens and I hope someday there will be some legal, permanent thing for all of us to stay here because all we do is work. Of course, everybody makes mistakes and there are some bad people. But most people really just want to work. I don't have a secure permanent permit to stay here. [Although his children are U.S. citizens, Edgar has Temporary Permit Status (TIP), which has to be renewed every eighteen months with the help of an immigration lawyer and the expense and paperwork that entails.] Who knows, if tomorrow, they say, "Okay, you guys, no more permits," we'd have to go back. So I'd like to have my own house in Guatemala and be ready. But if tomorrow they say, "Okay guys, you are now residents." That would be great. I would never go back to live. I'd travel and visit instead.

7 / Napa's Other Pleasures

Wine Train / Melodie Hilton

"I try to weave my stories so that people start dreaming. . . ."

Melodie Hilton is the director of marketing and public relations for the Napa Valley Wine Train. She also writes about wine, food, and travel for print and online media. She is petite, lively, and active—snowboarding, playing soccer in both a coed and an over-forty women's league, hiking, and generally participating in any "outdoor activity that puts you on the river or close to the earth." In recent years she has rebuilt her home, acting as her own general contractor, a challenge she believes everyone should tackle at least once in their lives.

———

I was born in Somerset, Pennsylvania, which is a very small town in the Appalachian mountain chain and relatively unknown before 9/11. Somerset County is where one of the planes tragically went down. So I am originally from cold hill country, but we didn't stay long because my father didn't like the snow and moved us to the South, which is where I grew up in the late '60s and early '70s. My father was a journalist, but also a musician. He told my mother when he married her that he wanted two little girls and planned to name them Melodie and Harmonie. I came first and got Melodie, which is a somewhat familiar name. But my sister was named Harmonie—not a common name at all for a child, especially a girl child growing up in the South. We'd meet other children and introduce ourselves, and they'd look at my little sister and say in a southern accent, "Your parents named you hominy? You're named after corn grits?"

My father worked for a newspaper called the *Playground Daily News* in Fort Walton Beach, Florida. I can remember as a small child playing under his desk on weekends, much like that picture of John John with JFK. I would keep my little knickknacks and stuff under his desk and play at his feet while in the background the old presses with the big webs [rolls of printing paper] would

Wine Train publicist and travel writer Melodie Hilton. *Courtesy of the Wine Train.*

be running. I would go back into the pressroom like a farm child playing in bales of hay and crawl on these webs and hide amongst them with my little sister. We grew up with the smell of ink, which is probably quite toxic, but I loved it. It's a smell that reminds me of my childhood and my father. I worked for him at many newspapers across the South including Athens, Tennessee, and right outside of Mobile, Alabama, where he had a little paper called the *8-Mile Whistler*. I did everything from working in the composition room, which no longer exists, to throwing papers in people's yards, which I was lousy at since I've never had a good arm. Over the years I learned a lot about working in community newspapers, so when I went to college and needed fill-in jobs, I was always able to get a good job in a newspaper, whether in a composition room, subscriptions—whatever.

When I was twenty I moved to Catalina Island [20 miles off the southern California coast]. I had gone there on holiday and fell in love with the place. Catalina is a nature preserve with goats and pigs and buffalo and indigenous fox, and great natural beauty. I had an amazing four years living in this idyllic island environment that was supported almost entirely by tourist dollars. In summer, people came over by the boatloads. We called them "cattle boats"— ten thousand people a day. I mean, it was just a tangle of bodies. It seemed like we served people relentlessly. At first, I had waitressing jobs. I'd get up early in the morning to serve pancakes and hot links at one little restaurant, then I'd go work at the beach restaurant, then I'd work at the Mexican restaurant. And at the end of the day, I'd fall into bed. We would do that for five months straight. But when all the tourists went away after Labor Day, we had the entire island to ourselves, all through the beautiful southern California fall and into the winter rainy season when the northeastern storms and Santa Ana winds would sometimes blow the boats right up onto the rocks. While I was waitressing, I went to the local newspaper every Friday to see if they had a job opening and one day they did. So for the next three years I was the production manager and typographer at the *Catalina Islander* back in the days when people were still setting type.

Catalina Island is an amazing place for people at the two ends of life. Families with young children enjoyed living there and did well. So did older people, but young people did not have good opportunities. Many would go to LA for school or work having learned to drive at 35 miles an hour or in a golf cart, and then were thrown into one of the world's largest car environments. They were totally unprepared. Catalina also had twenty-two bars in one square mile. When you are young and just having fun all the time with twenty-two bars, lots of parties, endless sun, beaches, and hiking, it can seem like that's all you need to do in the world. Life there is very casual. You'd go to one of the little stores or to the little Mexican restaurant and find a note on the door, "Gone Fishing," and they really would have gone fishing. I'd get in my skiff and find them out on the water. When I lived there, there was no cable TV. With only 2,200 residents, it didn't make economic sense. And they only had one little radio station. I'll give you an example of how small it was. When I moved there in '83 and met people I wanted to hang out with, I'd ask for their phone number so we could get together. They'd go, "Oh great. No worries, our number is 10." That's right! Their phone number had two digits. Only a few years before, the phone company still had an operator using a switchboard to connect calls. I believe it's now in the little museum that's located in the casino.

I moved off the island and came to Napa in 1986. A gentleman that I was seeing on the island had been born and raised in San Francisco, and he wanted to get married and start a family. We knew that Catalina Island was not the place for us to do that. So he invited me to look around the Bay Area. And, believe it or not, in Napa we found people that I knew from Catalina Island

and that he knew from high school in the city. And we loved it. Our alternative was Petaluma, but we loved Napa and I have been here ever since. Today I am single and live here with my seventeen-year-old son, twenty-one-year-old daughter, two dogs, two cats, and a turtle—all strays. I think when you buy a house, things just show up and live there, except for the children—I brought them with me.

When I first came to Napa I got a job at a little weekly newspaper called the *Napa Valley Times*. There were a couple of other weeklies in the community at that time: the *Sentinel* and the *Napa County Record*. I mostly covered education, business, and land use. I spent a lot of time at board of supervisors and city council meetings, where there was a lot of policy discussion about land use and the Ag Preserve and what to do to contain the spread of housing in an agricultural area. I learned quite a bit about land-use policies and from that experience started writing for wine trade publications. After writing about the business of the wine industry, I moved into food and wine and travel writing, which for me is much, much, much more of an affinity or feel-good job. It's all about having another good meal, another great glass of wine, exploring another fabulous place to stay, and all in the interest of telling people the story of what's here. I try to weave my stories so that people start dreaming, fantasizing about being here instead of sitting in traffic or at a meeting. No. They're enjoying the sun and sparkling wine and oysters at Bouchon at three o'clock on a Friday afternoon watching other relaxed people stroll by.

Here's a small story about that. I was sitting outside a café in downtown Napa, reading a book and eating my lunch when this man leaned over and said, "Excuse me, do you happen to have any recommendations for dinner? I just arrived in town and am visiting with my father." I said, "I can tell you about a lot of places. What do you want to hear?" He'd come from San Diego to San Jose for a golf tournament and wanted to spend some time visiting northern California. He had about three or four places he was interested in visiting, but after going online and reading some stories, he'd picked Napa. We began to date, and after I had known him for several months, we were talking about what had brought him to Napa. I said, "What were the stories you read?" They were mine. They were my online stories about Napa. I think that's a testament to talking and writing about what you love and enjoy and just expressing it.

I like to tell stories, but I also love engaging people on that level, hearing their stories. I actually get in trouble with my friends because I don't just like to talk about the weather. I want to talk about things that are intimate and personal. It comes from what my father did; he truly taught me my trade. He probably never knew how much of a hand he had in bringing me into the newspaper and writing business. Actually, writing is my least favorite part;

that's the hard part. I would rather pull my stool up to somebody's knee and listen to them talk about their passions. I love the opportunity to learn from people who are passionate about what they do.

While I loved being a print journalist and an editor, many of my friends saw the potential of the internet and continually cajoled me to join them in this new world. I was almost late to the party, making the jump from print to online just one year before the bubble burst. But once online I was able to expand my skills from writing to understanding the development of websites and, ultimately, online business systems. My interest was with the creative aspects, not just content, but in branding and marketing, and this eventually led me to my job here as publicist for the Wine Train.

The Wine Train is really unique. The train itself has four engines and a collection of early twentieth-century cars that are pure Americana. So often if we are interested in something that existed before us, we can only find it in a museum. The Wine Train gives people the opportunity to touch and feel something that at one point touched almost every American family—it's history that's still available for use. It also includes a contemporary restaurant operation in railcars that have been refashioned specifically for this activity. The train's main kitchen has a glass observation window that people can look through to see our executive chef and the sous chefs while they're preparing the food. We serve fine wines and cheeses, pancetta-wrapped fillets of salmon with amazing cream sauce, and much more all prepared in an onboard restaurant as good as any in Napa Valley. The dining cars are set up with two seating times, so that one group can dine on the northbound trip up the valley in the first seating. Then they retire to a parlor car to relax in comfortable chairs that swivel so they can look in or watch the scenery outside while they have their coffee and dessert. The guests going into the second seating have spent the first hour and a half in a different parlor car having cocktails and appetizers while enjoying the scenery and conversation. The train travels up the valley at about 15 to 20 miles per hour. To me, it offers almost everything Napa Valley has to offer: wine, food, the view, as well as a short-line railroad—a piece of history preserved.

The Wine Train brings a lot of people to the Napa Valley; about 130,000 per year go through our station. Some people come to Napa specifically for the Wine Train. Many people come for special occasions; anniversaries and birthdays are really big. Most of our visitors come from California, but we're also very popular with people from the Midwest, Florida, Texas, and New York. A fair amount of our clientele is international, including people from other countries who love trains, with Canada and Japan being on top. The Wine Train has become something of an iconic image. I just had a Japanese film crew shooting here. We are strongest in the thirty-five to fifty-five age group, but we're gain-ing among the thirty-year-olds. Maybe losing a little bit in the over sixty-fives. Not many people bring children, but twice a month we have family night. The parents come for the regular gourmet dinner, and we provide a professional day-care person and a meal and activities for the kids. Children love, love, love trains, but they hate, hate, hate long gourmet dining experiences.

Attire on the Wine Train started out a lot more elegant. I'm sure that if people look at some of the older pictures and brochures, they'd think that they need to dress up. But we welcome any style of dress; we want people to be comfortable. I saw one gentleman changing clothes in his car in the parking lot, out of his shorts and T-shirt and into khakis and a button-down. I actually sent him back out to re-change into shorts because it was summer and he was going to be in the open-air Silverado car without air conditioning.

The Wine Train runs about three hundred days a year. She's an old girl and needs to be carefully maintained. Parts are no longer available for most of these cars, so we go offline in January and part of February and just run on the weekends. The cars are taken off and their wheels are re-ground—like turning old drum brakes. It is incredibly heavy lifting since everything on these old cars is big and heavy. Our train master is a St. Helena boy who started working here weekends. His father was an incredibly gifted mechanic and taught him many things about engines. I just finished writing a wonderful profile on him for *The Lion Roars,* which is the Lionel Train collectors magazine. Our engineers are old hands. I suspect that many of them could easily be retired if they wanted to, but they love to drive trains. People can actually ride in the cab with the conductors and engineers. We allow that. They buy a ticket and sign a waiver; it's that easy. I was up in that cab right after I started working here and it was incredibly fun. It's very old-school and mechanical.

When the Wine Train was first proposed, there was a lot of opposition. Many residents and vintners were worried about its impact—the idea of disgorging hundreds of passengers all at once. How much of that remains today?

When I first started working for the Wine Train, some people asked me if the old animosity toward the train was still there. It seems to me—from just living here in the community—that most of the fracas has died down, if not died off. The early rift and millions of dollars in lawsuits aimed at preventing the Wine Train from disembarking rail users within the city limits of St. Helena seems to be long gone now. In fact, many vintners are now working closely with us and just this June [2009] the St. Helena City Council voted to support a trial which allows the Wine Train to provide passenger service to a special monthly event in the town. Right now, the agreement is limited to this special event, but it could be extended if both parties agree.

What do tourists say to you about the Napa Valley?

This is anecdotal, but one Friday I was on the train speaking with a farm family from Virginia who were very interested in the wind machines and frost control they saw in the vineyards. They have a much shorter growing season in Virginia. Here we have a fairly lengthy and benign growing season, one that other agricultural areas would die for. While they wage daily wars with Mother Nature, we expect an almost perfect season every year. I remember going to Virginia and visiting the wine country there and it started to rain during harvest. I thought, "Oh my God, it's raining!" because here it would have been a news story. There it happens so frequently that it was an expected part of harvest.

I had a friend who lived in Arizona and every time he came out here to visit, he couldn't stop talking about our flowers. Every time he came, no matter what time of year, there were flowers in bloom. It is easy to take for granted how colorful it is here. When I've been away, the harbinger of arriving home is when I cross the southern bridge and smell the fertile earth of the Napa River, in that southern reach where the land is laid out like fingers in the mud. It smells so wonderful, not hot and dusty or smelling of concrete.

I think those of us who live here forget how glorious it is. The first time a visitor drives up Silverado Trail and sees hot air balloons in the sky and practically has a wreck or has to pull over. We have one of the best ballooning corridors in the world. Surprisingly, this gets very little play. This is just an amazing environment.

Today many younger people who come here are foodies, and they are looking for authentic experiences. I ran into an adorable young couple from LA who own a Peruvian restaurant, and all we talked about was food. When I was younger, the people I knew were not as focused on food—food and gardens were not topics of conversation. But when I arrived in Napa it was different. There are so many chefs in the culinary schools here and so many people have gardens. Here's an illustration of what I mean. In Los Angeles I used to do dinner theater. My friends and I would go out to some sort of theater event and that was our evening. Then I moved to Napa, and the evening became a three- or four-hour meal. When I told my LA friends, they were like, "Oh my God, what did you do?" And I would say, "Well, we just went out to dinner." "Yes, but afterwards did you go to the theater? Did you go clubbing?" they'd ask. "Well, no, it was a four-hour meal. It was like seven courses." They were like, "What? You're kidding." Today, this is what I do for entertainment; the entertainment is the meal. It's the wine, it's the food, it's the conversation, and it doesn't have to have anything else. I've kind of forgotten what people in other places do on an evening out.

What do you enjoy about your work?

It is challenging. As somebody who now does marketing for a living, I have gone over to the dark side from journalism. In fact, when I first took the job some of my writer friends called and said, "Noooo. How could you? You betray us! You hack!" But this job is really an amazing opportunity. This is a brand [the Wine Train] that is unique and challenging—really challenging. On one side, we have absolutely no competition because there is no other Wine Train. But on the other side, people will not come unless we provide a really great experience. I also like it because I'm a bit of a gearhead. I love history, and the short-line railroad really appeals to me. The people who work here are great. They really care. Another big plus is that I don't have to drive to San Francisco to work. I can live and work in my own backyard—that's huge for me personally. I don't add to the congestion or the pollution, and I add to my family's health and happiness because if the dog gets sick or my child has to be picked up from school, I am available. I have a unique local job in a wonderful environment, and I get to be part of the community. It's a healthy balance. People who don't have this balance are on Prozac. They're in their car three hours a day and wondering why they're depressed.

I learned a long time ago to be grateful for what I do. Do you remember the 2000 Yountville earthquake, like a 5 or 6 on the Richter scale—something like that? Well, it shook up my little house pretty badly, broke dishes, broke windows, and knocked things about. I went in and sat down with the Small Business Administration loans and grants people in a big room with all of these desks. I had to bring in all of my tax returns and everything. The woman sitting at the desk across from me had been transferred in from another area by the government to help people process their claims. She's there to help us Napans make it through this little disaster we faced. So I am sitting at her desk, feeling very sorry for myself. My house is cracked up, it's a mess, and I can't afford to put in a lot of money to fix it up. She's going through my paperwork and says, "So, you *own* a house in the Napa Valley." I go, "Yeah, I do." She's looking through my tax returns and sees that I file a Schedule C because I write for a portion of my living, and she says, "And you're a writer." I go, "Yeah." She pauses and says, "You are a single woman and you're a writer and you have a house in the Napa Valley?" "Hmmm. I do. . . . God, that sounds good when you say it!" Here I am ticked off about things like the gallon of pickles my mother had brought over from Costco that exploded when it hit the ground sending pickle bombs all over the place, and this woman is thinking, "I'll take your pickles."

Massage / *Claude Smith*

"The energy that's in humans is the same energy that's in every-thing else."

Massage is one of the oldest healing arts: its earliest known use dates back three thousand years to China. Ancient Hindus, Persians, and Egyptians also used massage for many ailments. Hippocrates recommended rubbing and fric-tion for joint and circulatory problems. Today, there are two hundred forms of massage and bodywork whose benefits include increasing joint flexibility and therapy for chronic conditions such as arthritis and low back pain. But the most common reason tourists have for getting a massage is pleasure and relief from the stress and tension of everyday life. Many massage therapists work in the Napa Valley, with the highest concentration in the spa town of Calistoga. Lanky with long hair and a well-worn face, Claude Smith is one of the oldest and most experienced massage therapists in the region. He is also a talented painter.

———

I was living in New York City, where I grew up, sharing a big old brown-stone in Brooklyn. It was January in 1976 during a midwinter heat wave when all of a sudden for about four or five days it's like 70 degrees out and crystal-clear. I took the subway into Manhattan to go to SoHo, which for an artist was where everything was happening. I'd already graduated from art school and was trying to make a living at painting, but not doing great. I decide to take some mescaline. Here I am, tripping on mescaline, sitting on a stoop in SoHo, watching what felt like the entire art world parade by. Everybody was out: the artists, the art critics, the gallery owners—anybody who was anybody. Andy Warhol and his entourage were parading around. I'm sitting there very quiet watching all these social interactions and I'm thinking to myself, I'm never going to be able to do this. As a painter I'm dedicated, but to do that entire social thing suddenly seemed really distasteful. So I am sitting there trying to think of what else could I do. Then for no apparent reason, it came to me—in my altered state—that I could be a massage therapist. I'd never even had a massage and I didn't come from a family of warm, physical people. It was just a random, psychedelic thought.

When I got back to my brownstone in Brooklyn, I told one of my room-mates about my day in SoHo and about my idea of doing massage. He'd just returned from Vermont, and he says to me, "Ya know, I was just hanging out with this woman. She's a massage teacher. Her next set of classes starts February first and she needs a roommate." I got right on the phone and had a long conversation with her and in a week I was living in rural Vermont in the middle of winter with a person I don't know. On the first day, within five minutes of getting instructions and laying my hands on someone, I knew I'd done the right thing. I could just feel it. It was absolutely natural; my hands seemed to know exactly where to go. And here I am more than thirty years later still doing it.

The biggest thing about being a massage therapist is to be receptive, passionate, and caring. Maybe there's something in the artistic temperament—the way an artist observes and perceives and experiences the world—that crosses over into massage. Whatever it is, I had some degree of sensitivity, and the feedback I got from my classmates and teacher was that I was doing good stuff. So I felt very, very good. I learned Swedish and Japanese styles of massage, the two basic forms that everybody learns. After Vermont, I went to the New England School of Acupuncture to study Chinese medicine. Having gotten my feet wet, I thought to myself, "Okay, we're going to take it further." These were the very early days of acupuncture in this country. In fact, there were only two places where you could study it: the New England School and one in San Francisco. I dropped out of acupuncture after a year because within the established medical system there was really no place to intern or do a residency, but what I learned was invaluable to me in doing massage. Japanese pressure point massage, or Shiatsu, is based on the same system, so what I had learned was totally transferable. I can find spots that many massage therapists can't.

After leaving acupuncture school, I went to Toronto to try to find a Shiatsu teacher. Some people in a café in the Kensington market area suggested that I talk to this guy who lived down the street who was doing some neat healing. It's the dead of winter and it's practically a blizzard out. God only knows what I looked like. My hair was really long, and I was wearing a big black coat. I knocked on the door of this funny-looking house, and this Chinese man came out. I said, "I'm looking for a massage teacher." And surprise, he lets me right in. It was a very simple, spare place. We sat down, and he explains to me that he's a magnetic healer. He explained that he didn't touch people, he just held his hands an inch or two above their bodies and directed his energy into them through whatever power he's got. Then he demonstrated. I thought, "Okay, it's tangible. I can feel it." The term for it today would be "energy work." Anyway, he took me under his wing, and I started studying with him informally. His name was Yau Loong—just a regular, unpretentious guy who nobody knew about outside the Chinese community. He wasn't doing workshops. He wasn't doing speaking tours. But he was tremendous. Years later I had called him, and he says, "You might not believe me but this magnetic feeling energy can be projected long distance. Put the phone next to your face." Then he directed his energy to me and I could feel something completely wash over my body. It was amazing, and in time I incorporated it into my own massage work. Now when clients come to Calistoga and ask for "energy work," the receptionists know to direct them to me.

How I got to the Napa Valley is a weird story. I had moved to Woodstock, New York, with my girlfriend in 1979 and we went to hear this spiritual guy, Daniel Castro, talk. He was from Brooklyn and had spent a lot of time studying in India—kind of a tough guy, but very charismatic. He had a lot of compassion, and clearly he had some insight into what's going on with us as human beings. Anyway, I established a relationship with this guy and he asked me to come out to his community in Santa Rosa [California]. So we went out to visit, and it didn't take us long to know that we were not going back to New York. We moved into the community called the Darshan Yoga Society, and after the first year our son was born. It was more about meditating and dissecting what we are doing as human beings, trying to understand where our behavior comes from, than any ritualistic stuff. We had our own separate cottage, but there were people living together in joint households. The community had a clothing business to help support it. So suddenly I was the haberdasher—a new career. We lived there for a couple of years; the community splintered later, in either '83 or '84.

After we left the community, I became a baker, but I was still doing massage work and painting. I went on the arts and crafts circuit for a while, selling art and scarves that I had hand-painted, whatever, trying to make a living to support the three of us. In 1985, my wife and I separated. A while later I got jobs at several spas in Calistoga doing massage—a shift here, a shift there. I was working at a half-dozen places: the Calistoga Spa, the International Spa, Golden Haven, and Le Spa Français and some other places. Calistoga is a place where you can make a living doing massage. Not yet knowing the scene, I figured I'd try working at a bunch of places and see where I fit in best. It took me about a year to sort it all out. I dropped pretty much all my shifts except for those at the International Spa, which is where I settled.

The International Spa was different from the others, which is why I chose it. The owner, John Cashman, had been a massage teacher himself and only hired the best. I'm not talking about technically best; you always need good technique to be a skilled therapist. No, the quality that he was most interested in was having a good heart. He wanted people who really cared about people. It's not that I don't think all massage therapists want to do that; I think that's why most people go into massage therapy as a career. But not everyone has it, and just having good technique was not enough to get you a job there. He sold the business in '94 and opened another place called Lavender Hill Spa on the main drag [Highway 29] going into Calistoga. It's an old house converted into massage rooms with two separate outbuildings that are private bath houses. Lavender Hill has a sort of Asian identity. That's partially due to our owner being a practicing Buddhist. He has spent time in Thailand and China and still goes there often. On the walls we've got Chinese scrolls and Thai paintings. The gardens outside have a peaceful Buddhist look and feel. That might not work for some clients who want the locker room atmosphere, but for most people today the Buddhist thing is familiar and is no longer weird. I work at Lavender Hill on Friday, Saturday, and Sunday, which are the busiest days of the week. Each of my shifts is for six hours and each massage is an hour long with fifteen minutes in between. That gives the therapists enough time to get our clients up off the table and dressed and for us to run out of the room, wash up, change the sheets, and get our new clients in.

The Lavender Hill Spa owner decided we were going to be the spa for couples; that's what we hang our hat on. This appeals to a lot of people because many people come to the valley for a romantic weekend. Besides the massage rooms, we've got two private bath houses with side-by-side baths where you're left to yourself to do whatever you want. That's different from most other spas, which are like locker rooms with separate men's and women's sections—in those places, a guy might not see his partner for a couple of hours. So we do this side-by-side tub thing. And we don't make any distinction between married couples, unmarried couples, gay couples—it doesn't matter. We even have a couples room designated for side-by-side massages for people who can't stand to be apart from one another for more than an hour.

Our clientele comes from outside the valley but mostly within a hundred-mile radius which includes Sacramento, San Francisco–Berkeley, East Bay, South Bay, and San Jose. These are people who would rather do a long weekend just two hours away than get on a plane for a long weekend in New York or Santa Fe or wherever people go. There was a period after 9/11 when business was bad—the whole tourist industry took a pretty big hit—but now a lot of people are driving up for long weekends. As tourism has grown, Calistoga has gotten more upscale. It has more boutiques and things for tourists to do. The town is getting more and more tourist-oriented every year and that means more seasonal variation in business. Tourist time is summer and fall; in winter, things slow down and it's hard to make a living. But you always know that things will pick up again in the spring.

The spa business is a big part of what's going on in the Napa Valley. There are at least a dozen spas in Calistoga, which is a lot for a small area. And they're all competing with one another for clients. Massage is more popular now than it was ten or twenty years ago. Today each spa needs to establish an identity that distinguishes it from the other guys. The wineries are doing the same thing. Twenty years ago, you were a "spa" and you offered mud baths, you offered mineral baths, you had a pool, and you offered massage. All the spas were kind of the same. Now marketing is big, and everyone is trying to find an angle. You see ads for Winter Warmer Baths, Seaweed Treatments, Summer Refreshment Treatments, and on and on. The options change with the seasons. Take Valentine's Day: we've created a special package where we offer couples candy and a chocolate oil massage and other frills. At Lavender Hill we've had to constantly expand our menu, because clients are looking for newer and better services and we're of course trying to accommodate them. We started bringing in aromatherapy, started adding special herbal facials, and started adding Thai and hot stone massages—always trying to figure out what the new best thing was to offer. Honestly, I think there are too many choices. When clients come in today they have to choose among eight or ten different baths: "Do I want an aromatherapy bath or do I want a coconut Thai bath?" It's too much. It confuses people, and it can be intimidating. But the marketing seems to work, because it sets us apart from other places. The internet has become very important. When I ask my clients how they found out about this spa, most say they found our website. Today not only do you have to have a distinct identity, but it has to come across online. Twenty years ago there was no online.

We're not the most expensive spa in Calistoga, but we're not the least expensive either. We charge roughly $85 for the hour massage plus another $50 for the bath. So you're in for $135 before you tip the bath attendant or massage therapist. We get some customers for whom this is a very special occasion and they've set aside money just for it. Some people are celebrating an anniversary or birthday and it's an once-in-a-lifetime thing. They've come from wherever and they're going to have a nice dinner, stay at a luxury B&B, go wine tasting, maybe take the Wine Train, eat some great food, and maybe go hot air ballooning. And they're going to blow a few thousand bucks for three days in the Napa Valley. They're going to have the Napa Valley, northern California experience. Then there are other people for whom getting a massage is not a big deal, and it's not a strain on their budget. We get the full range.

What are your clients like?

At the spa, we get every type of body you can imagine. I've seen everything. I've worked on elderly people, people with no legs, dwarfs, people who weigh six hundred pounds, and guys who are seven feet tall. The one thing you don't get is children. Occasionally you might get a mid-teen and it's usually their first massage. Over the years the clientele has changed. Today they're younger, fatter, more spa savvy, and definitely more stressed. Everybody today seems to be under a fair amount of stress and it shows up in their bodies. Most people hold stress in their upper back, shoulders, and neck. When you start working on those areas, you can feel the tenseness. It's hard. It's not supposed to feel that way, it really isn't. Then you work on someone who doesn't seem to be stressed, and it's like, "My gosh! What are you doing in your life to counteract this [stress]?"

I don't care who I work on. My attitude is that no matter who comes into the spa, no matter what they look like, no matter how big they are, I'm going to give them a good massage. The key thing to getting a good massage is being receptive. The more receptive a person is, the better my massage is going to be. You can easily tell who isn't receptive because their jaws are clenched or their arms are rigid. People often don't know they're doing it; they can be completely unaware. I've had clients who just can't relax and will fight me for the full hour. Overall, I find women by their nature to be more receptive. You might find it surprising, but often really heavy women are more receptive because I am probably the only physical contact they have. In their normal day-to-day lives they get derision, they get judged for being big and obese. I have an hour to work on this person and the best thing I can do is accept and love them.

I can usually find positive qualities in most people; in fact, it's unusual when I can't find anything. Often I look at people's hands or I'll see something in their feet. I might point out how beautiful a client's hands are or that the shape of their fingers indicates a very creative person. And they'll go, "Wow, you can see that?" And then they'll tell me how they paint or sing. It's really fulfilling if you hit the right note, because people want to be seen and accepted and appreciated. If you can do that, the client will feel good about the whole experience.

If you're not already intuitive before becoming a therapist, you're likely to become more intuitive. Let me put it this way. I have to be able to read a body that I've never seen before in my life, and that I may never see again after the massage. When a client comes in, I have them sit down in the massage room, which is just big enough for a massage table and a stool. I have just a few minutes to ask them if they have any injuries, any medical conditions, any particular aches or pains or stresses that I should pay attention to. I ask them what kind of work they do, which can give me some clues. What we do occupationally usually shows up in our bodies. If a client is a waitress, she's going to be on her feet for eight hours a day carrying stuff with her arms extended. Now I know where to look for stress areas. Somebody who sits behind a computer or is doing sheetrocking or doing construction or whatever will have specific things going on in their bodies as a result of the work. Visually, I'm also trying to get all the clues I can to figure out how best to work on this body. What's their body language like? All this stuff is registering. I'm not calculating so much as just taking it all in. To be able to do a good job, you want to serve that particular person, not do a generic massage. Sure, I could go through the motions and bang out massages all day, but that's not what I'm here to do. And I wouldn't feel good about it if I did.

Those first few minutes with a client are also important because I'm establishing rapport. I don't know them and they don't know me. Look at me! I look like you could have dragged me out from under a bridge, and you're going to be on the table without any clothes on with me working on your body. Most clients feel vulnerable, and they've got to feel comfortable and have some trust in me. You get some women who have never been touched by a man other than their husband. For them a massage can be a really scary experience, and they may have a hard time relaxing. It's so foreign and weird to them that it's not pleasurable. On the other hand, you get some clients who test the waters to see how far you're willing to go. Most people understand that a massage involves taking their clothes off. I explain that they're going to be draped and not exposed, but now and then I'll get a client who doesn't want to be draped or only wants to be partially draped.[1] Sometimes I'll come back into the room, and the client will be lying face up naked, fully exposed. It's not an accident. These days though, most clients understand—at least at our spa—that they're here for a therapeutic massage and nothing more.

I don't think there's a spa in Calistoga that has not had an occasional problem with inappropriate behavior. I hear from my female counterparts that occasionally guys will do [sexual] stuff. I've even had guys try to do weird stuff with me. At one of the spas, I had one woman—totally outrageous—grab me and pull me down on the table. It was really weird because it was in a room where the walls don't go all the way to the ceiling, and her husband was in the next stall. It was awkward. It happens very infrequently, but when it does happen it's not good. The problems that people hear about usually involve male therapists taking advantage of female clients. That's totally unacceptable, and guys like that should be fired. It reflects badly on everybody. Women massage therapists are generally not predatory. Besides, you are much less likely to hear about a female therapist doing "extras" for male clients, because most men are not going to complain anyway. Secretly, I think every heterosexual male client is hoping against all odds that he will get that one female therapist who is willing to offer up some extras. I'm dead serious about this. In all the years I've been working here, I know of only one female therapist who has gotten fired, but many, many male massage therapists have been let go. And the only reason that the woman therapist got fired was because she was incredibly careless and indiscreet. She was way too noisy. By the way, I've never gotten sexually involved with a client. My basic ground rule is don't get involved. It's bad enough when you get involved with a co-worker. I did marry a bath attendant, but that didn't last very long. Bad idea.

The first thing I do when clients lie down on the table is put my hands on the soles of their feet. You can feel the energy of the whole body in the feet. You can tell whether this is an open or closed person, a contracted or receptive person. The feet don't lie. This has nothing to do with reflexology or any of that stuff. This is just something I have learned over thirty years of doing massages. Something else I've learned is that most people don't really inhabit their bodies. When you are working on them, you can tell. Some people haven't visited their bodies in years. It sounds stupid, but it's true. The human body is designed to move. If you're physically engaged, you're moving your body and finding outlets like sports, walking, or whatever. Eating well and being creative also help. I think creativity is a key factor in well-being. It doesn't matter what form the creativity takes; it can be painting, music, writing, cooking, or whatever. It's the creative part of us that makes the difference between a person who is contracted and a person who is expansive. People who are not engaged in some kind of creative process tend to be pretty shut down. That's become pretty evident to me.

I work intuitively; sometimes I can get an idea what's below the skin of the person I am massaging. I have worked on some people who I know have done some bad things. It's not anatomical as much as getting a feeling for what this person's life is like, for who the person is beneath the flesh and muscles. Sometimes I can draw conclusions about people without actually talking to them. But there are also plenty of surprises. I never know what is going to happen. Sometimes people just start crying. I'm working with them and I know I've hit a nerve, so to speak, when they just start sobbing on the table. Or they have some other physical manifestation. As a therapist, you have to be okay with that and not freak out. I'll ask, "Do you need a minute by yourself?" Or I might just simply let them do what they have to do with me being present. They'll talk about what's going on with them, about the stress they are under at work or at home. Sometimes it's simply the only time they have had to lie down in the middle of the day and not feel compelled to do anything. People can be very uncomfortable with doing nothing.

You never know how much people are going to talk during massages. Some people talk the whole time. Personally, I think it keeps them from relaxing. If it's just jabbering I don't get involved. But talkers can be fun, if they're interesting. Years ago, David Hockney, the artist, came to the spa with his partner. I am a fan of him so I juggled the appointment book so I could work on him. But David Hockney is stone deaf without his hearing aids, which of course he had taken out. So we had a silent hour except for me screaming at him to turn over. But he was very nice and easy to work on.

I use aromatherapy if I think it will be helpful. Clients who are anxious or depressed say that aromas lift their spirits and help them relax. Clients have about a half-dozen options to choose from. The oils are applied directly to the skin and get into the air once I start rubbing. I think it works sometimes. But I no longer think that all of the things that we're taught actually work. A lot of stuff is pretty bogus. And unlike probably 99.9 percent of massage therapists, I think American reflexology is nonsense. There's no scientific basis for it, period. Cultures from all over the world agree that working on the feet is a great thing, that it's relaxing and makes you feel good. Yes. But I don't buy that if you press a certain point on the foot it affects your liver or your pancreas or your kidneys or whatever. No way. Once I did some research on this, and I noticed the foot charts are different in different countries. If reflexology is for real, they should be consistent, the same in every country.

Some massage therapists like to use New Age music. I hate New Age music. I think it kills brain cells and over the long term it makes massage therapists stupider. Most clients don't want chanting, rattles, or drum music, and they don't want you waving crystals over them. They just want to get their muscles rubbed and relaxed.

Have you ever turned away a client?

Of the twenty-five thousand people I've done over the past thirty years, I've only refused to work on two. One was a woman from South America who couldn't speak English and was trying to convey to the staff that she could not have a man work on her. It was against her religion, it was way outside of what was acceptable for her. The receptionist and the bath attendants weren't getting it, and when I came in to do the massage the woman was petrified. She was all wrapped up, and I realized she could barely speak English. Since there wasn't a female massage therapist available, I told the receptionist to give her money back and let her go.

The other case was more interesting. I saw the couple in the reception room—huge guy about six-foot-four and a tiny wife. I bring the guy into the massage room. Remember, it's a little, itty-bitty room just big enough for the massage table. I've got a little boom box playing, probably classical music because I don't listen to New Age. I hate that stuff. Anyway, this guy comes in, and he tells me to turn the music off. I think, "Okay, this guy must know what he wants. He's one of those guys who wants an hour of total silence." I started doing my little question-and-answer period. He's visiting from the Bay Area. I think maybe he's a mechanic. Pretty soon, I notice he's starting to move out of the designated client area and coming around the table, so basically we're circling the table. He's clearly not happy. After we do one full circle around the table, it's clear that something here isn't right. He's got a lot of attitude behind the answers he gives me. Finally I ask him if he wants the massage and he says, "No!" So I ask him what he's doing here and he says his wife made him come in. I'm looking at this giant six-foot-four athletic body which could crush me with one hand and thinking, "How could his little wife possibly make him do anything?" He said all he wanted was to go back to the motel, watch the ball game, knock down some beers, and that would make him relaxed. So I went out to the receptionist and told her that I wasn't going to fight with this guy and to refund his money and get him the hell out of here.

I've got so many weird stories. I worked on a very unusual guy one time. I saw him and his wife out in the reception area, and the guy looked about sixty—like a military guy with a flattop haircut. When I got him on the table, the rest of him is like a twenty-eight-year-old athlete. I'm thinking this is highly unusual, and I'm intrigued. I've never seen a specimen like this, so I started asking him questions and I find out he sits behind a desk in Houston working in real estate. The only sports he plays are golf and a little tennis. I ask him about his diet. He says he eats whatever he wants. Now I'm getting kind of annoyed. So I cut to the chase and tell him that I've never seen anyone in my thirty years as a massage therapist in as good condition. He says it's part of his genetics and that he has a really positive attitude toward life. Well, I need to straighten this out because if this is what having a positive attitude will do, I am really impressed. Anyway, I finished the massage and I'm still baffled. I go out to the reception room, and his wife is already out there waiting. She's a grandma kind of person, certainly not the physical equivalent of her husband. She looks like she's in her mid-sixties and should be knitting. She looks at me and asks what kind of shape her husband is in with kind of a twinkle in her eye. I look at her: "Are you kidding?" She starts laughing and tells me how they just flew into Calistoga. Now you can't fly into Calistoga unless you have some kind of special clearance, so I asked her more. Finally, she tells me her husband can fly anywhere because he's one of the astronauts. I went, "Okay, now I get it." He would have been one of the astronauts in the early days of the space program when they were training these guys to be like Superman.

About two weeks ago some fairly large guys came in one night with their girlfriends and all the guys wanted massages. Some of them wanted deep tissue work. One change I've noticed is the number of people coming in for massage today looking for deeper work. They don't want the regular, old-fashioned Swedish massage. Even if they don't specifically ask for deep tissue massage, they want a firm massage, not just a nice, easy rubdown with oil. The problem for therapists is these hard massages are exhausting. Deep tissue work puts a lot of strain on your body, especially for female therapists working on big male clients. You really have to work much harder, and it can beat the shit out of you. Anyway, we had a new young female therapist on staff and she wound up getting assigned these guys. After two of them, I could tell she wasn't doing well, that it was becoming a rough night for her. We're down to the fifth hour of our shift, and another couple comes in and wants a deep tissue. So I told the receptionist, "Give the guy to me." I introduced myself, and he shouts out that he wants a woman massage therapist. I said, "You can either have a deep tissue massage or the cute girl, but you can't have both. Sorry." I'm not normally a smart-ass, but I couldn't help it. It was just one of those moments where I let loose.

Okay, here's a story. This is bad; I'm not proud of it, but I'll tell you anyway. This couple comes in. They look to be in their early thirties. The guy is very cocky, which I can tell by his physical presence and how he's swaggering. Generally, when clients come in, I shake their hand, look them in the eye, and introduce myself. This guy decided when I put my hand out to shake that he's going to break it. I assume to prove that he's more of a man than me, and he actually hurt me. This was a serious mistake. You don't mess with a massage therapist's hands. What was this guy thinking? I don't think he'd ever had a massage. We talked and he told me that I can do whatever I want, work as deep as I want, because I can't hurt him. He shouldn't have told me that because he was just asking for it. I decided I would take it upon myself to do all massage therapists a favor and make sure this guy never returned to a spa again. Like I said, I'm not proud of it. This was the one and only time I decided to hurt a client. The massage table is set down low and you're working with leverage. There are techniques, especially if you know pressure points, by using elbows and the weight of your body where you can hurt a person. Of course, our whole point is not to hurt people. Anyway, I just whaled on this guy and hurt him to the point where he told me to back off. I don't think he'll ever come back, and if he does, he'll ask for a woman. It was a bad moment all around and it took me a long time to get over it.

There are more women massage therapists than men. Not that it should be, but there is more demand for women massage therapists. More women than men get massages. You don't see groups of guys saying, "Hey, let's have a spa day out as pals." Women do that easily, and it's a fun day out for them. But having said this, spas are becoming popular with some men. But heterosexual guys mostly want women therapists and a percentage of women also feel safer with a female therapist. That's just the way it is. I would say that if there are forty massage therapists on staff here at the spa, thirty-five of them are women because that's what people want. So even though I have seniority, I won't get as much work as the women therapists. But being in northern California and

NAPA'S OTHER PLEASURES / 199

close to San Francisco, we do get a lot of gay clients who request male massage therapists, so this offsets some of the imbalance.

We get people who've never had a massage before. They have lots of questions, and for us they can be high maintenance. It can be funny, if you have a good sense of humor. If you don't, it's no fun at all. Actually, a client doesn't have to be a beginner to be high maintenance. Some people are just very needy. It's always too warm or too cold. They need an extra blanket or they don't want any blankets. The face cradle needs adjustment. Nothing is quite right. Overall, women tend to be more high maintenance than men. I might be a minute into the massage when a client will say, "So where did you get your training?" As if to say, "My therapist doesn't do it that way." I don't mind a straightforward question, but sometimes there is an attitude behind it. Sometimes I'll respond, "I got my training in prison." That usually stops that line of questioning; it scares them enough to make them shut up. Even though I tell them I'm kidding, they're not quite sure. Another kind of high maintenance person is the one who's oblivious to the clock. Massages are scheduled by the hour, so when you're done, you have to get up, get dressed, and get out—not fall asleep. Some people seem unaware that another client is coming in ten minutes after their massage.

With tips, you never know what's going to happen. Some people don't leave tips because they don't know it's part of the system. There is no law or requirement that the client must tip. But if you don't, it's like going to a restaurant and not leaving your server anything. In fact, the massage therapist is giving you a lot more personal, intimate service than your waitress ever does. I don't see any correlation between the quality of the massage or the experience clients have with the size of the tip they leave. Many people decide before they even come in what they're going to leave you—five or ten bucks no matter how good the massage. Overall, I'd say that 90 percent of clients give tips, and most of them give in the normal 15 percent range.

Tip money is important because it makes up a lot of our income. We don't get paid much relative to what the clients are charged. I make about 30 percent of what the client is charged. All spas are different, but I don't think any even have a 50-50 split. There are no benefits in this line of work, and we all work part-time, which is also why tips are so important. Tips make the difference between making $25 an hour or $40 an hour. That's big. A ten-buck tip is okay; twenty bucks is a good tip; forty bucks is exceptional. The biggest tip I ever got was $100. There were no unusual circumstances; the person just really liked the treatment and must've liked me. Holiday weekends are the worst for tips and for clients because they bring out the amateur clients. It's probably the same up and down the valley with restaurants, accommodations, and the wineries. I'm sure there's a difference between the people who know wine and know what they're looking for versus holiday people who are just out drinking or tasting and don't know a good wine from a bad one. It's the same with massage. A lot of people don't know a good massage from a bad massage. Most of the spas here give good massages, although there are a few places where I wouldn't let them put their hands on me.

Do massage therapists share any characteristics?

I think most massage therapists are compassionate and want to help people. You have to be in good shape physically, mentally, and emotionally. I have to admit that after I do five hours in a row I am beat. Now, after three days of work I need to rest. Mondays—because I work Fridays, Saturdays, and Sundays—I'm generally useless, I can't do anything. It's an overall physical exhaustion. Besides the physical strain, there's a lot of energy and emotional expenditure. At the end of the shift, I don't want to touch anybody. I don't want to talk to anybody. I don't want to be touched by anybody. It's good that I don't come home to a wife and kids, because it wouldn't work. All I want to do is crawl into a corner and not relate. It's important to get one massage yourself for every ten you give. It's therapeutic, good for the circulation, and good for loosening up the muscles and relaxing. And when you're getting a massage from another therapist, you sometimes learn a new technique or a whole different form that you can pick up.

I think massage therapists by their nature are fairly unstable and independent, but I also think that most people are neurotic and fucked-up. Massage therapists want to be their own bosses. They don't like being tied down and they like the flexibility of making their own hours. Some therapists can't fit into the spa scene because it's too regimented for them. They have to be on time and they have to be able to work within the system, even though it's not a hard system to work within relative to the real world. It's a short shift—six hours—but you have to be on time and good for all six hours.

Because massage therapists spend so much time working on bodies, they are more into health and healthy living and "New Age" health ideas. I don't know of many alcohol-drinking or cigarette-smoking massage therapists. They really don't go together. We can tell a client who's a smoker instantly during a massage. I mean "instantly." Remember we're in this very small room where there aren't any windows and not a lot of air circulating. I've been in a room when smoke is practically coming out of my client. When I start pressing on them, the room is permeated with the smell of cigarette smoke. And we're in the Napa Valley where people have been drinking. Somehow the interaction of a hot bath and alcohol, cigarettes, coffee, or whatever—it comes out of their skin. This affects therapists too.

After thirty years of doing massage, I think the most profound change in me is that I've become a whole lot more compassionate toward humans, about our lives and our bodies. No matter who comes in, I give them a good treatment. No matter how big or grotesque their bodies are, there is still something small, vulnerable, and soft inside. As I said before, I've tried to develop the ability to see that, to imagine every person as a baby and to tap into that. It's a totally different way of working with a client than having the idea that I am there to heal them by laying my hands on them. Clients, I think, have fairly high expectations of what a massage will do for them. If they've got chronic neck or back problems, they're hoping the massage therapist can give them relief. It's often unrealistic. We're not doctors, we're not chiropractors, and we're not osteopaths. I no longer hold the notion that I'm going to heal anybody. I am a massage therapist, period. But I do believe that if I can get my client completely relaxed, the body—which is a self-correcting mechanism—will do what it has to do to treat itself.

Looking back over the years, I've realized that one of the reasons I got into massage therapy was because it was a total contrast to the solo work of being an artist, of being in a studio by myself all day. Solo work requires contemplation and a lot of quiet time, whereas massage involves continual interaction one way or the other. I grew up in a family that wasn't touchy-feely; in fact, my mother was the kind of person who if she were an animal, she'd eat her young. I didn't learn about being warm, kind, and affectionate from my parents. It wasn't until I was an adult that I realized there was something absolutely missing.

If you would have told me back in 1976 that more than thirty years later I'd still be doing this, that I would have worked on twenty-five thousand people, I would have shrugged that off as impossible. No way. Now, here I am and retirement is nowhere in sight. Luckily I'm physically able to do it. Most therapists hit a burnout stage a few years into the job or they injure themselves and have to get out. But I'm blessed because after thirty years of work, I have no hand problems, no wrist problems, and no problems with arms or back. Nothing. That's highly unusual. If I had to do this work in my sleep, I could. I've done so many massages, my hands at this point can see, hear, and smell everything they need to. I don't have to think about too much, I trust my hands and know how much pressure to apply and when to let up. Because I don't have to think about it, that leaves lots of creative time. I think about all kinds of things while massaging; a lot has to do with art, thinking about projects that I'm working on and sometimes a light will go off in the middle of the massage and I'll find the solution. I think massage influences my artwork tremendously. It's deepened my sensitivity on all levels and made me think about the human condition, that we're all in the same boat together. It's also made me look at humans as not being separate from other living things in the world. The energy that's in humans is the same energy that's in everything else.

Hot Air Ballooning / *Joyce Bowen*

"Ballooning is like meditation."

In the 1970s there were fewer than five hundred hot air balloons in the United States, making it a unique activity and sight; landings drew curious onlookers. Although people are far more familiar with balloons today, their beauty and allure remain, and ballooning has become a popular activity for visitors to the Napa Valley. Joyce Bowen is the pilot and owner of Bonaventura Balloons. A Renaissance woman, Joyce has a graduate degree in ethnomusicology and has been a travel writer (she co-authored Frommer's first guidebook on Australia), a private music and school teacher, a design consultant, and a member of an all-woman fire brigade, as well as a licensed commercial pilot. Her hillside home is filled with traditional and exotic musical instruments, textiles, baskets of obsidian and flint arrowheads, and books which reflect her fascination with travel and other cultures. Although Joyce is based in the Napa Valley, she also leads international balloon trips.

———

I've always had an affinity for flying. My father was an FAA [Federal Aviation Administration] official and co-owner of a small plane. I was about five the first time I got to fly in it. And even after all these years I still love the feeling—the freedom of flight. I've always liked things that feel like flying, whether diving off high diving boards or riding horses. I moved to Napa in 1971 after studying and traveling abroad for long periods and became very involved in the community, eventually meeting friends who were just getting started in ballooning. They asked me to help them, and I became a member of their ground crew. I'd been ballooning a few times on the weekends for fun. At the time, I was teaching piano and a few classes at Napa Valley College and working as a design consultant for a builder in the valley. I was also a single parent raising two children.

I fell in love with ballooning and ended up going to flight school to become a commercial pilot. I bought my first balloon in 1983 with the help of a hefty loan, and started my own company—Bonaventura Balloons. "Bonaventura" is my Esperanto—a combination of Spanish, French, and Italian—for "good adventure." Becoming a balloonist takes a lot longer than you would think, especially here because you can only fly one hour a day before the winds pick up. The weather has to be just right to fly a balloon; you can't take chances. The best time for ballooning is at sunrise because that's when it's

Joyce Bowen.
Photograph by
Vi Bottaro.

calm and cool and manageable. In other places, like Arizona or Texas, you can also fly in the late afternoon before sunset; and the weather out there is also good for ballooning in the winter. The main flying season here is from April through October. Not much flying goes on in the winter; March is an especially high wind month. But half of the year it's pretty stable. The valley's airspace is somewhat protected by the mountains and that's what makes it a nice place to fly, along with the beauty of the valley.

What is the work of a balloonist like?

With my routine, you're never done. If you're conscientious, trying to create an experience that's special and magical for your passengers, it's like preparing a Broadway show. I can say that because I have directed musicals. There's a lot of backstage work. And because it's FAA aviation, the preparation and the follow-up are massive, with lots of record keeping. It's also expensive. We use propane in the aircraft, but that's not the major cost. There are layers of insurance, overhead, FAA-required maintenance, vehicles registered with the PUC [Public Utilities Commission], employees who are required to have drug and alcohol testing, workman's comp, and more. Then there's the public relations and hospitality side of the job. There's no other piloting job in the world where you are entertaining and talking to your passengers at the same time as you are flying.

When I'm going to take people out, I check the weather the night before. And I check it again in the morning. I need to know my exact wind directions on the compass at different levels. I'm always checking the weather. What time I get up depends on sunrise. Sunrise varies over a two-hour period during the year, 5:30 to 7:30. We'll start getting ready at least an hour before that. My crew may need to be picked up or else I'll meet them at the launch site. My crew varies; some are students who have the summer or a semester off, but I've also had folks like an artist who wanted something active to do and a writer working on a book. Some have grown up in the valley, others are new. Either way, many of them have told me it was the best and most fun job of their lives.

A member of my crew or I will meet the guests, and then drive them to our chosen launch site. We give them a historical narrative on the way. While the balloons are being set up by the crew, I brief my passengers so that they'll know a little bit about the experience and what to expect. People think there's going to be a lot of speed, action, noise, more like a glider or fixed-wing airplane or a helicopter, but it's totally peaceful. Of course I also talk about safety—how important it is to listen to the pilot, to watch out for ropes and parts. I also talk about the history of ballooning, and I have a notebook with copies of old etchings. Man's first flight was actually in a balloon, whereas most people think of the Wright brothers. They don't realize that in 1783 the Montgolfier brothers, French papermakers originally, launched a hot air balloon with no pilot: their passengers were a sheep, a duck, and a rooster. A few months later they were able to send up two passengers on a twenty-minute flight with a huge crowd looking on from the Palace of Versailles. One of the reasons I insist on a briefing and some history is so that people have respect for the sport. I consider this part of my mission. Many of my guests have thanked me for it. They have often started out thinking that ballooning is like a carnival ride, not realizing that these are FAA-regulated aircraft.

Standing the balloon up is a dramatic and photogenic process. People love it, and we love them to be a part of it. I have eight balloons of different sizes, from a one-man all the way up to a ten-passenger. The maximum number I take, however, is eight people. It's nicer to take four to six, and that's what I usually do. With ballooning it's all about weight, not the number of people. But four to six passengers creates a more intimate experience. For me, flying a balloon is so much like making music, following a melodic line or creating a song. All my balloons are named, mostly musical names: *All That Jazz, Calypso, Salsa, Baby Jazz.* The one-man balloon is *Joie de Vivre.* I also have *Dancer, Hakusan,* and the *Duchess of Burgundy*—she's a deep burgundy color with scallops like petals. I guess all balloons are "shes," like ships.

Once my passengers are in the balloon, I give them another short briefing, then there's liftoff, and that's magic. Sometimes we blow soap bubbles because the bubbles will fly along with us. Whether it's slow or fast, it's awesome every time. It doesn't matter how many times you've done it. Every launch and every balloon flight is different and beautiful. I usually take off a bit on the slow side because you never know if you have someone who's a little bit afraid. Some people who are petrified of heights but have gotten their courage up to go ballooning are thrilled—they'll say things like, "Wait till my kids hear this! I'm up in the air." Sometimes you get squeals of delight. Sometimes the reaction is just an awed "Oh, my gosh!" The feeling is so gentle. You're just silently gliding and moving as if on a magic silk carpet. I think that's one reason people aren't afraid. It's just not scary.

One day might be very, very calm and so I can go for a little height. Sometimes we're looking at Mount Tamalpais or Mount Diablo or Mount St. Helena—looking all over the place. You can see everything like an eagle or a hawk. The view is so immaculate. It's so cleaned up; nothing mars it. You're not looking through anything like a scratched airplane window—and the view is 360 degrees, all around you, and in the clear fresh air. If there is too much high wind above the mountains, I'll stay low, and we'll watch the grapes grow, look at the rabbits and the foxes on the ground, and pick leaves. Everything seems so close. It's like we're in the middle of a painting and can reach right out and touch everything. On every trip, winds permitting, I try to do both a little bit of low flying and a little bit of high flying so my passengers get the intimate and the broad view.

What do you mean by picking leaves?
Ballooning is filled with traditions. Picking leaves from the treetops is a ballooning tradition, but I couldn't tell you how it began. The idea is to pick the leaf off the top of a tree that you wouldn't have been able to climb and therefore wouldn't have been able to reach and then put it under your pillow so your dreams will come true. So we cruise along slowly, just barely close enough so they can reach out and try to get a leaf. Once I gently swooped so low out in the countryside that my passengers were able to reach out and pick a couple grape leaves from an end grape vine at the edge of a vineyard. It had long fronds coming up several feet—this was after harvest—and they were so thrilled. They

actually framed them together with the verse that I recite as a blessing at the end of each flight, which is another ballooning tradition. It goes,

The winds have welcomed you with softness
The sun has blessed you with its warm hand
You've flown so high and so well
May the gods join you in your laughter
And set you gently back into
The loving arms of Mother Earth.

They sent it to me with a thank-you note. I hear from people like that a lot.

Ballooning requires a real kinesthetic sense, a subtlety that is unlike any other kind of piloting, where you just get in the plane and turn the instruments on. Flying a balloon requires more constant focus, but it's also a lot more forgiving because you're going slower. Still, you need to watch and evaluate almost every minute. You have to feel what's going on with the balloon, the air, and Mother Nature. When you're flying, you search for and follow a wind layer. That's how you get your directions. You don't have an engine that gives you any direction, but you can move easily up or down into or out of the layers. You have to do it by sensing what you're dealing with. You have to consider a lot of factors, especially when you're getting ready to land: ambient temperature, the elevation, the weight of the people, the location and terrain, potential landing areas, wind speed.

In the Napa region we only want to fly with very calm air because we need to have absolute control over the landing. You've got to be able to tack up and down like a boat would tack, only it's three-dimensional. You're looking down from high above at an infinitesimally small place from that distance. It's all concentration and focus. In some places, such as Ireland or England, pilots fly with a bit more wind because they are forced to; it's always more windy and they have more open spaces. I've flown and landed in Mongolia at 30 knots, and the same in Dubai. I've flown over our mountains at 40 knots, but I had low, calm wind conditions on the ground or else I never would have done it. Balloons can fly as fast as the wind; they've gone around the world now at up to 200 miles an hour. But you need to be able to control the landing, and in Napa landing places are precious few and far between.

Flights usually last about an hour, but since I only do one flight a day, it might last an hour and a half. It depends on the circumstances. I have to locate a place to land within the right amount of time, and—as I've said—a lot depends upon how strong the wind is and other factors like increasing temperatures, thermals, fuel, and weight. Sometimes there's a box wind, where you can go south or north and make a U-turn, come back and circle around. It's called a box wind because of the shape you outline. This is one thing that makes Albuquerque, New Mexico, so popular and famous for the biggest balloon meet in the world. They have a reliable box wind, so pilots can navigate to targets and play around.

What are your passengers like? And what are they most curious about?

Most of my clients are Americans, but I have guests from many countries—many of them learn about us from guidebooks or the internet. The type of person that is attracted to ballooning is just the best—inquisitive, intellectual, and interesting for the most part. Part of the program I have offered for more than twenty years is breakfast after the flight at Meadowood or Rancho Caymus Inn. I usually have breakfast with my passengers, and sometimes we sit there for a few hours and talk and become friends.

During the flight, people often ask about the vineyards and wine production. Depending upon their interest and knowledge, I'll go into that—you know, I'll talk about pruning, trellising, the seasons, the grape varieties, and what the wind machines are for. Some people are really interested in Napa Valley history. I was on the board of the Napa Valley Museum for many years and have an interest in the valley's history. I've taught classes about Napa's Native Americans, and I enjoy sharing a little bit of Indian lore, which they love. Some people are interested in the fact that I've lived here this long and seen all the changes. When I moved to Napa Valley, nobody had heard of the little dead-end road I live on, even people who grew up here, and now my neighbors are Robin Williams and Boz Skaggs. People always like to hear about celebrities, and many ask me about who I have flown.

I often get asked how I got into ballooning. It's pretty unusual to have a woman pilot. Probably less than one in five pilots is a woman, and most of them are private pilots. When I was younger, I'd get comments like, "Oh, a woman driver." In those days I'd often wear a type of flight jacket with lots of balloon pins—something so that when people looked at it they knew there was a lot of experience there. I think some people are still uneasy about a woman pilot. I can sense that sometimes. That's another reason I give my passengers a full briefing beforehand. It lets them know I've been around. I try to throw out enough background so that they realize there *is* a background and also so it's more interesting for them. I let them know I've received special invitations to fly in exotic places from Mongolia to Bhutan, the Philippines, Malaysia, Burma, western China, India and Sri Lanka, Turkey, Dubai, Austria and Switzerland, France, Ireland, England, Mexico, Chile, Colombia, Venezuela, Brazil, and more. After that, I can see them just fall into the routine and they're really pleased. I have to protect the experience for them and for me; I'm not going to put up with male chauvinism. I have flown with some cocky men. Most of them end up being fine, but they don't realize at first that ballooning is FAA aviation and that you have to have a pilot's license and to have gone through ground school and flight school. I actually have more experience in varied and challenging flying than most of the male pilots I know.

Some people are interested in the technical side of ballooning, particularly people who are pilots or are mechanically oriented. Some people are just intellectually curious and want to know how lift works and how you steer. The principles of ballooning are pretty simple to explain, but it's the finesse and the combination of factors you're dealing with that creates the complexity. Men and women ask basically the same questions. Women are maybe more apt to also ask, "Do you have children?" or they'll comment on my earrings, which I've often gotten in other countries. Some people are quiet and just into the wonder of the experience, and I try to be totally sensitive to that. Other people are busy visiting with each other. Sometimes they exchange numbers and addresses after the excursion.

Some visitors are into their own personal dynamics. People often go ballooning to celebrate a special occasion like an anniversary, a birthday, or a surprise wedding proposal. I've performed a number of weddings over the years; I'm a licensed, nondenominational minister. I've also done funerals on the ground and in the air. One very special one involved scattering the ashes of Venerable Master Hsuan Hua, the Dalai Lama of the Dharma Realm Buddhists. He had written in his will that his ashes should be scattered to the winds by air. After several live interviews, I got the job. I've even done a divorce flight. A couple decided they were going to do something fun for their last activity together. They were still on good terms, despite the fact that she'd caught him making out with another woman by Coit Tower in San Francisco. They told me the whole thing and had a great sense of humor. It was quite amazing. Their flight with me was like their formal closure, and it was totally successful.

One celebration was the ninetieth birthday of a local man, a retired minister. His wife and several elderly friends had gotten him the balloon flight and all came to watch. He was incredibly spry and had a great time, so I said, "You've got to come fly with me for your hundredth birthday." And he did! Another flight involved a proposal that almost didn't happen. The valley was clear, but there was fog at the Oakland Airport. I'd arranged for a friend of mine to fly to Napa from Oakland in a small plane trailing a banner that said "Katie, will you marry me?" He was also going to make smoke rings around us. Well, he got delayed by the fog, and I had flown around for almost an hour before I heard him coming. As he flew around us with all the bells and whistles, the gentleman dropped to his knees and proposed. She clearly didn't know what to say. I hovered over what was then Inglenook Winery for the longest time and was beginning to worry about my fuel. She still didn't say yes. Then it was almost 8 AM and folks were arriving at the winery to work. They looked up and got excited when they saw the plane circling around us and yelled, "Say yes! Say yes!" When she saw the ring, I remember she said, "Oh, my gosh. Did you sell the house?" I finally had to say, "We'll need to land soon!" So she said,"YES!" It turns out that it was April 1st and she was afraid that it might be an April Fool's joke. They have come back to see me and have even sent me birth announcements.

I generally enjoy talking during the flight and answering questions, but sometimes it's difficult. If I've flown every day for twenty days, I can get tired answering the same questions. I'll try to focus the passengers on enjoying the flight instead. It always seems like when I'm getting ready to land and really need to focus, people start asking me even more questions like, "How did you get into ballooning?" If there's no quick answer, I just have to cut them off and brief them on their positions for landing. I want them to be holding on and I want them to stay in the basket. Most people don't realize how important weight is, even though we stress it in the briefings before the flight. I have to be able to sense exactly what the balloon is going to do, and one person's weight can make a lot of difference. So I don't want someone hopping out of the basket to take pictures as soon as we touch down, sending me back up into the sky again after I've made a beautiful controlled landing.

This reminds me of something that can be disruptive on a flight. That's when a passenger moves very brusquely or is really clumsy aloft. A balloon makes a fabulous, stable camera platform normally. But if someone shifts their weight abruptly it can ruin someone else's photo opportunity. A lot of people who come with me are into photography, including famous professionals and filmmakers. I'm an avid photographer too and am apt to have my camera on board. I'm always stimulated and inspired by what I'm seeing and I'm still taking pictures after twenty-six years of flying. So I ask people to be sensitive about this. But if they're not and they're oohing and aahing and loving the experience, what can I do?

Once we get down, the crew squeezes the air out of the balloon and packs it up like a parachute. After I have checked everything, I celebrate with my passengers. Sometimes we have champagne right then, if we've landed in an appropriate place. And I honor them with their aeronaut pin, so they have their "wings." Or we'll go back to Rancho Caymus Inn or Meadowood, if they're having breakfast there, and celebrate. We always celebrate. It goes back to the tradition of man's first balloon flight in France and celebrating with Champagne. Ballooning is very much associated with wine country. I even tease my passengers sometimes about having chosen the right place to fly. Because we're in Napa Valley we are sure to have great "champagne." If we were in Mongolia, they'd have to drink fermented mare's milk followed by vodka.

I have many friends who were originally clients. Some are on a kind of informal waiting list to go on international tours with me—as my energy and time permit. In 1996 I started taking groups of eight to ten people to France to fly in Burgundy. I've also organized ballooning tours in Costa Rica, Burma, Mexico, Turkey, and a few other places as well. I love the international trips. Sometimes in remote places, it can feel a bit like "the gods must be crazy," if you remember that film. We just drop down from the sky, and people look at us in wide-eyed wonder. I love the magic of it. It's like a return to the magic of childhood when you'd raise your arms out and flying actually seemed possible. I used to dream about doing that when I was little; I think most people world-wide have dreamed of flying. I've been privileged to have some amazing experiences upon landing. I'm often given food and invited to participate in whatever event is happening. And I've been given many small but wonderful gifts like the little treasured ring a ten-year-old girl in Mongolia gave me. Children have sometimes chased the balloon's path for miles over country roads, bridges, and fields on their bicycles until I landed.

Has ballooning in the Napa Valley changed much over the years?

I think Napa Valley has developed a bit of a schizophrenic personality over the four decades I've been here. There have been huge changes in the valley, and there are widely differing opinions about how to deal with them. Still, I always love coming home no matter where I have been. This is indeed a beautiful part of the world, and I feel blessed to have lived here most of my life. And I enjoy being part of something that gives people so much pleasure and that is used to represent the valley. Balloons can now be found on almost every publication or ad representing Napa, from the *Wine Spectator* to *National Geographic* magazine, to Victoria's Secret and even hospital and real estate ads. Balloons have done a lot to help promote the valley to the outside world. I've been on the Travel and Food channels, PBS, BBC, NHK Japan, World IMAX, and many others. Jancis Robinson is famous in the wine world and produced a film with us, as have Burt Wolf and Michael Chiarello. Diane Sawyer, Charles Gibson, and Josh Groban did a *Good Morning, America* transmission from a Bonaventura balloon at Niebaum-Coppola Winery [now Rubicon]. Yet ballooning has become far more difficult in the valley politically. It has become like a political football which is tossed around by various factions who really don't understand how we work and don't want to. Some people don't want to encourage any tourism, and they've made it very difficult for us to find places to land. Yet I can't tell you how many times over the years folks in the valley have told me, "When I look out and see balloons in the morning, I know it's going to be a good day!" or the many people who, upon seeing us land, have brought out coffee and even breakfast, not to mention wine and cheese. This is the kind of hospitality that I wish all of the Napa Valley was known for.

Bike Tours / Brad Dropping

"Cycling helps clear my mind. It's almost like yoga to me."

First developed in nineteenth-century Europe, bicycles are now ridden world-wide for transportation, sport, and pleasure. Bicycle touring has a long history in Europe, but only comparatively recently has it become a popular leisure activity in the United States. Bicycle tour companies can now be found at many tourist destinations. One of the world's largest—Backroads—got its start in the Napa Valley in the 1970s. Napa Valley Bike Tours opened its doors in 1987. Its current owner, Brad Dropping, was always an avid cyclist but did not convert his passion into his work until he visited the Napa Valley in 2004.

——

My involvement in cycling goes back to my early childhood. When I was older, I raced motorcycles, but I got out of that because it was expensive. I met my wife at college, and after graduating we ran a mortgage business in Atlanta. It was long hours, a lot of wining and dining, and not much exercise. I had started putting on weight in college, but afterwards it just got worse. I stopped carving out any time for health and exercise. I went from 175 pounds to 237 pounds. I began having health issues and went to the doctor, who told me I needed more exercise in my life and that I had to start eating better. At the same time, my sister gave me a book called *Body for Life* which had a twelve-week program where you balanced out your carbs and your proteins. It taught me to eat five to six snacks a day rather than big meals and to exercise every day. That program worked very well for me; in twelve weeks, I went from weighing 237 pounds to 197 pounds.

A guy in my neighborhood raced mountain bikes, and I started talking to him. To make a long story short, I got into mountain biking for health reasons and because of my childhood biking experiences. In fact, I got into it very heavily and entered the racing scene, where I did fairly well. Cycling became my passion again. It was also fun exercise, and I lost another fifteen pounds without trying. I started entering a twenty-four-hour mountain bike race where you race for twenty-four hours on a closed-circuit track, going around as many times as you can. The winner is the person who goes around the most. The race was always in October, and the month before, my wife and I would come out to Napa Valley to celebrate our wedding anniversary without the children. It was our "husband-and-wife-only getaway vacation."

We came every year and fell in love with Napa. Because it was always the month before this major cycling race, we'd rent bikes and I'd train. We always got our bikes from Napa Valley Bike Tours, and in 2004 we decided to do one of their organized tours on our anniversary. Little did we know that the owner had just put the business up for sale. We'd been thinking about leaving Atlanta. We'd been there for twenty-six years and wanted a change. We disliked the hot and humid weather, and it rained a lot. Mountain biking in the mud is not fun. The climate in Napa is great with cool mornings, warm days, and no rain for six months of the year. We just made up our minds that morning that someday we'd move to Napa. Later that day, we met the owner of the bike company. He explained that he was just tired of working seven days a week. The more we talked to him, the more it seemed a great fit for us. We did have some financial concerns. We were a family of four, and our house in Atlanta was valued much lower than it would have been in Napa, but we wanted to move badly. Fortunately, we'd been pretty good savers in Atlanta and had a big enough nest egg to make such a crazy move.

It was rough for about six months, but slowly business improved. We bought the business in January 2005, and since then we've been able to increase the company's revenues by seven times. I've changed a number of things. One thing that I saw in the previous owner was that he was burned out because he was doing everything, including guiding the tours. He loved cycling and he still cycles, but there's a lot more to running this business than taking people out on bike tours. There's payroll, accounting, administration. There are vendor relationships, government issues, employee issues. It's a full-time job just running the business, and he was running it *and* doing the tours as well, working seven days a week.

We now have three little kids (three, nine, and thirteen), and they want me home at five and at least one full day a week. So I hired people right off the bat to guide the tours and focused my time on building the business. When I took over there was just one full-time person, plus one on-call guide and an on-call van driver. Now I have twenty-seven people; five are full-time. I have three full-time guides who come to work every day during the peak tourist season, and a bunch of other people who are on call. They work when we have big tour groups. I'd never had any experience running a bicycling vacation business, but I'm a quick learner and it has worked out great.

What kind of people rent bikes or go on bike tours in the Napa Valley?

I'd say 95 percent of our clients are tourists, not cyclists. We also get some locals, but most of our customers are tourists. Most of them are from out of state and they're here for a convention or just a getaway vacation. We don't get

Napa Valley Bike Tour employee reloads bikes at Saddleback Winery.

that many families, although we do have children's bikes. This valley is more romantic than it is family-oriented. I wish it was perceived to be more kid-friendly, but the basis of the valley is wine and wine is romantic and adult. Most of our clients are couples who've come for a special occasion—an anniversary, a birthday—or just to get away.

Most people are probably in their mid-forties to mid-fifties, which may have to do with wine being popular in this age group. But also I think a lot of people we get fit the pattern I've experienced in my own life. They were active when they were young, then they went through a period where they were inactive, then they woke up in their mid-thirties and said, "Oh, my gosh! What am I doing to my body?" Then they got back into fitness. Cycling is a great fitness vehicle for people in their thirties, forties, fifties, and up. It's easy on the joints, easy on the body. And it's usually easy to find a place to cycle. You put cycling together with wine, great food, and romance, and you've got the ultimate adult vacation. Plus you have a great way to burn up those carbs.

About 10 percent of the tourists we get are foreigners, a lot from the UK and Canada. One wonderful thing about our business is that our clientele, whether they're foreigners or Americans, tend to be really easygoing. They're definitely not pretentious, although we get people who have bought and sold businesses and made millions. Sure, there's always a rotten apple or a black sheep every once in a while, but for the most part we're blessed with really great customers.

Our clients are probably a bit different from the typical wine tourist. Today is a perfect example. Very few people would get out and ride on a misty, drizzly day like today [in March]. But the couples that were here riding today were fine with it. Because most of our clients are couples, the sex ratio is virtually 50-50 male-female. When it comes to groups, it leans toward women. Many come to Napa for a girls' weekend out or whatever. They may have been at college together or used to live together or worked together on their first job, and now they're just getting together again. Napa tends to be a destination for that kind of thing. Cycling has become very popular with women in the past several years. Ten years ago, there were no bicycles specifically designed for women, but now every bike manufacturer has them.

We don't get many groups of guys going out on tours. I use the analogy of a party. When you go to a party, the guys tend to cluster around the beer while the women are into wine. Maybe if we cycled to all the brewing companies in the area, we'd attract more guy groups. Hmm, maybe that's a good idea. I think wine just has more of a romantic feel to it and a bunch of guys don't want romance with each other. Also, guys may be more inclined to organize their own tours, without our help. And they may want a little more hard-core riding. Our tours are definitely not hard-core. They are aimed at the tourist, not the cyclist. If we threw a couple of "manly" things on our website, like hard-core riding or king of the mountain, or some type of attraction for the testosterone of the nation, we might bring up our guy numbers. We can only grow so fast, but all of this stuff is in my vision.

People often compliment our guides on how well they handle groups and how knowledgeable they are about the valley. I think they also appreciate the wineries we pick to visit. No offense to the Mondavis and the Beringers of the world, but anyone can find those places without our help. The experiences that a visitor gets there are totally different than the experience they get at a small boutique winery. We take our guests to smaller wineries that they might not ever get to. We pick wineries that have friendly staff, great ambiance, and, of course, great wine.

What is the routine like for people going on a bike tour?

We ask everybody to get here at 9:30 AM. We go through the paperwork with them and all the un-fun stuff like bike sizing, orientation with the bikes, and the rules of the road. That takes about a half an hour. We try to have no more than ten people on a tour for a couple of reasons. First, it's easier to have ten people cycling single file than a group of twenty-five, who could create a big jam on the roads around here. Secondly, we like to keep the guide-to-customer ratio down. It's just like a party. If you have ten people, there's good conversation and you get to talk to everybody. If there are thirty people, you probably won't get to talk to everybody.

We have a van that follows behind on every tour. It's there to transport guests who don't want to ride the whole way and to carry the wine that riders buy at the wineries we visit. We don't push our guests to purchase wine, but we do encourage it because they are not likely to find the same wine at their grocery store or wine shop at home. We've had a few people in their sixties and even seventies who don't want to ride the whole time. But we also had a lady who was seventy-six and here with her daughters. They rode three straight days with us. I can't imagine my grandmother being on a bike for three days.

Our tours are on flat terrain. We try to go about twenty miles a day. We've found that twenty miles allows a good mix of riding and wine tasting. It works out to be about two hours of cycling spread out between the four wineries we visit. In effect, we have "intervals"—a series of three- to five-mile bike rides with rest stops at a new winery in between. We stay at a winery for thirty-five to forty-five minutes, depending on the group and the tasting room staff. Then we get back on the bike for another three to five miles. At the third winery, we have a catered picnic-style lunch. We try to pick a winery where we can eat outside and overlook the vineyards. A local deli does the catering and it's great food—a seasonal salad, cheese and fruit tray, olives, hummus, and an assortment of sandwiches. One of the tasks of the van driver is to keep everyone's water bottle filled up while they're at the wineries. We try to keep people hydrated. Usually we're back here sometime between 3 and 5 PM. We don't really push people, so the return time just kind of evolves.

Occasionally we'll get four, five, or six friends going on a tour. That obviously affects the dynamics of the group of ten since one-half of the group is already friends. But by the end of the day, you'd think the entire group had been friends forever. Sure, in the beginning, some people are reserved and quiet, but that breaks down very quickly on a bike trip. We had one couple in their early forties, and the husband ran his own mutual fund company in health and sciences technology. Anyway, he was a goofball. He always had people laughing, and he loved to pick on any person who seemed negative or pessimistic. I think it was a challenge to him to get that person out of their shell. It was like, "Life is short, dude. Chill out." He was very humorous and was even able to get this one really gloomy guy going. Everybody was smiling when they came back at the end of the day.

One thing we tried this year is offering half-day tours. I felt there were a lot of people in the valley who had come because of a conference in the morning or maybe a spa treatment in the afternoon and who couldn't burn up a whole day cycling. So, we tried offering half-day formats. Logistically, it was a bit of a nightmare in the beginning, but we've worked it out and it has become a popular option. Overnight trips are also something that we've fine-tuned this year. We offer them on scheduled dates, but we also give people the option of starting them whenever they want. With most bicycling-vacation companies you have to conform to their time window. It's regimented and a lot of times just doesn't fit into people's schedules. We wanted to be different, so we created a "Ride, Wine, and Dine" vacation package in which people can start any day of the week and go for as many days as they want—total flexibility. It's been popular. It's kind of fun going from town to town and staying at a different place every night.

We also have a package we call "Wine to Waves" that has an adventure element. We start in Yountville and go out to the ocean on a five-day trip—through Sonoma, then out to Bodega Bay, up the coast and following the Russian River, into Healdsburg, then into Calistoga, and back down the Napa Valley to Yountville. This one is more oriented toward cyclists than just tourists. We provide some options within this. Maybe one spouse is less of a cyclist. Often it's a she, and she can choose just to ride the bike until lunch and then get in the van and be driven to the resort and hang out at the pool and wait for the group to get there later in the day. Also, people can choose to ride as little as fifteen to twenty miles or as much as a hundred miles every day. Most groups do thirty to forty miles.

Who are your tour guides?

Most of my guides are retired or have full-time jobs with flexible schedules. One guide is a retired Chevron executive who lives at the Napa Yacht Club and owns a second home in Tahoe. He's an avid cyclist. He's sixty years old and in incredible shape, only 7 percent body fat. He also pours wine at one of the wineries around here and is a ski instructor at Squaw Valley and kind of hangs out at his cabin much of the winter. He has the life many people dream of, but he's not pretentious. He's got his priorities straight. Until two months ago he didn't even own a car, but he owns a $7,000 bicycle.

Another guide used to be a firefighter in Chicago. He is forty-eight and married a woman who lives in Yountville. He is the organizer of an urban adventure racing event called the Wild Onion. Most adventure racing is hike, bike, and kayak, but he took the format and adapted it to an urban situation in Chicago. They climb the stairs at the Sears Tower, for instance, instead of hike. They run through the city. They canoe through the city and so on. It's very popular and it's televised on ESPN. He's a pretty neat guy. We have another full-time guide who is a single mom with three children. She used to work in the wine industry in a tasting room, and is very knowledgeable in that area. She's personable and loves interacting with the guests. We also have several guides who are teachers, which is perfect for us because they are free to work during the summer when we're most busy. Most of the guides are in their forties and up.

When nobody wants to work, I have to. A perfect example was Thanksgiving Day: we had six people who wanted to ride and nobody wanted to work that day except one guide—a retired schoolteacher. He was fine as long as it was a half-day tour, but I had to come in and help him get through that day. Everything worked out, although it was no fun leaving my family that day. As a business owner, you're always the person who does the stuff that nobody else wants to do. But overall it's been nice making a living in the cycling-vacation industry.

Are accidents a concern?

Not as many accidents as you would think. An outsider might think, "Oh great, you're bicycling on the roads in Napa Valley where everyone's drunk because they're going to tasting rooms." Well, as you and I know, that's not the case. Yes, there might be the occasional drunk person, but for the most part the wineries are good at managing their guests and giving a correct tasting pour versus a drinking pour. People aren't going around drinking wine at the wineries, they're tasting wines. A lot of people don't realize that until they get here. I wish I could prove to everyone that cycling here is not dangerous.

The business will be twenty years old this January, and based on the information I received from the previous owner, there had only been one mishap—with a woman while out in Carneros. There was a really sharp turn and a cargo truck had cut the corner too tight, and she got scared because she wasn't an experienced cyclist and went off into a ditch. Unfortunately the ditch was about four feet deep and it was not clean. It was in kind of a wooded area and she hit herself pretty hard and broke both wrists. And I think she was in a coma for a couple days. And she wasn't even traveling fast. She was just meandering down the road, and this guy scared her and she just dove into the ditch. She's okay now.

Does weather have much influence on the tourists' experiences?

I think the weather affects all people's experiences. I hate rain and I hate temperatures below 60 degrees. Moving from Atlanta where it was always quite hot—if it got below 75 degrees, I'd get cold. Now that I've been here a couple of years, I'm pretty good down to 50 degrees. It's only then that I start getting a little grumpy. I think that's true with our guests too, but it really depends on where they're coming from. We have guests from all over the world. This time of year, we get a lot of people from Florida, and for them Napa is cold. But for Canadians, the weather is nice. It all depends on where people are from and on the person. I don't like to wear a lot of extra clothing when I ride. I wear bicycle shorts, a jersey, and a helmet and I'm gone. If I have to wear arm and leg warmers or a jacket or layer up, it's not as fun for me. I think that holds true for visitors as well. But again, it depends on where they're from and what they're used to. I have a cousin in Michigan. He came out here in January when it was raining all the time and had a great time here. I was freezing.

How much equipment do you have?

Altogether we have 254 bikes—road or touring bikes and mountain bikes. We have to have a lot of bikes because at times we have big groups. Last year we had one group of 154 people—a management company having their annual meeting in Napa—and they just wanted to bike from point A to point B.

Renting is great for people who don't want a guide or to be with other people. Some people just want to ride for an hour or two and not do any wine tasting. Some are hard-core cyclists who want to go out riding all day. People rent from us for all kinds of reasons, especially being here in Yountville, which is a walking town. There are nearly four hundred resort and hotel rooms here, so it's a great location to have a bicycle rental. And we're centrally located in the valley. Plus there are vineyards within two blocks of us. It seems to be a younger crowd that rents. We do get a lot of young Bay Area people coming up for the day and renting bikes, and a lot of people from Stanford and other colleges.

What are your feelings about development in the valley?

Development is a big issue for me. I don't want our roads to get any busier than they are now, and I'd love for our roads to be in better shape. A road that is in great shape for a car isn't necessarily in great shape for a bike. Highway 29, for instance, is maybe adequate for a car, but it is not adequate for a bike because it's lost its smooth coat in many places. We really need more roads with bicycle lanes. The big news is that the first steps have been taken in creating a multi-use path for biking, walking, and rollerblading that will eventually go all the way from the Vallejo ferry terminal up the valley to Calistoga—about fifty miles. The Vine Trail will connect hikers and bikers to San Francisco. The first section of the trail was just dedicated here in Yountville, financed mainly by the federal stimulus package. It's going to take a while to complete, but it will be a great amenity and not just for tourists because a lot of locals will be using it as well. I give Napa County a lot of credit for doing a great job controlling growth in this valley and preserving the agriculture here, preserving the wine country.

Cycling in California is more accepted than I think it is in other areas of the country. Perhaps because there are so many cyclists in California. If you're driving a car, you probably have a relative who is a cyclist. In Georgia, I did not ride my bike on the road—I just didn't. Cyclists were not as welcome on public roads there. Here I'm very comfortable riding on the roads. Even the migrant workers are very accommodating to cyclists.

Cycling has definitely changed my life, especially my health. I don't know that I'd go so far as to say that I'd be dead now without it, but I'm definitely a much happier person because of cycling. Cycling helps clear my mind. It's almost like yoga for me. It helps me spiritualize and come back into balance, to see what's most important in life. I was in the rat race for so many years of my life when it seemed to be all about the dollar. Working in cycling has saved me from that—I'm getting ready to go on a mountain bike ride today even though it's drizzling. It's just something that keeps me in balance. I think it makes me a better father, a better husband, and a better boss.

Art Gallery / *Paul Thoren*

*"Even though people come from all over the world and have differ-
ent personalities and different tastes, they all are enamored with
the Napa Valley experience."*

*When people travel, they often bring back a memento of their trip. In addi-
tion to wine and conventional souvenirs, some people purchase art. Paul
Thoren is the owner of Gallery 1870 housed in V Marketplace in Yountville.
Originally called Vintage 1870, the complex of specialty shops, galleries, and
a wine-tasting room was the first major tourist development in Yountville. It
was created in the former Groezinger Winery, an imposing three-story brick
building built in 1870. Paul's gallery, unlike high-end fine art galleries in the
valley, is aimed primarily at tourists.*

*In his late fifties, and built like a baseball catcher, Paul is the eldest of
eight children. He was raised in a small community on the Columbia River
and had not yet learned to read or write when he entered third grade after
his family moved to the larger town of Elgin, Oregon. He caught up quickly,
however, and soon was involved with choir, the marching band, and sports.
By the time he was a senior in high school, he was an Oregon state wrestling
champion. Paul runs Gallery 1870 with his wife, Kathy, and their daughter,
Kassia.*

———

Getting into the art business was kind of an accident. It started when my
daughter Kassia was going to UC Davis and working part-time at a Thomas
Kinkade gallery. At the time, I had retired after twenty-eight years as a manager
in the Kmart Corporation and wanted to do something else. When an opening came up where my daughter worked, she encouraged me to look into it.
I took the job. I certainly didn't have a background in art; my undergraduate
degree was in business and economics. But I'd always had an interest in collect-
ing—antiques, old cars, stamps. Not having a degree in art might bother some
people, but not me. Actually, I don't know of many gallery owners who *do* have
degrees in art. It's mostly a business. Besides, I have always been interested in
learning as much as I can about any business I'm in, and that's what I did at the
Kinkade gallery.

I enjoyed learning a whole new field, and I've always liked working with
people. When you are showing art to people you get to see where their passions
are and to learn how they perceive things. I liked the job and I happened to be

Galley owner Paul Thoren.

in the right place at the right time. I had been working at the Thomas Kinkade gallery for two years when the owner decided to sell Gallery 1870 in Yountville. At the time I was learning a lot about artists in the Napa Valley, especially those who did vineyard and wine-related themes, which are so important to the tourist market. Having grown up in the country, I appreciate what grape growers do. I understand all the work that's involved in making a living off the land. I also really appreciate the romance and the beauty of wine art even though I don't drink wine myself. I never developed a palate for it.

After I crunched all the numbers, I decided to make an offer on the gallery. My wife, Kathy, was out of town, and when she returned home it was a bit of a surprise. I've had to learn a lot but it has been fun. For example, I had a client who bought a painting of a French bistro. After I wrapped it up and presented it to her, she gently told me that I had been mispronouncing the composition's name—"Paul," she said, "It's *Shay*, not *Chez*." You never know as much as you think you do, and once in a while you just have to laugh at your own mistakes.

The art hanging on my gallery walls is definitely geared toward the visitor market because it's wine-related. That's a strategic decision. When most visitors come into the valley, they're interested more in buying Napa landscapes and scenes than in buying contemporary abstract or impressionistic works or fine art pieces. That's why I consider my gallery a traditional gallery. It's traditional in the sense that it presents what people recognize and can relate to in their own life experiences. Our sales have been excellent, up 25 percent since we took ownership.

What have you learned about the tourists who visit art galleries?

Well, many want art that relates to the experiences they have in the valley. Even though people come from all over the world and have different personalities and different tastes, they all are enamored with the Napa Valley experience. They talk a lot about the vineyards and how they carpet the valley floor and run up the hillsides, the bucolic feeling of this place, and the magnificent wineries which are each so different from one another. Often they want to buy a work of art that reminds them of these scenes and their experience here. When visitors tell me where they're from, I often have something to share with them. If they say they're from Washington, D.C., I might say, "Oh my gosh, that's where the Senators used to play and my grandfather [Byron Speece] played for them." If they say they're from Nashville—well, my grandfather played baseball there, too. If they're from Texas—well, I lived in Texas as part of my corporate career. It's the same for Idaho and Washington and other places in California. Finding a little something in common with people helps you establish a connection with them. It's not phony because I really do like meeting people. I've always felt that I'm able to develop rapport with almost anybody once I find out something about them.

I enjoy talking to visitors about what they've seen and done in the valley. Most people like telling you about their experiences and sharing their opinions. Sometimes they want advice, like recommendations on wineries and where to go for good food. I'm happy to tell them, and I know that when they leave here and go to a winery or to a restaurant and someone asks them where to go in the valley to find art, they are going to say, "Go to Gallery 1870." They'll remember the friendliness and might stop back in the gallery on their way home and maybe make a purchase.

Some folks coming into the gallery are at the start of their Napa vacation, and I can see in their faces that they've been stressed. Maybe they are coming off an intense business cycle. If I see them again at the end of the trip or halfway into it, it's pretty obvious that they've started to mellow out. Napa will do that to you. And that's where art comes in. People can take that feeling back home in a painting. Recently a couple from Belgium came through the gallery, and we struck up a nice conversation. I was able to tell them about some of the special Napa Valley wineries represented in the paintings. I was able to send them on some complimentary tastings and gave them some fine dining recommendations. A few days later they returned, wanting to buy a painting that would remind them of their experience, and they wanted me in a photo taken with them. It was nice and it meant a lot to me to have been able to make their trip memorable.

Some visitors will commission a painting to commemorate their visit to the valley. We just did that with this one [*pointing to a large canvas*]. It's a compilation of several images that the client saw during her visit to the valley and that she wanted to include in one painting. She wanted a particular landscape but with the reds and oranges of fall foliage, and she wanted a few barns placed in the foreground and some overarching branches framing the scene. This is the image of the memory she wants to bring home.

What's your daily routine like?

My day begins about eight or nine o'clock when I start getting the gallery ready to go. Sometimes I need to do some framing or cleaning before I open. As the day moves on, I'll check my e-mail again and again. Sometimes I move art around to different places on the walls to mix things up and keep the look fresh. During the day, I will follow up on people who have come into the gallery and are looking for something in particular. There is always work to be done on a show we are planning. All the while, I try to remain available to visitors walking into the gallery. You need to be ready to go out and meet people or else you risk losing a sale. Typically, I don't get home until about 7:30 PM. It's a long day, but I do love the work and the people I meet.

Is there anything in your background that prepared you for dealing with tourists?

Well, I've always had a strong work ethic, probably dating back to my childhood. I was a paperboy from the fourth to the tenth grade. I grew up in the small community of Elgin, Oregon. I had to get up early, often in the cold, to get my papers and deliver them. That was when I first started meeting people because I'd have to go to their house to collect the money each month. I was voted the hardest worker in my high school graduating class. After high school, I went to college at Eastern Oregon State, now Eastern Oregon University. That's where I met my wife, Kathy. We've been married thirty-six years now. After graduation, I still had the same work ethic. By then I'd probably had, at the least, fifteen different jobs—farm jobs, ranch jobs, lumber jobs. I'd learned that if you worked hard you could get to where you wanted to be. It may sound odd now, but my goal was to get a job with the Kmart Corporation.

In the '70s Kmart was very big and really doing well. In my senior year I went to Washington to visit my girlfriend, Kathy, and stopped in at the Kmart store. I told the manager that I wanted to be considered for the management training program after I graduated. I must have made an impression on him because he arranged an interview for me with the district manager on the other side of Washington. As soon as I graduated, I drove five hours for the interview and I got the job. The manager said, "Show up Monday morning for work." So I drove five hours back home, loaded up all our stuff, and we moved there two days later. I worked for Kmart for twenty-eight years, mostly as a store manager, and I enjoyed it. But I worked hard. Christmastime at Kmart meant working a minimum eighty hours a week. It's a tough deal, but you know that's part of the job and you do it. When I purchased this gallery, I applied that same work ethic to it.

Is there a strategy to selling art to tourists?

To sell art you have to be friendly, almost to the point where you are not trying to sell anything but simply having a conversation with them. It's also important to be observant in order to judge people's level of interest. You have to know when the time is right to step in and provide them with more information. Going into an art gallery is like going to school or being in a class. It's difficult to absorb all the information at one time. When someone comes into my gallery, it's important to give them time and be sensitive to how much information they really want. Just like the winery workers who serve tourists in tasting rooms, you have to be sensitive to how much information your visitor wants. You have to learn to listen carefully. You may want to just give them a seed, something of interest that they can mull over. I like to find out what they've done in the valley and what they really have enjoyed about their experience. This will tell me what kind of art may trigger an emotional memory of their visit. Having a good conversation and having a positive experience in the gallery help people reach the point where they will consider buying a painting.

Like most things, timing is important. It can make a difference whether my customer has just arrived in the valley or is on his or her way home. If they've just arrived, they will often say, "We're going to be around for a few days. We'll think about it and come back." You hear that a lot and you hope they *do* come back, but of course many don't. Conversely, when people are leaving the valley, they may feel some urgency to find a painting to take home. In general, when visitors are looking for art, it's better if they've already eaten lunch or dinner because it's easier for them to focus if hunger isn't gnawing at them or if they're not worrying about getting to their dinner reservation on time. If they come just before a meal, they may see art on the walls they like, but they are not going to make the decision to buy.

A lot of people who come into the gallery are only interested in browsing. They're really not buyers. But you shouldn't judge them too quickly, because people can surprise you. I've had people who just came into the building to buy some popcorn down the hall and then ended up buying a painting from me. So I try never to prejudge my visitors. Some people buy on the spot. Others come back many times before making a purchase. But because I'm in a tourist market, a lot of my clients want to buy art now, before they go home.

You can also spend a lot of time with someone and they don't buy anything. People often use the same phrases when they don't want to buy, to exit the gallery gracefully, such as "I like it but I've got to go home and measure my wall first" or "We really have to think about it because one of us likes it, but the other one isn't crazy about it." I try not to pin them down because they really have to make up their own minds. I much prefer to have a conversation with them so I can understand what they're looking for, what size, and maybe what price range, and then steer them in that direction.

Are there any patterns in what tourists buy?

Most people who come in like landscapes. Wine still-life compositions are popular too. You get an idea what people are going to like by watching what they're first attracted to. More often than not, most people go first to a painting that they really like. That tells you something. When couples come in, some split up and go off in different directions. Others look at the paintings together and discuss them. I also get a lot of couples where just one person comes into the gallery, while the other is shopping elsewhere in the building. Guys will come in and look at the art, while their partners are shopping for clothes or shoes or something else in the building. Women also come in alone while their husbands are at a conference or playing golf. Overall, I think it's women who are usually the most serious about buying art. A woman will say, "I'd really like to have this piece hanging over the fireplace." She's already decided where in her home she wants to put the painting. Men are less likely to think that way. Men are more likely to be responsible for the wine cellar.

How do you choose the artists you exhibit?

Most of the artists I show were already in the gallery when I bought it. I don't spend a lot of time looking for new artists like some gallery owners do. However, people do frequently mail me their portfolios. In order for me to take on a new artist, I would have to eliminate someone else or reduce the amount of wall space I assign to that artist or to each artist. If I did that, I'd be screwing up some long-term relationships. I know that down the road the point may come when one of my artists no longer fits. Tastes change and there may be a time when visitors coming to the valley are less interested in wine-related still lifes, for example. I don't think that's going to happen, but you never know. Some galleries like to follow the trends and add new artists. That's fine, but you risk stepping on the toes of the artists you already have.

When I sell a painting, we have to ship it to the buyer about half the time because we're in a tourist market. Not everybody can carry a painting home with them on the plane or even in the trunk of their car. Occasionally with southern Californians, a customer will drive six or seven hours back here to pick up art, but more often we ship it to them.

Most tourists are one-time buyers. They are only going to buy one piece. It's the memory piece of their trip. Locals will often come back and buy other works. I have heard that the industry average is that when people buy a piece of art, they'll come back and buy three more pieces from the same gallery over their lifetime. I have a few local clients who have bought eight or nine paintings from me.

Do tourists ever haggle over the price?

Maybe one out of every twenty clients will try to bargain. They'll say, "What's your best deal?" I swear that nine times out of ten, the person who does this is a car dealer. I say, "You must be a car dealer," and the guy says, "How did you know?" I say, "Hey, I understand totally where you're coming from." With some art I *can* be a little bit flexible on price, because some artists are flexible. But other artists are not. My paintings range from as low as $200 up to $20,000.

The art business, like tourism, is seasonal. In March I can go three or four days without selling anything. I don't get discouraged, because I know there are going to be slow times and that over time sales average out. We've done pretty well since we opened and all the new development of high-end hotels and resorts and world-recognized restaurants in Yountville is bound to keep the tourists coming and give us business.

Do you have plans for a second retirement?

I'm not sure if I'll ever get tired of selling art. My daughter, Kassia, who recently received her MBA and was the person who encouraged me to take that first part-time job at Thomas Kinkade, is now my director of marketing and business development. It's nice to see the gallery create an opportunity for her.

In 2006 I received a magazine from Denver in the mail. It's called *Mountain Living Magazine* and inside they listed the top twenty galleries in the West. Somehow their readers in the Denver market had selected this art gallery as one of the top twenty. I looked at the list and there were galleries in Santa Fe and all over, but we were the only one in California. They also had voted on their top ten resorts, and Auberge du Soleil was number two. On their list of the top restaurants was the French Laundry. I've had clients staying at Auberge du Soleil, eating at the French Laundry, and then coming to Gallery 1870. I can't ask for better than that, and it just came out of the blue. Totally unexpected.

8 / Tourism, Quality of Life, and the Future of Napa

*W*hat effect does wine tourism have on the Napa Valley? What economic benefits does it bring, and what about its impact on the social and cultural life of the valley? Are residents better or worse off today because of tourism? These questions have seldom been posed for wine regions, especially in the United States, where wine tourism is only now beginning to receive scrutiny from social scientists. In this final chapter, we look at these issues in the three decades since wine tourism in Napa became a mass phenomenon.

Wine Tourism's Economic Impact

Wine and wine tourism together have made Napa County far more affluent than any of California's other rural counties. In 2005, the wine industry produced 8.5 million cases of wine which yielded $8.1 billion in revenue and generated $1.4 billion in wages.[1] That same year, tourists to Napa County, according to a study by Purdue University's Tourism and Hospitality Research Center, contributed $1.3 billion to the local economy.[2] With a population of just 134,000 people, the nearly $11 billion in revenue generated from wine production and wine tourism in 2005 represented over $82,000 for every man, woman, and child in Napa County. Although at first glance the wine industry appears to contribute nearly seven times as much as tourism to Napa's economy, without tourism there would be far less interest in Napa's wines and, of course, fewer sales. Many small and mid-sized wineries can't survive without visitors. "Having visitors is how you build brand loyalty," says Barbara Insel of Stonebridge Research, who is the leading researcher for the Napa Valley Vintners, "and it's how you get people to identify with the region. Unlike other agricultural products, wine always comes from a particular place, so if you want people to buy your wine it's important for them to visit and know that place." Conversely, take away the wine industry and Napa would have very little tourism.

Both the wine and the tourism stimulate other sectors of Napa's economy. Much like dropping a stone in a pond, they have a financial "ripple" or what economists call a "multiplier effect." Vineyards and wineries generate indirect employment through their demand for agricultural equipment (such as irrigation equipment, chemicals, and fertilizer), supplies (such as barrels, pumps, tanks, bottles, and labels), and affiliated services (such as warehousing, office, and financial services). People who are employed either directly or indirectly by both the wine and tourism industries spend a significant portion of their payroll dollars on local goods and services like food, clothing, housewares, and health care. As these tourism and winery payrolls work their way through the local economy, they support other jobs that have no direct relationship to either industry. According to the Purdue study, more than 100 different Napa Valley businesses are at least partially supported by tourist spending and 17,000 jobs owe their very existence to tourism.[3] Napa residents also benefit significantly from the millions of dollars that are injected into the local economy from indirect business taxes, especially retail sales taxes and the "transient occupancy tax" (TOT) collected by hotels and inns from every overnight visitor. While in 1974 there were just 644 rooms in the entire valley available for visiting tourists, by 2010 that figure had increased nearly tenfold to 6,000. "If it wasn't for tourists," says Nancy Levenburg, who as president of the St. Helena Chamber of Commerce is a tourism booster, "every man, woman and child in Napa County would have to come up with an extra $1,000 in various taxes each year to make up for the revenue that we would lose without it. That's a very big number." In short, tourism helps pay for the services and amenities that contribute to the high quality of life enjoyed by most Napa Valley residents.

Napa's Changing Demographics

The growth of wineries and wine tourism has changed Napa's population profile. The desirability and cachet of the valley has brought affluent newcomers not merely to visit but also to live. Many are retirees and active professionals from San Francisco who reside at least part-time in the valley. The new wealth created during Silicon Valley's dot-com boom in the mid- and late 1990s also contributed, enabling some Californians to purchase a second or third home in the valley. This, coupled with the growing prosperity of the owners and top managers of Napa's wine and tourist industries, has given Napa County a high median family income ($80,112 in 2008) compared to the entire state ($70,029 in 2008). This is especially true of Napa's up-valley towns—Yountville, St. Helena, and Calistoga. The county's population profile has also gotten older. The median age of its residents has increased from 32 in 1970 to 39 in 2008, and the percentage of its population over the age of 65 years is now 15 percent, compared to 11 percent for all of California.

The arrival of people capable of paying top dollar for a home in the valley has driven up the cost of housing. Many native Napans who earn respectable but modest incomes have been forced out of the local housing market. They include young families; hospitality, agricultural, and winery workers; service providers like firefighters and police; and even teachers and young professionals. A 2005 study found that less than one-quarter of Napa County households could afford to purchase a median-priced home.[4] The same affordability issues affect renters. The result is that many workers must live outside the valley and commute to their jobs. Ironically, while tourism has helped contribute to the overall prosperity of the valley, most jobs in the tourism industry are so low-paying that most employees cannot afford to live there.

Napa County also has too few houses—what town planners refer to as a poor "jobs-to-housing ratio." The town of St. Helena, for example, has two jobs for every dwelling.[5] A carefully planned community should have a relatively even ratio of jobs to housing, which would allow most people who work in a community to live there. The shortage of affordable housing is a particular problem for many Hispanic residents, who tend to be more recent arrivals and to work in lower-income jobs. Many are forced to live in crowded conditions, often with several families or individuals sharing. Or, they must live outside the county, where housing is cheaper but the resulting commute can take an hour or more. In commuting, they add to the valley's traffic, air pollution, and greenhouse gas emissions. Even some of the old-timers say that their children have left the valley to find affordable housing. "I hate what's happened," says Isabel Regusci, a native Napan and owner of Regusci Winery. "They've wrecked it for our kids. There is so much outside money [buying homes] that our kids can't afford to live here."

The arrival of affluent newcomers has driven up the cost of living in other ways. They can afford to pay high prices for the services of architects, craftsmen, carpenters, painters, plumbers, and others, inflating the cost of these services for everyone. The cost of Napa labor is now comparable to that of Marin, the wealthiest county in the United States. For many Napans, the high cost of living is a strain. Some older residents describe themselves as land rich, but cash poor.

Minorities have always played a vital role in Napa's culture and economy, beginning in the late nineteenth century with Chinese laborers, followed a few decades later by Italian immigrants, and after World War II by Mexicans. Since the 1950s, Mexicans have provided nearly all of Napa's agricultural field labor. Today, a quarter of Napa County's population speaks Spanish as their primary language.[6] Most Mexican laborers prior to the 1970s were seasonal migrants who returned home once the harvest was over, but since then many have stayed on to become permanent residents of the valley. Over the last thirty years Napa County has gone from having one of the lowest percentages of persons of Hispanic descent among the Bay Area's nine counties (9 percent in 1980) to having the highest percentage (30 percent in 2008). Many former agricultural workers have left vineyard work and moved into construction, landscaping, and the hospitality sector, creating a demand for more agricultural labor from Mexico. Changes in the labor requirements in Napa vineyards due to the transition from "grape growing" to "fine wine growing," which requires more cultivation and canopy management of the vines, have also created more demand for agricultural labor. As one winery owner explains, "I now have enough vineyard work to keep my guys [Mexican laborers] busy most of the year, instead of just half the year like before." It is uncommon today to find anyone working in the vineyards or in restaurant kitchens, cleaning hotel rooms, or doing the "environmental housekeeping" of tending winery grounds, roadside plantings, and town parks who is not Hispanic.

Changing Appearance of the Valley

When Robert Mondavi opened his new winery in Oakville in 1966, the valley's agriculture was still fairly diverse. Prunes, walnuts, pears, hay, barley, Christmas trees, wheat, cattle pasture, and dairy all competed with vineyards. Since then vineyard acreage has expanded dramatically and at the expense of all other crops. As the demand and prices for Napa grapes reached new heights, vineyards began to climb up the hillsides, replacing many stands of native oak woodland. Concern about Napa's changing hillsides—the loss of native vegetation, the change in scenery, and especially the soil erosion on new hillside vineyards which was silting up the valley's streams and the Napa River—led some locals to form Concerned Citizens for Napa Hillsides (CCNH) to lobby for preservation and better environmental control.[7] In 1991, following several damaging landslides, Napa County enacted ordinances to limit and control hillside developments in order to reduce erosion.

More disturbing than hillside vineyards to many residents today are the large houses that have been built on the hillsides. They began to appear in the 1980s and '90s, most built by wealthy newcomers, many of whom live in the valley for only a few months or weeks of the year. Author James Conaway refers to them in his writings as "muscle houses" or "houses on steroids," and to their owners as "city slickers" and "cocktail farmers." His book, *The Far Side of Eden,* deals in part with the battles between these newcomers and local Napans who want to preserve the valley's landscape, viewshed, and open space. Resentment of outsiders and new residents is a common phenomenon, especially when the newcomers have more money than most locals and appear to have little understanding of or respect for traditional land uses, as is sometimes the case in Napa.

The mountain ranges that physically and visually contain the Napa Valley on both sides and create its north–south orientation may be Napa's most important feature. While vineyards and farm buildings visually establish the valley's agricultural nature, it is the mountains that frame and thus create much of its real beauty. In the opinion of nearly everyone who grew up or has spent many years living in the valley, visually prominent hillside and ridge-top homes and mansions have degraded the viewshed. In the words of Napa tourism consultant Erica Ercolano,

> A lot of those big houses are eyesores, just ostentatious. I think the Johnny-come-latelies arrived here not understanding what we are all about and what made the valley attractive for them to come here in the first place. It's not hard to look at what's happened to other beautiful California valleys and see what too much growth and careless development have done to them. If you ignore that, you're likely to repeat the same mistakes with the same consequences here.

Conaway argued that these newcomers have been "indifferent to the past" and often hostile to making "even the smallest sacrifices for the general good . . . Even if gratifying their desires meant wrecking views for others and sullying the way of life that had attracted them in the first place."[8] In the words of St. Helena's city planner Greg Desmond,

> I have a difficult time with most of the hillside estates that are visible from the valley floor. They detract from the intent of the agricultural preserve and take away from the unique agricultural heritage and open space that the county has been struggling to retain. . . . I am not an anti-development advocate but I am a true believer in appropriate development.

Calistoga native and postman Nick Triglia composed a song that expresses his scorn for wealthy seasonal hillside residents. Called "Geekin for the Weekend," it begins, "Gee, I think I'll buy a winery and will call my house a château. Call my dog Pinot, and drive a pickup with a winery logo."

Our survey of tourists, in contrast, revealed that very few visitors were bothered by Napa's hillside development. This may be because most visitors did not know the valley when the hillsides were pristine, unscarred by development. Napa resident anthropologist Rue Ziegler explains it this way:

> Most visitors simply don't realize that out of the nine Bay Area counties, Napa is an anomaly. We are the least urbanized, most opposed to sprawl, and the most dedicated to preserving the agrarian landscape.

This has given us tremendous benefits; so when the people who live here see any encroachment on what was a very purposeful land-use policy, it is very disturbing. Visitors are usually unaware of this history, and of how incredibly fragile all this [Napa's environment] is and the risk posed to everyone by insensitive development.

For most tourists, Napa is still markedly rural in contrast to the cities in which they live.

Tourism and the Quality of Life

In terms of its impact on daily life, traffic congestion is the most serious consequence of tourism for valley residents. Five million tourists visit each year. This means an average of 14,000 people per day over the course of the year, but visitor traffic is seasonally skewed with the quietest period from November to April. During the peak tourism season, which occurs during the September–October grape harvest or "crush," as many as 40,000 to 60,000 people may be on Napa's roads on the weekends. The valley's major thoroughfare, Highway 29, which narrows above Yountville to a two-lane undivided road, can slow to a crawl on weekends and during the weekday rush hours. According to one study, the highway north of Yountville had reached its "practical capacity" in 1973 when the tourist boom was still in its infancy. When cars, limos, and agricultural vehicles idle or drive at less efficient speeds, fuel is wasted and pollutants are spewed into the air. Traffic also creates noise and forces drivers—workers, tourists, and locals alike—to spend more money on fuel.[9]

Weekday traffic, especially during rush hours, is caused less by tourists than by commuting workers; this itself is related to tourism. One up-valley resident characterized the traffic problem in a letter to the *St. Helena Star* newspaper this way: "It is a witch's brew composed of too much available alcohol, farming vehicles and tractors, rubbernecking tourists, a wine industry needing to ship or receive a commodity product on 18 wheelers, bicyclists, and landscape panoramas that draw the eye away from the roadway."[10] The same writer decried that "the pastoral beauty of the valley we work so hard to preserve is being destroyed by the traffic and the millions of cars. . . ." While overstated, the letter expresses the sentiments of many. Many locals now avoid Highway 29 when it is most congested, which often means staying home or taking alternative but longer routes when they do go out. Agriculture relies on the road system to move workers and products from vineyard to winery and from winery to market, and is also impacted by the congestion. Roads clogged with visitors and commuting workers slow down agricultural operations.

At the outset, we assumed that the volume of traffic during Napa's peak tourist season, combined with drivers who are wine tasting, would result in a high rate of auto accidents. We also assumed that many collisions would have serious, even fatal, consequences due to the large oak and eucalyptus trees that line portions of Napa's roads, and the curves and narrow bridges that exist in other places. For years we had heard stories about horrific accidents, and we knew two people who had been involved. We also listened to Napans accuse tourists of drinking too much and causing accidents. So it was a surprise when the head of the regional office of the California Highway Patrol (CHP), Mark Rasmussen, told us that their data show that the collision rate and the incidence of DUI on Napa County roads is no greater than elsewhere in the state.[11] "DUI and accidents are more often caused by ag workers who've had too much Budweiser, than visitors to tasting rooms who've had too much wine," another CHP official told us. Our own three-month analysis of DUI arrests reported in the Napa newspapers arrived at the same conclusion; the vast majority of those arrested had Napa addresses. Traffic analysts, such as Tom Vanderbilt, who wrote *Traffic: Why We Drive the Way We Do (And What It Says about Us)*, do not advocate removing trees from highway margins, and not only because that would reduce the scenic beauty of many roads. Rather, the presence of trees, which leaves drivers with little room for error, probably slows them down. No doubt the slower speeds of motorists caught in Napa's high-season traffic congestion also lessens the damage when collisions do occur.[12]

Residents complain frequently about today's traffic. In reminiscing about her high school years during the 1970s, JoAnne Lincoln said there was so little traffic in the seven miles between St. Helena and Oakville that "we often tried to see how far we could drive on the wrong side of Highway 29 without having to move over for an oncoming car. Sometimes I could get most of the way home." Congestion, like hillside development, is more irritating for Napa's residents than for visitors who mostly come from metropolitan areas and are accustomed to heavy traffic. Nonetheless, it does negatively impact their experience. Creeping along Highway 29 and through St. Helena wastes precious vacation time. Moreover, "They don't want to deal with the traffic or listen to traffic noise at night," adds Vicki Baxter, former president of the Yountville Chamber of Commerce. "They've come to the Napa Valley for its rural charm and to get away from the hustle and congestion of the metropolitan environments most of them are from. They've spent a lot of money to come here and they don't want to deal with it [traffic]!"

Tourism's Impact on Local Services

Tourists frequently increase the demand on local services in the places they visit, to the detriment of the local population. In trying to assess whether this was the case with wine tourism in the Napa Valley, we focused on St.

Helena, the largest up-valley town. In 1983 it commissioned a study to examine the impact of tourism, including its consequences for police, fire protection, and parks and recreation.[13] This provided us with a baseline with which to compare today's situation. According to the St. Helena police department, tourism has had no measurable effect on St. Helena's crime rate, in contrast to many tourist destinations, particularly those in less-developed societies, where crime (notably theft, prostitution, and drug sales) generally increases with the arrival of tourists. Napa's visitors, who are older, better educated, and wealthier, are less likely to commit crimes while on vacation than the younger, less affluent tourists who visit many other locations, including Napa County's popular Lake Berryessa. In St. Helena the major public safety issue, according to the police, is traffic congestion. The size of the police department actually declined between 1984 and 2010, from sixteen to thirteen people, while the number of wine tourists visiting the valley doubled.

The only impact tourism has had on the town's fire services has been the extra time it takes firefighters (all of whom are volunteers) to drive through traffic to reach the fire station, which is located on Main Street, and get their equipment in order to respond to an emergency. Nor has tourism had a noticeable impact on the town's parks. Wine tourists, who typically do not bring their children to the Napa Valley, are less likely to make use of local parks than other categories of tourists. In addition, some wineries provide their own green space and even picnic areas. In sum, assuming that St. Helena's experiences are fairly typical of other Napa Valley towns, wine tourism has not had an appreciable negative impact on local services. Indeed, the sales and local taxes tourist-oriented businesses pay help finance town improvements such as better street lighting, sidewalks, attractive signage, well-appointed libraries, and parks.

Some health-care and social programs have benefited substantially from wine tourism due largely to Napa's famous wine auction, Auction Napa Valley, which attracts many wealthy collectors who pay to attend and bid on wine donated by Napa vintners. It raises millions of dollars annually for charitable causes. In 2010, the thirtieth annual auction, attended by 850 bidders and vintners, raised more than $8.5 million.[14] Events include a daytime food and wine festival with entertainment; a barrel tasting and auction; a gala evening live auction for special lots of wine, dinner, and entertainment; and various bidders' luncheons and dinner parties at vintners' homes and wineries, all of which give participants behind-the-scenes experiences with America's top winemakers and chefs before the bidding starts. A simultaneous online E-Auction is held with international bidders dueling in real time with bidders on-site. One auction participant in 2000 bought a vertical vintage (different vintages of the same wine from the same winery) from the Harlan Estate for $700,000; another paid a half million dollars for a single imperial (six-liter bottle) of 1992 Screaming Eagle Cabernet Sauvignon. The auction has earned more than $80 million since its inception in 1981 for valley hospitals, children's health care, and non-profit youth and housing programs that, according to Napa Valley Vintners, "help maintain the health and well-being of the valley community."[15]

The Transformation of Main Street

The arrival of large numbers of well-heeled tourists with money to spend has transformed the Main Streets of all the up-valley towns. Many family-owned shops that served local needs (such as groceries, furniture, plumbing supplies, auto parts, clothing, and household notions) have given way to specialty shops catering to tourists and to the valley's newer wealthy residents. These include art galleries, jewelry stores, expensive clothing boutiques, interior decorators, and expensive spas. The increased demand for retail space on Main Street has driven up rents to the point that they are no longer affordable for most of the traditional, local-serving businesses. Those stores that still sell the basics have usually added product lines that appeal to the tourist trade. Steve's Hardware on Main Street in St. Helena, for example, which has been in business since 1878, now sells, along with nails, paints, tools, and fishing tackle, gourmet cookware and grape- and wine-themed gift items. Some local-serving businesses have only survived because they own their buildings.

The transformation of Main Street, which began noticeably in the 1970s, was in a few short years beginning to alarm local residents. St. Helena's tourism self-study in 1983 included a number of comments from locals like the following: "Tourists—let's welcome them graciously, feed them well, and lodge them comfortably, but we must be drastic, clear minded, and even belligerent about directing St. Helena's destiny. No, you can't have our town."[16] On the upside, the new Main Street businesses and their attractive shop fronts have given Yountville, St. Helena, and Calistoga a prosperous look and new vitality. Many local residents, of course, still shop on Main Street, and some enjoy browsing in its new boutiques and art galleries, but as one town official noted for St. Helena, "Yes, there are some folks in the town that can afford that stuff [art and boutique clothing], but they're typically not the ones that live here year-round."

Nowhere has the transformation of Main Street been greater than in Yountville (population 3,100), which one of us knew well in the pre-tourism 1960s because of frequent visits to a ranch owned by family friends. The town today is a tourist destination in its own right with several luxury inns and world-famous restaurants, notably the French Laundry, considered by most food critics to be one of the top restaurants in the United States. Yountville is also home to French-owned Domaine Chandon, another highly esteemed winery and restaurant, and to the Napa Valley Museum and the Lincoln Theater, which since a $22 million restoration has become the foremost performing arts center in the valley. On most mornings, brightly colored hot air balloons can be seen taking flight from the edge of town. In 2009, *Sunset Magazine,* the premier guide to life in the West, included Yountville in its list of "The 20 Best Small Western Towns" in America.[17] But prior to the rise of tourism in the late 1970s, Yountville was a dreary agricultural backwater and adjunct to a large residential institution for military veterans—the Veterans Home of California. Yountville's only services then were a diner operated by "hippies" in a small building that had previously housed the Greyhound Bus station, a small general store, shacks that provided housing for agricultural workers, and several dingy bars and brothels whose main clientele were the 1,100 vets living nearby. In the words of local anthropologist Rue Ziegler, "The place was practically a slum. It has gone from being an eyesore to being a trophy village. And its renaissance is entirely an artifact of tourism."

While none of the old-timers we interviewed would deny that Yountville is a much improved place, many are not happy about other changes in the valley. This response is not surprising given the role nostalgia plays in people's lives, but some of their discontent contains a legitimate critique. They miss the old stores, or what some refer to as "normal stores," that sold the basics. They find the new specialty shops too "cute" and expensive and say they offer little that interests them. The many fine restaurants that have opened are said to be too expensive to patronize for more than a special event. Some people refer to the changes taking place in up-valley towns as the "Carmelization" of Napa Valley, a reference to the popular central California coastal town of Carmel, which is prized for its scenery, rich history, and art galleries, but is also overrun with tourists and the specialty shops, restaurants, and hotels that cater to them. With just over 4,000 residents, Carmel is smaller than St. Helena (population 5,950), but has fifty galleries and jewelry stores, a "celebrity sightings" tab on the chamber of commerce's webpage, and quaint yet tourist-prompted city codes like the one that bans the wearing of high heel shoes without a permit— aimed at preventing tourist lawsuits arising from tripping accidents caused by the town's irregular sidewalks that have been pushed up by tree roots. (Carmel police do not actually enforce the ordinance.) Carmel is a model of tourist development that St. Helenans do not wish to emulate.[18]

One unexpected consequence of the changes on Main Street (combined with the problems created by traffic congestion) has been a reorientation for many locals away from the mid-valley towns—St. Helena and Yountville—and toward the city of Napa, especially for shopping. Similarly, those living near

Calistoga, as well as some St. Helena residents, now often travel to Santa Rosa to shop, a thirty-minute drive over the mountains. As lifelong Oakville residents and octogenarians Bob and Gayle Navone explain:

> St. Helena is where we went to high school. It's where most of our friends are. And it's where we would go out, but not now. There aren't many normal stores left . . . everything there is for the tourists. It's become like Carmel, with outrageous prices. It used to take ten minutes to get there [a distance of five miles] . . . now you have to plan on a half hour or more.

It seems that traveling away to shop diminishes residents' sense of community.

Many older residents claim there are "fewer things to do" in the new Napa Valley. Their social life, which once revolved around informal social gatherings like picnics and barbecues at friends' homes, swimming in the Napa River, holiday parties at the Grange Hall, Kiwanis and Rotary meetings and lunches, and weekend drives or rambles in the countryside, has been diminished by the changes in the valley. They also feel that they have lost the freedom to roam and explore the valley at will, without concern for trespassing. The expansion of vineyards, especially on the hillsides, fencing, and the arrival of new owners from urban settings who are not accustomed or comfortable with letting people "trespass" on their land—apparent from their "statement" gates with entry codes—has closed off places they once walked. "When I was a kid in the 1950s," remembered the late local historian Kathy Kernberger,

> You could roam all over these hills. The only rule was to be back by dark and close any gate securely behind me. You didn't want to let out anyone's horses or cows. You could trespass on private property and no one cared in those days. You can't do that today because nobody wants you on their land. Many people have fences and no one makes it easy for you to walk on their land. In the past, there was an implied sense of responsibility to others that you don't see much today.

Eighty-one-year-old Louie Pometta of Oakville, who has enjoyed hiking in the nearby Mayacamas Mountains all his life, says, "Now, people look at you and think, 'What are you doing here?' I say, 'I'm taking a walk.' 'Well do you live around here?' All these questions. That didn't happen when we were kids. You didn't see that." In the words of another Napa native: "As a young kid we used to go down to the river a lot. That was beautiful. We'd dam up a section and make a swimming hole . . . our families would have picnics there. Just about everything we did for fun was in the river. Today, you can't get down to the river, and if you do, someone will come along to investigate and tell you to get out."

Not all Napa residents, of course, feel as strongly or as negatively about the changes that have taken place in the valley. Young and middle-aged Napans are more likely to recognize the many benefits that development and tourism have brought. Many are enthusiastic about the range of produce and specialty items available in upscale grocery stores and the many art galleries in up-valley towns that are fun to browse in, and the independent bookstores that Calistoga and St. Helena can now support. "Now when you go out to lunch, chances are that you're getting really fine food; sometimes you are eating at a world-class restaurant," notes local author Lin Weber about the new dining opportunities in St. Helena. "And it's the same thing in the tasting rooms, where we have the opportunity now to taste world-class wines."

The valley's many artists, notably painters and photographers and to a lesser extent potters and sculptors, who may sell their work in Main Street galleries, benefit directly from tourism since it is primarily visitors who buy their work. In turn, artists enhance Napa's identity as a desirable tourist destination by enabling visitors to have a richer experience through their visits to galleries, exhibitions, and open houses.

Local Attitudes toward Tourism

Overall, what do Napans think of tourists and of tourism? Opinions vary, of course, as the previous discussion shows. Not surprisingly, most people who work in tourism and the industries that directly benefit from it are inclined to view it favorably. Nearly everyone has at least some appreciation of the economic benefits tourism brings, and this makes most people tolerant, if not supportive. But residents are also aware that tourism comes with costs, such as traffic congestion, that inevitably impact their lives; tourism has also contributed to the changing character of their communities. At other tourist destinations, social scientists have found that there is a relationship between the number of tourists and the amount of local resentment toward them.[19] As the flow of tourists into a region increases and they begin to overwhelm local facilities—roads, downtown streets, stores—the resident population is naturally strained. "For many folks," reports Yountville mayor Cindy Saucerman,

> tourism is fine, but please don't let me be inconvenienced. If someone gets stuck in traffic going through town, or they can't find a parking space when they pull into the grocery store because there are a lot of people in the parking lot who are not residents, they don't like it. People don't like being put out and when they are put out, it colors their opinion about the people [tourists] who are causing it.

"Some people flat out don't like the tourists," admits one Yountville resident. "It's the attitude, 'I'm here. It's great. I like what's mine and I don't want it ruined by others.' It's NIMBYism. They like the place just the way it is, that's why they moved here and they don't want it to change." According to Mayor Saucerman, the Yountville City Council and planning commission meetings are frequented by people who think this way: "They got their slice of heaven, and now they'd like everybody else to go away and not change anything." Even among tourism's biggest boosters, however, there is concern that too many tourists and too much tourism-related development will detract from their quality of life.

Attitudes toward tourism also appear to vary among the valley's towns. The city and town councils of Calistoga and Yountville, which was barely a town until the recent tourist boom, have strongly encouraged tourism through promotional marketing. St. Helena, on the other hand, has always been cautious, if not "tourism phobic," in the words of one town official. St. Helena's skepticism about tourism was reflected in the language of a 1983 report which characterized tourism issues as "frequently surrounded by controversy and sometimes sharp polarization of views . . . [and] . . . mistrust . . . and non-cooperation between various groups and individuals in the valley."[20] And when St. Helena updated its general plan in 1993, there was strong interest in developing policies that the city could use to promote "locals-serving" businesses as opposed to those that primarily catered to tourists, although not everyone agreed. As town planner Greg Desmond explained, "Some local folks who showed up at public hearings stated that art galleries, jewelry shops, and the like were businesses they were interested in seeing in the community, while other locals pointed out that the individuals interested in these high-end businesses were folks who did not reside in the community year-round. Both are locals."

Recently, the St. Helena City Council has shown signs of rethinking its coolness toward tourism. "It's not just been the recession," continues town planner Desmond, noting that the city has been feeling the impacts of tourism without realizing the revenue benefits.

In 2008 Calistoga and Yountville each took in $3.4 million in TOT or hotel taxes, more than double St. Helena's revenue of $1.56 million.[21] After keeping a tight cap on the amount of visitor accommodation in town and opposing a proposal to develop a sixty-room hotel (to be called Vineland Station) for years, the St. Helena City Council finally approved it in 2009, and by a large margin. And after fighting the Wine Train when it was first proposed in the late 1980s and succeeding in preventing its passengers from disembarking in St. Helena, the city council, with support from St. Helena's business community, in 2009 began allowing Wine Train passengers to get off in town for a once-monthly event called "Cheers! St. Helena." It is expected, however, that this "trial" will lead to a further loosening of restrictions. Despite these new overtures, St. Helena, which has always prided itself on being the agricultural heart and service center of the valley, is unlikely to ever embrace tourism with the same enthusiasm or on the same scale as Calistoga or Yountville. St. Helena seems unlikely, for example, to allow new downtown tasting rooms as neighboring towns have done or to grant permits for new businesses that would cater to tourists with smaller budgets. "St. Helena is very sensitive to the agricultural heritage and character that make this such a unique community," says planner Greg Desmond. "We are not interested in becoming another Yountville or Calistoga. I believe that the direction we are heading in with the current General Plan will allow the community to evolve in a manner that benefits both locals and tourists without compromising the uniqueness of this place."

Tourism and a New Appreciation of Napa Valley

One effect of wine tourism in Napa has been a change in how locals "see" the valley. With five million visitors, mostly college-educated and affluent, arriving each year to enjoy the beautiful landscape and "enchanting lifestyle," Napans have developed a greater appreciation for where they live. Today most locals believe that the valley is a special place. This wasn't always the case. One vineyardist recounted that his father in the 1960s and '70s thought nothing of leaving junk cars in the field surrounding his house just off Highway 29. "There really wasn't much regard for the valley in the 1960s. We didn't think of it as being special, as being any different from any other rural place." Rue Ziegler, who has interviewed many Napa old-timers in doing ethnohistorical research, says,

> In the past, I don't think anyone sat here and said, "Wow, what a fabulous place we live in," mainly because they were working too damn hard just trying to keep their heads above water . . . trying to get through those terrible triple whammies of phylloxera, prohibition and depression. When I'd say to them, "It's so beautiful here," they'd kind of look at me funny because they didn't really think of it that way.

It is their children, argues Ziegler, whose appreciation for the valley has changed the most. Those born after World War II did not grow up with the privations of their parents and because they did not have to leave school early to work on the farm or take a wage job to help support their family, most were able to finish high school or go to college. Afterwards, most moved away for work, but after a while some returned and it was then they realized how "nice" and affluent the valley had become. In the words of one returnee, "It wasn't until I came back, after being away for six years in Illinois that I realized what we had." In our conversations with Napans it is often the "newcomers" who express the greatest appreciation for the valley today.

Napa's Tourism and the Development Balancing Act

What does the future hold? Will Napa continue to be a wine tourism mecca? Or will it lose its standing as tourists seek out new wine regions or turn to new activities? Will it decline in popularity because of overdevelopment? Or will Napa continue to avoid the overdevelopment that has afflicted so many other tourist destinations and thus retain its appeal? As someone once remarked, "Tourism is a bit like mustard on a hotdog. A little bit makes the hotdog better, but nobody likes mustard sandwiches." Some of the early academic literature on tourism described a developmental cycle analogous to birth, growth, maturation, and decline for many tourist destinations.[22] Geographer R. W. Butler's Tourism Area Life Cycle model (1980) outlined five distinct stages of growth that most mass tourism destinations experience: exploration, involvement, development, consolidation, and stagnation. During the "exploration" stage, a destination is relatively unknown and only small numbers of visitors arrive. Then as word spreads about its appeal, its amenities are improved and expanded, and more tourists arrive. In this early stage, tourists are generally welcomed by local residents who willingly interact with them and informally treat them as guests. But as numbers increase, the contact between tourists and locals inevitably becomes more impersonal and formalized. As the numbers continue to grow, local resources and infrastructure can no longer keep up with the volume of visitors, and the destination exceeds its "carrying capacity." Social or environmental stagnation or both set in, and the characteristics that once made the destination appealing and accounted for its success—the enthusiastic welcome and hospitality of locals, its pristine and uncongested environment, and the lack of gross commercialization—disappear. At this point, many popular tourist destinations decline as travelers seek new and more attractive places to visit.

At present, wine tourism in the Napa Valley is healthy and growing, but there are areas of concern and signs that it has reached its carrying capacity up-valley. Neighboring Sonoma Valley is trying to promote this perception and capitalize on it by advertising itself as the wine tourism destination that is, in contrast to Napa, "down-home and less congested." One warning sign of tourism overdevelopment is when the business community and local government begin to make decisions that favor the interests of tourists over those of residents. Some Napa Valley residents, especially those who live up-valley and have lived there the longest, argue that this is already happening on the "new" Main Streets, with shops aimed at tourists crowding out those serving locals. Other upscale tourist destinations like Carmel, once a delightful place to live, have crossed that line and today suffer from too much tourism. As many visitors comment, "Great place to visit, but I wouldn't want to live here." So far, few visitors to Napa say this.

While it is difficult to reliably measure many of the impacts of Napa's tourism industry on the valley, one fact is abundantly clear: the future of Napa's wine tourism and industries rests entirely on the fate of the Agricultural Preserve. The land-use restrictions the Ag Preserve created have protected the valley's vineyards from development and thereby preserved the foundation of its tourism industry.[23] Without Napa's verdant vineyards, open space, rural character, and beauty, tourism would surely decline. While the Ag Preserve has been under pressure since its inception from those wanting to develop or subdivide the land for profit, and it is constantly being chipped away by "parcelization" (notably, landowners making special claims based on historical land usage in order to subdivide their parcels for housing), it is not in any imminent danger of being overturned. However, several circumstances could change this. If the valley were to become significantly warmer due to climate change, it would become less suitable for growing the premier grapes for which Napa is famous. A prolonged economic recession or a pest infestation which causes widespread and repeated crop failures could also threaten the Ag Preserve. Either of these scenarios could drive grape growers and vintners into bankruptcy, which could make county officials and voters vulnerable to pressures to rezone the valley to allow development.[24] If that were to happen, the valley could be transformed, with open spaces and agricultural land converted into housing subdivisions, private "ranchettes," and commercial strip malls. At present, such dire scenarios are unthinkable to most Napans, who regard the Ag Preserve as sacred. Doing away with it would be akin to killing the goose that laid the golden egg. But similarly unthinkable scenarios already have played out in many parts of the United States.

The importance of Napa's agricultural landscape and open space to the experience of tourists was made abundantly clear in our 2007 tourism survey. When we asked visitors what made their visit a "memorable experience," over 40 percent identified some aspect of the landscape or the general beauty of the valley first.[25] Clearly, preserving the beauty of the valley is essential to Napa's popularity as a tourism destination, and nothing would threaten this more than having the valley's towns sprawl into the surrounding agricultural land, and having further hillside housing development.

Whatever the future of tourism, the growing congestion on Napa Valley's main arteries needs to be ameliorated, not just for visitors but for the quality of life of its residents and workers. Napa County projects that traffic will increase on Highway 29 by up to 70 percent by 2030.[26] Widening Highway 29 is not an option, as it would allow still more people to visit the valley and seriously diminish the valley's bucolic, small-town feel. County and state officials have been considering possible solutions for years, including light rail, expanded bus service, and special tourist or shuttle buses. So far, all of these ideas either have encountered opposition from landowner or farm interests or have proven impractical (for example, there is insufficient ridership and funds to make light rail sustainable). The major cause of rush-hour congestion, which is the lack of affordable housing for Napa's workers, must also be addressed. As long as there is too little affordable housing—both for purchase and for rent—much of Napa's workforce will have to commute into and out of the valley each day.

Some road improvements already have been made to ease the congestion and improve safety, notably widening the roadway shoulders and putting in center left-hand turn lanes to allow traffic to more easily enter and exit the main roads. These improvements have been enthusiastically received and made the roads safer, but they have not reduced the number of drivers on the roads. For now at least, Napans and visitors alike may just have to get used to greater congestion.

Solving the traffic quagmire is also important if Napa is to reduce its greenhouse gas emissions. The "heat-sink" effect of the extra infrastructure (buildings, roads, and parking lots) built to accommodate tourism also contributes to local climate change.[27] Research by climate scientists Greg Jones and Gregory Goodrich, among others, has discovered that temperatures in the Napa Valley in recent years have risen by one to two degrees Fahrenheit on average.[28] Tourism is a climate-sensitive industry. Changes likely to result from global warming, such as water shortages, extreme weather, a loss of biodiversity, reduced landscape aesthetics, and increased natural hazards and incidence of vector-borne diseases can all negatively impact tourism (not to mention residents and local businesses).

Climate often determines a tourist destination's seasonality. Any contraction or lengthening of the tourist season has implications for the profitability of different tourism enterprises. As climate change becomes more evident, some popular holiday destinations will decline while others are expected to improve. Tourists are highly mobile and freely shift their vacation destinations. Clearly, in the decades ahead climate change will demand adaptations by all the stakeholders in Napa's tourism.

No one can be certain what Napa's future will be, but we believe there is cause for optimism. Napa's planners at both the county and city levels seem determined, often passionate, about preserving the valley's historic rural character and of minimizing the impact of development. These goals are evident in the county's and cities' new general plans and became apparent in our interviews with planners and elected officials. Napa County, for example, currently has in place legislation, programs, or serious proposals to protect the hillside viewshed, encourage the reuse of historic buildings, preserve stone bridges and stone walls constructed before 1920, and develop hiking trails and a bicycle path stretching the length of the valley. The county also opposes the construction of new billboards and supports the removal of the few existing ones that remain in the valley. It is also trying to strengthen public awareness of cultural and historic preservation through education and public outreach. In short, local government appears committed to promoting historic and cultural resources as one means of maintaining Napa's identity as the nation's premier winegrowing region and a top tourist destination.

By way of illustration, one of the county's new initiatives is the development of a multi-use trail and bikeway to be called the Vine Trail. It will stretch from Calistoga in the north to American Canyon in the south, with a connection to the Vallejo ferry terminal. Tourists and locals would be able to take the ferry from San Francisco across the bay to Vallejo and cycle from there to Napa and then to its up-valley towns. Over eighty wineries and most of the valley's most significant scenic and historic resources, such as the Old Bale Mill, would be accessible to cyclists on the bikeway. Although not suitable for all tourists, the Vine Trail could nonetheless enhance tourism without increasing road congestion. Construction of the first section of the Vine Trail began in Yountville in 2010.[29] The valley's geographical compactness and relatively flat terrain, along with its temperate climate, make it an ideal place for cycling, both for recreation and transportation. At present, highway-speed traffic and the absence of designated bike lanes discourage many residents and visitors from taking their bikes out on the main roads. Many Napa parents, who fondly recall cycling all over the valley during their youth, now prohibit their children from riding near the main roads out of concern for their safety. For tourists the Vine Trail would provide an activity besides wine tasting, and one which planners predict will encourage some visitors to spend an extra day in the valley. Bike tourism in the Napa Valley, as we saw in Brad Dropping's narrative, has been steadily increasing each year.

Whatever the future brings, for the present there is no doubt that wine tourism, while certainly not an unqualified blessing, has helped make the Napa Valley prosperous and contributed to the diversity of the valley's social and cultural life. Has it made Napa a better place to live? For many residents, especially old-timers, the answer is no; but for tourists and new residents alike, the answer is almost always yes.

ACKNOWLEDGMENTS

During the five years this book was intermittently in progress, many people helped out. We owe much to wine industry insiders Jim Lincoln, Michaela Rodeno, Craig Root, Voelker Eisele, and Ellen Flora; to local anthropologist Rue Ziegler; and to Morgan Gmelch for their insightful comments on drafts of chapters. Their suggestions have made this a better book and have helped us avoid some embarrassing mistakes. We also owe an intellectual debt to geographer Sandy Nichols on farmworkers, to anthropologist Kenji Tierney on food and many other topics, and to town planner Greg Desmond for a planner's perspective on the impacts of tourism.

We are grateful to many other people who spoke to us at length about their lives and experiences in the valley. Among them are Don Buller, David Hellwig, JoAnne Lincoln, Catherine Luke, Robert and Gayle Navone, Louie and Jeannette Pometta, John and Una Raymond, Isabelle Regusci, Cindy Saucerman, Julie Siler Flynn, Nick Triglia, Wendy Ward, Kim Waddell, Lin Weber, and John Ziegler. Many thanks are also due to our agent, Rob Wilson, and colleagues and friends who provided guidance, encouragement, or just a patient ear: Lars Bjorkman, Tom Curtin, Alfredo DeHaro, Israel DeHaro, Jim Eder, Rob Elias, Liv Eskola, Walt Gmelch, Jerry Handler, Dave Jaeger, Shannon Jaeger, Amy Joseph, Gerard Kuperus, Jeannine Laverty, Marjolein Oele, Teresa Meade, Richard Nelson, George Sheldon, Andor Skotnes, and Candace Sommers. Mark Salvesterin and Jim Pappas suggested good "oldtimers" to interview. The reference librarians at the St. Helena Public Library were always helpful.

The University of San Francisco and Union College provided the environments in which the ideas in this book could develop, financial support, and student research assistants. Special thanks are owed to USF student Diane Royal who transcribed tapes, critiqued narratives, and was a valuable sounding board. Smith College student intern Carolyn Hou provided excellent comments on the final draft. Union students Sara Callahan, Vanessa Dumonet, Cristina Liquori, Sarah Melton, and Katie Newingham assisted with the research in a variety of ways and often entertained us as well. We are grateful to our excellent editor, Rebecca Tolen, an anthropologist herself, and her assistant, Peter Froehlich, for their enthusiasm for this project and for walking this book through the labyrinth of publication. David and the late Kathy Kernberger, Andrew Lincoln, Charles O'Rear, Vi Bottaro, the Wine Train, Opus One Winery, Napa Valley Vintners, and Domaine Chandon Winery kindly provided photographs to supplement our own.

Finally, our deepest gratitude goes to the eighteen narrators in this book who generously gave us their time and trust. In them we discovered some amazingly gifted and dedicated individuals, and their stories opened an important window onto the workings of the Napa Valley. We hope they will not be disappointed with the result.

Authors' Note

Unless otherwise noted, all quotations are from interviews we conducted specifically for this book. We've often "tidied up" what people said since spoken conversation, with its hesitations, false starts, grammatical slips, and momentary confusions, rarely reads intelligibly when presented verbatim. In the narratives, we have been careful to maintain people's characteristic voices and, of course, the meaning of what they said. The narrators were all given their edited narratives to check for mistakes and for final approval.

All photos without credits were taken by the authors.

NOTES

1. The Napa Valley—a Brief History

This chapter relies heavily on the following sources, unless otherwise specified: For Napa Indians—Robert F. Heizer, "The Archaeology of Central California: The Early Horizon," *Anthropological Records* 12(1) (1954), "The Archaeology of the Napa Region," *Anthropological Records* 12(6) (1953): 225–314, and "Indians of the San Francisco Bay Area," *Geologic Guidebook of the San Francisco Bay Counties* (San Francisco: California Department of Natural Resources, Division of Mines, Bulletin 154, 1951); C. Hart Merriam, "The Indian Population of California," *American Anthropologist* 7(4) (1905); and Lyman L. Palmer, *History of Napa and Lake Counties, California* (San Francisco: Slocum, Bowen & Co., 1881). For first settlers and early resorts—William F. Heintz, *California's Napa Valley: One Hundred Sixty Years of Wine Making* (San Francisco: Scottwall Associates, 1999); Denzil Verardo and Jennie Verardo, *Napa Valley: From Golden Fields to Purple Harvest* (Northridge, Calif.: Windsor Publishing, 1984); Charles Sullivan, *Napa Wine: A History*, 2nd ed. (San Francisco: Wine Appreciation Guild, 2008); John Doerper, *California Wine Country*, 3rd ed. (New York: Fodor's Compass American Guides, 2000); and Lin Weber, *Old Napa Valley: The History to 1900* (St. Helena, Calif.: Wine Ventures Publications, 1998); for wineries and Prohibition—Heintz, *California's Napa Valley*; C. Sullivan, *Napa Wine*; Lorin Sorenson, *Beringer: A Napa Legend* (St. Helena, Calif.: Silverado Publishing Co., 1989); D. and J. Verardo, *Napa Valley*; and Lin Weber, *Roots of the Present: Napa Valley 1990 to 1950* (St. Helena, Calif.: Wine Ventures Publications, 2001); for the Agricultural Preserve and post-1960s—James Conaway, *The Far Side of Eden: New Money, Old Land, and the Battle for Napa Valley* (New York: Houghton Mifflin Harcourt, 2002); Sullivan, *Napa Wine*; and Rue Ziegler, "Round Pond: The History of a Napa Valley Estate," unpublished manuscript, 2006.

1. Quoted in C. Hart Merriam, "The Indian Population of California," *American Anthropologist* 7(4) (1905): 605. By 1880 they are estimated to have numbered 50 in the Napa Valley; only one full-blood Wappo—Laura Fish Somersall of Geyserville—was reputedly still alive in 1976, according to Yolande Beard in *The Wappo: A Report* (St. Helena, Calif.: self-published, 1977).

2. Francis Farquhar (ed.), *Up and Down California in 1860–1864: The Journal of William H. Brewer* (New Haven, Conn.: Yale University Press, 1930), 222 and 215.

3. From John Russell Bartlett, a commissioner for the U.S. and Mexican Boundary Commission, who described the valley in the 1850s in his personal narrative.

4. Farquhar, *Up and Down California*, 224.

5. Heintz, *California's Napa Valley*, 29.

6. Charles Nordhoff, *California for Health, Pleasure and Residence* (New York: Harper and Brothers Publishers, 1873), 219.

7. Linda Heidenreich, *"This Land Was Mexican Once": Histories of Resistance from Northern California* (Austin: University of Texas Press, 2007).

8. William Ketteringham, "The Settlement Geography of the Napa Valley," master's thesis, Stanford University, 1961.

9. Quoted in George Williams, *Hot Springs of Northern California* (Carson City, Nev.: Tree by the River Publishing, 1997), 271.

10. Lin Weber, personal communication.

11. Recounted in William Heintz, *California's Napa Valley: 160 Years of Winemaking* (San Francisco: Scottwall Associates, 1999), 198.

12. Weber, *Roots of the Present*, 56.

13. Sorenson, *Beringer*, 92.

14. Michaela Rodeno, personal communication.

15. Julia Flynn Siler, *The House of Mondavi* (New York: Gotham Books, 2007), 39.

16. Ziegler, "Round Pond," 2006.

17. Heintz, *California's Napa Valley*, 119.

18. Sorenson, *Beringer*, 140.

19. Ibid., 140–41.

20. Ketteringham, "Settlement Geography," 167.

21. Environmental Science Associates (ESA), *A Study of Tourism in St. Helena* (Novato, Calif.: n.p., 1983), 14.

22. The restaurant at Domaine Chandon, opened in 1977, was the first "top flight" restaurant in Napa Valley.

23. Environmental Science Associates, *Study of Tourism*, 14.

24. Sullivan, *Napa Wine*, 322.

2. The Tourism of Taste

1. Robert Mondavi, *Harvests of Joy: How the Good Life Became Great Business* (New York: Houghton Mifflin Harcourt, 1999); and James Lapsley, *Bottled Poetry: Napa Winemaking from Prohibition to the Modern Era* (Berkeley: University of California Press, 1997), 47–51, 137.

2. Charles Sullivan, *Napa Wine: A History*, 2nd ed. (San Francisco: Wine Appreciation Guild, 2008), 289.

3. Wilfred Wong, "Wine Shopping the Millennial Way," *Vineyard and Winery Management* 33(5) (2007): 10–12.

4. Wine Market Council, "2008 Consumer Tracking Study" (at www.winemarket council.com; accessed June 16, 2009) and "2009 Consumer Tracking Study" (at www .winemarketcouncil.com; accessed March 25, 2010).

5. Liping Cai and Joseph Ismail, *Napa County Visitor Profile Study* (West Lafayette, Ind.: Purdue University Press, 2006).

6. In 2006, the median household income in the United States was $46,000.

7. With the help of two student assistants in the summer of 2006, we surveyed 161 tourists outside Napa Valley winery tasting rooms. Because it was an opportunistic sample, the results of the survey should be considered suggestive rather than definitive, although they are consistent with other studies.

8. Gary L. Peters is credited with coining the term "winescape." See his *American Winescapes: The Cultural Landscapes of America's Wine Country* (Boulder, Colo.: Westview Press, 1997).

9. See Rachel Kaplan and Stephen Kaplan, *The Experience of Nature: A Psychological Perspective* (New York: Cambridge University Press, 1995) and *With People in Mind: Design and Management of Everyday Nature* (Washington, D.C.: Island Press, 1999); and Howard

Frumkin, "Healthy Places: Exploring the Evidence," *American Journal of Public Health* 93(1) (2003): 1451–55.

10. From the Rutherford Ranch website: www. rutherfordwines.com (accessed June 25, 2006).

11. Environmental Science Associates, *Napa Valley Tourism Project* (San Francisco: ESA Planning and Environmental Services, 1984), 9.

12. As of August 25, 2009, there were 313 producing wineries in Napa County and an additional 104 wineries which had been approved but which were not yet producing—a total of 417. Nine more applications were pending at that time. Trish Hornisher, Napa County Planning and Development office, e-mail, August 3, 2009. As of March 2010, 377 wineries were members of Napa Valley Vintners (www.napavintners.com; last accessed March 25, 2010).

13. One of the winery's owners, Kathryn Hall, was ambassador to Austria between 1997 and July 2001.

14. Quoted in Larry Walker, *The Wines of the Napa Valley* (London: Mitchell Beazley, 2005), 89.

15. Oh Sang Kwon, Hyunok Lee, and Daniel A. Sumner, "Appellation, Variety, and the Price of California Wines," *Agricultural and Resource Economics (ARE) Update* 11(4) (2007); available online at www.agecon.ucdavis.edu.

16. Liz Thach and Tim Hanni, "Wine Marketing for Diverse Palates," *Vineyard and Winery Management* 34(1) (2008): 30–34.

17. Diane Ackerman, *A Natural History of the Senses* (New York: Random House, 1990), 13.

18. A Vinturi is a relatively new device that fits over the top of a wine bottle and quickly aerates the wine using a pumping action.

19. This discussion comes largely from Jamie Goode, "Wine and the Brain," in *Questions of Taste: The Philosophy of Wine,* ed. Barry C. Smith (London: Oxford University Press, 2007), 79–98, and Thach and Hanni, "Wine Marketing for Diverse Palates," 30–34.

20. Daniel Zwerdling, "Shattered Myths," *Gourmet,* August 2004.

21. Thach and Hanni, "Wine Marketing for Diverse Palates," 30–34.

22. Pierre Bourdieu, *Distinction: A Social Critique of the Judgement of Taste* (London: Routledge, 1984).

23. See Suzanne Gannon, "Where the Good Life Demands Grape Views," *New York Times,* Sept. 13, 2007.

24. Quoted in www.thenapavalleyreserve.com (accessed Sept. 26, 2010). See also Dennis Myers, "Gold in the Fields—the Very Reserved Napa Valley Reserve," *Colorandaroma.com* (May-June 2008). Available online at http://writingchef.com/lifestyle_new/Napa_Reserve.pdf (accessed Oct. 20, 2010).

25. See Franck Vigneron and Lester W. Johnson, "A Review and a Conceptual Framework of Prestige-Seeking Consumer Behavior," *Academy of Marketing Science Review* 1999 (1): 1–23; available online at http://www.amsreview.org/articles/vigneron01-1999.pdf (accessed Sept. 5, 2010). Much of modern advertising is built upon Veblen's ideas.

26. Walker, *Wines of the Napa Valley.*

27. Kwon, Lee, and Sumner, "Appellation, Variety, and the Price of California Wines."

28. The film *Mondovino* (Jonathan Nossiter, Diaphana Films, 2004) examines the globalization of wine, including the effect wine critic Robert Parker and wine consultant Michel Rolland have had on the industry.

29. Cai and Ismail, *Napa County Visitor Profile Study.*

30. According to wine industry analyst Barbara Insel, quoted in Stacy Finz, "Wineries Pouring It On to Lure Upscale Clients," *San Francisco Chronicle,* March 19, 2006, A1, A4.

31. Even today, only a small part of total U.S. wine sales are handled through direct shipping. Most states have strict laws on direct shipments of wine, and delivery is prohibited in certain states or areas within states.

3. Consuming Place

1. Quoted material comes from Lucy Long (ed.), *Culinary Tourism* (Lexington: University Press of Kentucky, 2004) and Barry Glassner, *The Gospel of Food* (New York: Ecco, 2007). See also C. Michael Hall and Liz Sharples, "The Consumption of Experience or the Experience of Consumption? An Introduction to the Tourism of Taste," in *Food Tourism: Development, Management and Markets,* ed. C. Michael Hall et al. (Chatsworth, NSW: Elsevier Australia, 2003), 13; and "Study: New York One of Top 'Food Tourism' Destinations," Feb. 19, 2007. www.1010wins.com (accessed May 14, 2007).

2. This information comes from a 2007 study of culinary tourism conducted by the International Culinary Tourism Association (ICTA) in partnership with the Travel Industry Association of America (TIA) and *Gourmet* magazine. See Samantha Gross, "Traveling to Eat: Food Tourism Grows in USA," USA Today online, Feb. 19, 2007. Available online at www.usatoday.com/travel/destinations/2007-02-19-food-tourism_x .htm (accessed Oct. 20, 2010).

3. Gary Alan Fine, "You Are Where You Eat," *Contemporary Sociology* 30(3) (2001): 231.

4. Thomas Keller, *The French Laundry Cookbook* (New York: Artisan, 1999), 3. Longenecker is quoted in Marion Edward, "The Rise of Culinary Tourism," Nov. 6, 2006 (www.hotelinteractive.com/article.aspx?articleID=6528; accessed Jan. 30, 2007).

5. According to the Napa County Economic Impact Study, restaurants received $265 million in direct spending from tourists compared to $184 million for the wine industry: Liping Cai and Joseph Ismail, *Napa County Visitor Profile Study and Napa County Economic Impact Study* (West Lafayette, Ind.: Purdue Tourism and Hospitality Research Center, 2006), 20.

6. See Eric Schlosser, *Fast Food Nation* (New York: Houghton Mifflin, 2001); Jane Goodall with Gary McAvoy and Gail Hudson, *Harvest for Hope* (New York: Warner Books, 2005); David Kamp, *The United States of Arugula: How We Became a Gourmet Nation* (New York: Broadway Books, 2006); Michael Pollan, *The Omnivore's Dilemma* (New York: Penguin, 2007) and *In Defense of Food* (New York: Penguin, 2009); Mark Bittman, *Food Matters: A Guide to Conscious Eating* (Simon & Schuster, 2008); Barbara Kingsolver with Steven L. Hopp and Camille Kingsolver, *Animal, Vegetable, Miracle: A Year of Food Life* (New York: Perennial, 2008); and Karl Weber, ed., *Food, Inc.* (New York: Public Affairs, 2009).

7. Paul Freedman (ed.), *Food: A History of Taste* (Berkeley: University of California Press, 2007), 26–27.

8. Carolyn Lochhead, "Organic, Local Farms Get a Boost from USDA," *San Francisco Chronicle*, April 15, 2010, A-1.

9. See Carlo Petrini, *Slow Food: The Case for Taste*, trans. William McCuaig (New York: Columbia University Press, 2003), and Bruce Pietrykowski, "You Are What You Eat: The Social Economy of the Slow Food Movement," *Review of Social Economy* 62(3) (2004): 307–21.

10. Napa Valley Vintners website, www.napavintners.com (accessed June 27, 2010).

11. Cary de Wit, "Food-Place Associations on American Product Labels," *Geographical Review* 82(3) (1992): 323–30.

12. David Graves, quoted in Janet Fletcher, "Napa Valley Restaurant Scene Is Cooking," *San Francisco Chronicle*, Aug. 1, 1998, A1.

13. See John Doerper, *California Wine Country*, 3rd ed. (New York: Fodor's Compass American Guides, 2000), 14.

14. Quoted in Fletcher, "Napa Valley Restaurant Scene Is Cooking," A1.

15. Quoted in Mira Advani Honeycutt, "After the French Laundry, What?" *Los Angeles Times*, April 10, 2002.

16. These restaurants included Hiroshi Sone's Terra (St. Helena) in 1988; Grant Showley's Showley's at Miramonte (St. Helena) in 1990; Jonathan Waxman's Table 29 (Napa) in 1991; Jeremiah Tower's Stars Oakville Café (Oakville) in 1993; Thomas Keller's French Laundry (Yountville) and Jan Birnbaum's Catahoula (Calistoga) in 1994; and Ken Frank's La Toque (Rutherford, now in Napa), Philippe Jeanty's Bistro Jeanty (Yountville), and Thomas and Joseph Keller's Bouchon (Yountville) in 1998.

17. According to the Napa Valley Vintners, 37 out of 389 member wineries have in-house chefs (see www.napavintners.com; accessed May 6, 2010).

18. Amy Trubeck, *The Taste of Place: A Culinary Journey into Terroir* (Berkeley: University of California Press, 2008).

4. From Vine to Wine

1. A 2005 study of 6,790 farmworkers on Napa County farms found that 99 percent were from Mexico. Fifty-five percent of these were "regular" workers (working seven months or more), 19 percent were "seasonal" (working three to six months), and 26 percent were "temporary" (working less than three months). In terms of demographics, 96 percent were men and 4 percent were women. Their average age was 35, with one-third being over 40 years of age. They had been in the United States an average of 13 years and in Napa County for an average of 9 years. About 60 percent reported being "undocumented." Richard Mines, Sandra Nichols, and David Runsten, *California's Indigenous Farmworkers*, Final Report of the Indigenous Farmworker Study (IFS) to the California Endowment, 2010. Available online at http://indigenousfarmworkers.org/IFS%20Full%20Report%20_Jan2010.pdf (accessed Sept. 4, 2010).

2. The starting wage for unskilled fieldworkers in Napa was about $9 an hour in 2010, which exceeds the current Mexican minimum wage for an entire day. More experienced fieldworkers earn $13.50 per hour, and vineyard supervisors are paid upwards of $20 per hour on average, while a foreman earns slightly less than $20 an hour.

3. Sandra Nichols, *Saints, Peaches and Wine: Mexican Migrants and the Translation of Los Haro and Zacatecas in Napa, California*, PhD diss., University of California, Berkeley, 2002.

4. Winiarski sold Stag's Leap Wine Cellars to a partnership of Washington-based Ste. Michelle Wine Estates and Tuscan vintner Piero Antinori in 2007, so the winery is now corporate owned. But the Winiarski family retained ownership of its Arcadia vineyards.

5. Les Médocaines is one example. It comprises four female chateau owners in Bordeaux who jointly market their properties and wines and also offer tourist programs such as cooking classes and food and wine pairings.

5. Touring and Tasting

1. Companion planting uses plants that contain natural substances (e.g., in their roots, flowers, leaves) that repel harmful insects or attract beneficial ones. It is a form of pest control and helps create a balanced ecosystem.

6. Food and Fine Dining

1. Keller cooked at La Rive, a small French restaurant in upstate New York, for three years during the summers and then moved to New York City, where he became *poissonnier* at the Polo Restaurant. In Paris he apprenticed at Taillevent, Guy Savoy, and Le Pré Catelan.

2. Upon returning to New York he was hired as the chef de cuisine at La Reserve. Three years later he and Serge Raoul opened Rakel in Tribeca. Following the stock market crash, he left rather than "compromise my quality and standards" in order to lower prices by replacing the restaurant's stylish cuisine with a more moderately priced bistro fare as his partner wished to do.

3. French Laundry sous chef Timothy Hollingsworth (now executive chef, or chef de cuisine) was tutored by Keller and Keller's own mentor, master chef Roland Henin; he won the gold medal at the USA semifinals in 2008 and went on to compete at the Bocuse d'Or finals in Lyon in 2009, placing sixth, the highest position ever garnered by an American. This international competition has been likened to a "culinary Olympics."

4. With a partner Keller had started a small business, EVO Inc., producing olive oil.

5. Keller has every new employee at the restaurant read Chef Fernand Point's book *Ma Gastronomie*. Point is recognized as the father of nouvelle cuisine, and Keller considers his ruminations about food and commitment to cuisine "extraordinary." Point believed that it was the duty of every good *cuisinier* to transmit everything he has learned to the next generation, a path Keller is following.

6. Keller often uses pop culture reference points and traditional foods to inspire him. His version of "macaroni and cheese" is butter-poached lobster and mascarpone-enriched orzo. "Bacon and eggs" is a soft-poached quail egg served on a spoon with crumbled bacon on top.

7. California is the first state to pass a law banning the sale and production of foie gras from force-fed animals; it will go into effect in 2012. In Defense of Animals has picketed a couple times in front of the French Laundry to protest its serving of this gourmet delicacy. See "Protesting Force Feeding for Foie Gras," *Yountville Sun*, May 13, 2010, p. 4.

8. Keller's views on this are criticized by those who object to the energy use entailed in transporting food long distances. These critics believe it is important to support the growth of local agriculture and to put money in local farmers' pockets so that they have an economic incentive to grow a variety of plants and animals. Some also have pointed out that the concept of cuisine is based on the use of a limited set of locally available and regionally common ingredients.

9. Plans for the twenty-room inn, and with it the required low-cost housing units, were dropped in August 2009.

10. Keller has a signature line of Limoges porcelain tableware by Raynaud, called Hommage in honor of Fernand Point; he also helped design a collection of silver hollowware by Christofle and has lent his name to a line of knives by MAC. He has been a consultant on two films—*Spanglish* and *Ratatouille*—and has appeared on television numerous times.

11. *Sous vide* cooking involves the use of two new appliances: a vacuum machine (to seal food tightly in a plastic bag) and an immersion circulator (in which the food is cooked at a precise temperature in a water bath). The technique is sometimes used to compact the cells of a food in order to create a new texture for a familiar food as well as to intensify flavor. But usually it is used to allow a chef to slow-cook food to perfection in a water bath with the flavors sealed in. The technique was developed in France in the early 1970s, much refined and then introduced in 2000 to Keller and other chefs by Chefs Gerard Bertholon and Bruno Goussault of Cuisine Solutions.

7. Napa's Other Pleasures

1. Besides providing a boundary, draping also helps keep the client warm, which aids in his or her relaxation. In some countries, draping requires that certain areas, such as the genitals on both genders and the breast area on women, be covered at all times. In the United States draping is a standard of the profession, while in other parts of the world, including Asia and parts of Europe, it is not practiced at all.

8. Tourism, Quality of Life, and the Future of Napa

1. "Economic Impact of Wine and Vineyards in Napa County" report, 2005. See also the Napa Valley Visitor Profile and Economic Impact Study. An executive summary of the report can be found at http://www.napavintners.com/downloads/visitor_profile_study.pdf (accessed Oct. 16, 2010).

2. See "The Napa Valley Visitor Profile Study, 2005–2006," p. 12. A study prepared for the Napa Valley Vintners, which looked only at the impact of wine tourists specifically, reported $714 million in wine tourism expenditures in 2006, or about half the figure of the Purdue University study; see Joseph Ismail and Liping Cai, *Napa County Visitor Profile Study and Napa County Economic Impact Study* (West Lafayette, Ind.: Purdue Tourism and Hospitality Research Center, 2006), 2. While their statistics refer to the economic impact made by all tourists, over 80 percent of Napa visitors were found to have come primarily for the wine.

3. A lower figure of 10,210 jobs (2006) was reported in another study, Stonebridge Research, *Economic Impact of the Napa Valley Wine Industry, 2008.* An estimated 8,000 people are directly employed in the wine industry.

4. See "The Napa Valley Visitor Profile Study, 2005–2006." A single wage earner in 2005 had to earn over $21 per hour for a full-time, 40-hour-per-week job to afford the average-priced housing in the county, yet the mean wage in Napa at that time was under $14 an hour.

5. "St. Helena General Plan Update—Housing Element," 2009, p. 6.

6. "Napa County General Plan—Ag and Land-Use Element," p. 7. According to the U.S. Census, in 2008 25.2 percent of Napa County residents spoke a language other than English in the home.

7. William Friedland, "Agriculture and Rurality: Beginning the 'Final Separation'?" *Rural Sociology* 67(3) (2002): 354.

8. James Conaway, *The Far Side of Eden: New Money, Old Land and the Battle for Napa Valley* (New York: Houghton Mifflin Harcourt, 2002), 2.

9. Some officials have wanted to widen Highway 29, but experience elsewhere has shown that widening roads only provides more capacity, which enables more traffic, producing little or no change in congestion.

10. *St. Helena Star,* April 12, 2007.

11. Interview with Mark Rasmussen, head of the Napa region of the California Highway Patrol.

12. Tom Vanderbilt, *Traffic* (New York: Alfred A. Knopf, 2009), 207.

13. Environmental Science Associates, *A Study of Tourism in St. Helena* (Novato, Calif., 1983), 6–7.

14. "Big Bucks Back at Wine Auction as Revelers Drop $8.5 Million," *Yountville Sun,* June 10, 2010, pp. 2, 10.

15. From the webpage of the Napa Valley Vintners, the nonprofit trade association that hosts the annual community fundraiser Auction Napa Valley, popularly known as "the Wine Auction."

16. Environmental Science Associates, *Study of Tourism in St. Helena,* 12.

17. See "Top 20 Small Towns in the West," *Sunset Magazine,* March 2009, 26–40. The magazine's editors based their selection on "a sense of connectedness," where people "commute less, know their neighbors," and "follow their passions," in addition to general information on each town, including population and median home costs.

18. Environmental Science Associates, *Study of Tourism in St. Helena,* 13.

19. Philip Pearce, "The Relationship between Residents and Tourists," in *Global Tourism,* ed. William Theobald (Burlington, Mass.: Elsevier Science, 2004), 135.

20. Environmental Science Associates, *Napa Valley Tourism Project* (San Francisco: ESA Planning and Environmental Services, 1984), 1.

21. "St. Helena Economy Is Hurting, Worth Healing," op-ed, *St. Helena Star,* Aug. 12, 2009.

22. David Weaver and Laura Lawton, *Tourism Management* (Milton, Queensland: John Wiley and Sons Australia Ltd,, 2000), 308.

23. The Land Trust of Napa County, a nonprofit organization founded in 1976 that has over 1,500 members, has also been a major force in protecting open space. By 2009, the Land Trust had preserved forever over 52,000 acres (or about 10 percent of the county) of agricultural and natural land in Napa County through conservation easements, property transfers, and land donations.

24. At present the most likely cause of such a catastrophe would be a crop infestation on the scale of the earlier phylloxera plagues. Napa agriculture is always on the

lookout for any signs of an insect called the glassy-winged sharpshooter, a large leafhopper which arrived in California accidentally in shipments from the southeastern United States, and for the European grapevine moth which appeared in the valley in 2009.

25. The easygoing, relaxed lifestyle of Napa ranked second at 23 percent, wine and wine tasting was third at 12 percent, and dining fourth at 7 percent.

26. "Napa County General Plan—Circulation" (Napa, Calif.: Napa County, 2007).

27. North–south winds from the San Francisco Bay area bring pollutants into the valley, where they become trapped by atmospheric conversions and topography and create conditions conducive to the formation of ozone, adding to an already high ozone and particulate concentration created by automobile traffic in the valley.

28. Information on the effects of climate change on the Napa wine industry come largely from an interview with Napa Farm Bureau president and vineyard manager Jim Lincoln and from Paul Franson, "Weathering Climate Change," *San Francisco Chronicle,* Oct. 24, 2008, pp. F1–2.

29. The Vine Trail will connect to the Bay Trail (a five-hundred-mile shoreline trail around the San Francisco Bay) and the Ridge Trail (connecting and preserving the ridges and open space surrounding Bay Area communities).

A GLOSSARY OF WINE AND VITICULTURE TERMS

Aging

Wines that are stored properly undergo a number of transformations. In red wines, ideally, the color can change from a rich purple to a lighter old-velvet red and the flavors can soften and lengthen. The primary chemical change has to do with tannins, which can be responsible for an astringent quality in red wines. As they fall out of the liquid, the flavor can soften, leaving behind the more majestic characteristics of the fruit. In many white wines, which do not begin their lives with a high tannin content, the primary changes are a browner color and a stronger flavor, the result of a process often described as caramelization.

Appellations

An appellation is a geographically based name for a wine-growing region that is believed to show unique characteristics of soil, climate, and more. In the United States, appellation names such as Napa Valley are approved by the Bureau of Alcohol, Tobacco, Firearms and Explosives (ATF). The term "sub-appellation" is used informally to refer to a smaller appellation wholly contained within a larger one.

Astringent

The "puckerish" quality of high tannin content, which has the effect of drying out the mouth. Many young red wines are astringent because of tannin.

Balance

Harmony among the wine's components: fruit, acidity, tannins, alcohol. A well-balanced wine possesses the various elements in proper proportion to one another.

Body

The weight and texture of a wine; it may be light-bodied or full-bodied. Often refers to alcohol content.

Botrytis cinerea

A mold that attacks certain grapes, producing honeyed sweet wines like Sauternes and late-harvest Rieslings.

Bouquet

The complex of aromas that develops with age in fine wines; young wines have aroma, not bouquet.

Brix

Term used to measure the sugar content of grapes, grape juice (must), or wine. Grapes are generally harvested at 20 to 25 degrees Brix. This results after fermentation in alcohol content of 11.5 to 14 percent.

Bud Break

The stage of the growing season, usually early spring in the Napa Valley, when tiny shoots emerge from their buds.

Buttery

Descriptor for rich flavor and smoothness of texture, somewhat akin to the oiliness and flavor of butter. It more often refers to oak-aged white wines than reds; many Chardonnays and white Burgundies are said to have buttery aromas and flavors.

Canopy

The part of the grapevine that is above ground, in particular the shoots and leaves.

Closed

Young, undeveloped wines that do not readily reveal their character are said to be closed. Typical of young Bordeaux or Cabernet Sauvignon, as well as other big red wines.

Complex

Multifaceted aroma and/or flavor. Most great wines exhibit a combination of flavor and aroma elements.

Cooked

Wines that are overripe.

Corked

Wine that is "corked" has been contaminated by its cork stopper and takes on an unpleasant moldy aroma and flavor sometimes described as "wet cardboard."

Crisp

Fresh, brisk character, usually with high acidity.

Crush

The time of year when Napa Valley is harvesting and crushing its fruit. "Crush" specifically refers to putting newly picked grapes into a "destemmer," a machine that destems the fruit and crushes it, releasing juice from the berry.

Dry

Opposite of sweet; somewhat subjective in that tasters may perceive sweetness to varying degrees.

Earthy

Smell or flavor reminiscent of earth. A certain earthiness can be appealing; too much makes the wine coarse.

Enology

The study and science of wine making.

Estate-bottled

To use this label, the wine must contain only grapes grown in the named appellation on land controlled by the bottling winery, and it must be made in one continuous process at the site of the winery.

Fermentation

A chemical process in which yeast consumes the sugar in juice, converting it into alcohol and carbon dioxide. In red and white wine production, the carbon dioxide is released during fermentation, while in the production of sparkling wine, the carbon dioxide is trapped, producing bubbles.

Finish

Aftertaste, or final impression the wine leaves; it can have a long finish or a short one (not desirable).

Grafting

The process of physically connecting two plants or pieces of plant tissue together so that they grow as one. In viticulture, grafting is often used to join a rootstock with a vine variety.

Green

A wine made from unripe grapes that is tart and lacking fruit flavor.

Herbaceous

Aromas reminiscent of fresh grass or hay are said to be herbaceous or grassy, as in certain Sauvignon Blancs; also the green pepper character of some Cabernets.

Legs

The viscous rivulets that run down the side of the glass after swirling or sipping, a mingling of glycerin and alcohol.

Long Finish

Fine wines should have a long and satisfying finish, or aftertaste.

Maceration

Maceration is the steeping process that comes after the grapes are crushed. During this period, the juice spends time in direct contact with the skins and seeds, so that important characteristics are transferred to the finished wine.

Malolactic Fermentation

Part of the vinification process when the tart-tasting grape acid malate is converted by lactic acid bacteria into softer-tasting lactate. It produces a rounder, fuller mouthfeel.

Microclimate

The unique climate and geographical conditions of a designated area, such as a vineyard, within a wine region.

Nose

The smell of the wine; it may have a "good nose" or an "off-nose," meaning defective odors.

Oxidized

Flat, stale, or sherry-like aroma and flavor; spoiled as the result of overexposure to air.

Phylloxera

A small aphid that feeds on and fatally damages vine root systems.

Pierce's Disease

A fatal disease caused by bacteria borne by the blue-green sharpshooter or glassy-winged sharpshooter, a leafhopper insect. The bacteria transmitted by the sharpshooter multiply and eventually block the vine's water-conducting systems.

Rootstock

The root system to which a vine variety is grafted.

Sharp

Biting acid or tannin.

Sparkling Wine

This bubbly wine is traditionally made from Pinot Noir, Chardonnay, and Pinot Munier grapes. When made in the Champagne region of France, it's called Champagne.

Steely

Firmly structured; with a taut balance tending toward high acidity.

Structure

The way a wine is built; its composition and proportions.

Tannin

A natural component found to varying degrees in the skins, seeds, and stems of grapes. Tannin is most prominent in red wines, where it creates a dry, puckering sensation in young reds of concentrated extract; it mellows with aging and drops out of the wine to form sediment. It is a major component in the structure of red wines.

Terroir

French for "soil," the physical and geographical characteristics of a particular vineyard site that gives the resultant wine its unique properties.

Trellis System

The supporting framework on which a vine is trained to grow.

Unfined

A wine to which nothing has been done, including filtering, to remove suspended solids.

Varietal

A wine made from a single grape source, such as Chardonnay, Cabernet, or Merlot.

Variety

A particular type of grape, such as Chardonnay, Cabernet, or Pinot Noir.

Velvety

Smooth and rich in texture.

Veraison

The stage of the growing season when young green grapes soften and turn either yellow or red in color depending on the variety. In Napa Valley veraison can occur from late June through mid-August.

Vintage

The year in which a particular wine's grapes were harvested.

Vintner

A person who produces wine.

Viticulture

The study and practice of growing grapes.

Yeasty

A bready smell, sometimes detected in wines that have undergone secondary fermentation, such as Champagne; very appealing if it is not excessive.

Sources: Barbara Ensrud, "A Wine Taster's Glossary"; Jim Lincoln, viticulturalist, Beckstoffer Vineyards; and www.sallybernstein.com/beverages/wine/wine_glossery.htm.

BIBLIOGRAPHY

Ackerman, Diane. *A Natural History of the Senses.* New York: Random House, 1990.

Beard, Yolande. *The Wappo: A Report.* St. Helena, Calif.: self-published, 1977.

Bisson, Linda, et al. "The Present and Future of the International Wine Industry." *Nature* 418 (Aug. 2002): 696–99.

Bittman, Mark. *Food Matters: A Guide to Conscious Eating.* New York: Simon & Schuster, 2008.

Bourdieu, Pierre. *Distinction: A Social Critique of the Judgement of Taste.* Cambridge, Mass.: Harvard University Press, 1984.

Brosnan, Kathleen. "Grapes or Crabgrass: Suburban Expansion, Agricultural Persistence, and the Fight for Napa Valley." In *Cities in Nature: Urban Environments in the American West; Essays in Honor of Hal K. Rothman,* ed. Char Miller. Reno: University of Nevada Press, 2008.

———. "The Root of Your Family." *Environmental History,* April 2007.

———. "'Vin d'Etat': Consumers, Land, and the State in Napa Valley." In *The Golden Grape: Wine, Society, and Globalization; Multidisciplinary Perspectives on the Wine Industry,* ed. Gwyn Campbell and Nathalie Guibert. London: Palgrave Macmillan, 2007.

Carmichael, Barbara. "Understanding the Wine Tourism Experience for Winery Visitors in the Niagara Region." *Tourism Geographies* 7(2) (2005): 185–204.

Chrzan, Janet. "Dreaming of Tuscany: Pursuing the Anthropology of Culinary Tourism." *Expedition* 49(2) (2007): 21–29.

Cohen, Erik, and Nir Avieli. "Food in Tourism: Attraction and Impediment." *Annals of Tourism Research* 31(4) (2004): 755–78.

Coleman, Simon, and Tamara Kohn. "The Discipline of Leisure: Taking Play Seriously." In *The Discipline of Leisure: Embodying Cultures of "Recreation,"* ed. Simon Coleman and Tamara Kohn. New York: Berghahn Books, 2007.

Conaway, James. *The Far Side of Eden: New Money, Old Land and the Battle for Napa Valley.* New York: Houghton Mifflin Harcourt, 2002.

Cook, S. F. "The Aboriginal Population of the North Coast of California." *Anthropological Records* (University of California) 16 (1956).

Csikszentmihalyi, Mihaly, and Eugene Rochberg-Halton. *The Meaning of Things: Domestic Symbols and the Self.* Cambridge and New York: Cambridge University Press, 1981.

Dean Runyan & Associates. *Planning for Travel and Tourism, Napa County.* Portland, Ore., 1990.

de Wit, Cary. "Food-Place Associations on American Product Labels." *Geographical Review* 82(3) (1992): 323–30.

Doerper, John. *California Wine Country*. 3rd ed. New York: Fodor's Compass American Guides, 2000.

Environmental Science Associates (ESA). *A Study of Tourism in St. Helena*. Novato, Calif., 1983.

———. *Napa Valley Tourism Project*. San Francisco: ESA Planning and Environmental Services, 1984.

———. *City of St. Helena 1993 General Plan*. San Francisco, 1993.

———. *City of St. Helena General Plan Update: Environmental Impact Report*. San Francisco, 1993.

Farquhar, Francis, ed. *Up and Down California in 1860–1864: The Journal of William H. Brewer*. New Haven, Conn.: Yale University Press, 1930.

Federal Writers' Project. *California: A Guide to the Golden State*. New York: Hastings House, 1933.

Fine, Gary Alan. "You Are Where You Eat." *Contemporary Sociology* 30(3) (2001): 231–33.

Finz, Stacy. "Wineries Pouring It On to Lure Upscale Clients." *San Francisco Chronicle*, March 19, 2006.

Fletcher, Janet. "Napa Valley Restaurant Scene Is Cooking." *San Francisco Chronicle*, Aug. 1, 1998.

Franson, Paul. "Weathering Climate Change." *San Francisco Chronicle*, Oct. 24, 2008.

Freedman, Paul, ed. *Food: A History of Taste*. Berkeley: University of California Press, 2007.

Friedland, William. "Agriculture and Rurality: Beginning the 'Final Separation'?" *Rural Sociology* 67(3) (2002): 354.

Frumkin, Howard. "Healthy Places: Exploring the Evidence." *American Journal of Public Health* 93(9) (2003): 1451–55.

Gannon, Suzanne. "Where the Good Life Demands Grape Views." *New York Times*, Sept. 13, 2007.

Getez, Donald. *Explore Wine Tourism: Management, Development and Destinations*. New York: Cognizant Communication Corporation, 2000.

———. "Critical Success Factors for Wine Tourism Regions: A Demand Analysis." *Tourism Management* 27 (2006): 146–58.

Glassner, Barry. *The Gospel of Food: Everything You Think You Know about Food Is Wrong*. New York: Ecco, 2007.

"The Global Drinks Market: Impact Databank Review and Forecast." 2009 edition. Available online at www.winespectator.com/contentimage/wso/pdf/GLOB09-toc.pdf (accessed Oct. 20, 2010).

Goodall, Jane, with Gary McAvoy and Gail Hudson. *Harvest for Hope*. New York: Warner Books, 2005.

Goode, Jamie. "Wine and the Brain." In *Questions of Taste: The Philosophy of Wine*, ed. Barry C. Smith, 79–98. London: Oxford University Press, 2007.

Gower, Eric. "Growing a 4-Star Garden." *San Francisco Chronicle*, Sept. 12, 2010.

Heeger, Jack. "U.S. Wine Consumption Up." *Napa Valley Register,* Jan. 20, 2008.

Heidenreich, Linda. "History and Forgetfulness in an 'American' County." PhD diss., University of California, San Diego, 2000.

———. *"This Land Was Mexican Once": Histories of Resistance from Northern California.* Austin: University of Texas Press, 2007.

Heintz, William F. *California's Napa Valley: One Hundred Sixty Years of Wine Making.* San Francisco: Scottwall Associates, 1999.

Heizer, Robert F. "The Archaeology of Central California: The Early Horizon." *Anthropological Records* 12(1) (1954).

———. "The Archaeology of the Napa Region." *Anthropological Records* 12(6) (1953): 225–314.

———. "Indians of the San Francisco Bay Area." *Geologic Guidebook of the San Francisco Bay Counties.* San Francisco: California Department of Natural Resources, Division of Mines, Bulletin 154, 1951.

Hodgson, Robert T. "An Examination of Judge Reliability at a Major U.S. Wine Competition." *Journal of Wine Economics* 3(2) (2008): 105–13.

———. "An Analysis of the Concordance among 13 U.S. Wine Competitions." *Journal of Wine Economics* 4(2) (2009): 1–9.

Honeycutt, Mira Advani. "After the French Laundry, What?" *Los Angeles Times,* April 10, 2002.

Ismail, Joseph, and Liping Cai. *Napa County Visitor Profile Study and Napa County Economic Impact Study.* West Lafayette, Ind.: Purdue Tourism and Hospitality Research Center, 2006.

Jacobstein, Bennett. *California's 58 Counties.* Fremont, Calif.: Toucan Valley Publications, 1999.

Joanes, Ana Sofia, dir. and prod. *Fresh.* 2009. www.FRESHtheMovie.com.

Jordan, Jennifer. "The Heirloom Tomato as a Cultural Object: Investigating Taste and Space." *Sociologia Ruralis* 47(1) (2007): 20–41.

Kamp, David. *The United States of Arugula: How We Became a Gourmet Nation.* New York: Broadway Books, 2006.

Kant, Immanuel. "Objective and Subjective Senses: The Sense of Taste." In *The Taste Culture Reader: Experiencing Food and Drink,* ed. Carolyn Korsmeyer. New York: Berg, 2005.

Kaplan, Rachel, and Stephen Kaplan. *The Experience of Nature: A Psychological Perspective.* New York: Cambridge University Press, 1995.

———. *With People in Mind: Design and Management of Everyday Nature.* Washington, D.C.: Island Press, 1999.

Keller, Thomas, with Susie Heller and Michael Ruhlman. *The French Laundry Cookbook.* New York: Artisan Press, 1999.

Kenner, Robert, dir. *Food, Inc.* Magnolia Pictures, 2009.

Ketteringham, William. "The Settlement Geography of the Napa Valley." Master's thesis, Stanford University, 1961.

Kingsolver, Barbara, with Steven L. Hopp and Camille Kingsolver. *Animal, Vegetable, Miracle: A Year of Food Life.* New York: HarperPerennial, 2008.

Kostrzewa, Susan. *Wine Enthusiast Magazine.* N.p., 2007. Web. March 10, 2009. http://www.winemag.com/buyingguide.com.

Kwon, Oh Sang, Hyunok Lee, and Daniel A. Sumner. "Appellation, Variety, and the Price of California Wines." *Agricultural and Resource Economics (ARE) Update* 11(4) (2007). Available at www.agecon.ucdavis.edu.

Laird, Charlton Grant, ed. *Webster's New World Dictionary and Thesaurus.* 2nd ed. Cleveland: Wiley Publishing, 2002.

Lamont, Michelle, and Annette Lareau. "Cultural Capital: Allusions, Gaps and Glissandos in Recent Theoretical Developments." *Sociological Theory* 6(2) (1988): 153–68.

Lanchester, John. "Scents and Sensibility: What the Nose Knows." *New Yorker,* March 10, 2008.

Lapsley, James. *Bottled Poetry: Napa Winemaking from Prohibition to the Modern Era.* Berkeley: University of California Press, 1997.

Leach, William. *Land of Desire: Merchants, Power and the Rise of a New American Culture.* New York: Vintage, 1994.

Lehrer, Adrienne. "Talking about Wine." *Language* 51(4) (1975): 901–23.

Line, Les. "Can Napa Valley Survive Success?" *Audubon Magazine* 91(6) (1989): 68–73.

Long, Lucy, ed. *Culinary Tourism.* Lexington: University Press of Kentucky, 2004.

Maloney, Field. "Beer in Headlights." *Slate,* May 30, 2007. Available online at http://www.slate.com/id/2167292 (accessed June 3, 2007).

Martin, Glenn. "Napa's Farm Workers." *San Francisco Chronicle Magazine,* Dec. 19, 2004.

Matasar, Ann B. *Women of Wine: The Rise of Women in the Global Wine Industry.* Berkeley: University of California Press, 2006.

McCool, S. F., and G. H. Stankey. "Managing for the Sustainable Use of Protected Wildlands: The Limits of Acceptable Change Framework." Paper presented at IV World Congress on National Parks and Protected Areas, Caracas, Venezuela, Feb. 10–21, 1992.

McCoy, Elin. *The Emperor of Wine: The Rise of Robert M. Parker, Jr., and the Reign of American Taste.* New York: HarperPerennial, 2005.

McCracken, Grant. *Culture and Consumption: New Approaches to the Symbolic Character of Consumer Goods and Activities.* Bloomington: Indiana University Press, 1988.

McKee, Irving. "Historic Napa County Wine-Growing." The Wine Institute for the Wine Advisory Board, n.d.

Menefee, C. A. *Historical and Description Sketch of Napa, Sonoma Lake and Mendocino.* Napa, Calif.: Reporter Publishing Co., 1873.

Mennell, Stephen. "Of Gastronomes and Guides." In *The Taste Culture Reader: Experiencing Food and Drink,* ed. Carolyn Korsmeyer. New York: Berg, 2005.

Merriam, C. Hart. "The Indian Population of California." *American Anthropologist* 7(4) (1905): 594–606.

Mitchell, Richard, C. Michael Hall, and Alison McIntosh. "Wine Tourism and Consumer Behaviour." In *Wine Tourism around the World: Development, Management and Markets*, ed. Michael C. Hall et al. Oxford, UK: Butterworth-Heinemann, 2000.

Mines, Richard, Sandra Nichols, and David Runston. *California's Indigenous Farmworkers: Farmworkers*, Final Report of the Indigenous Farmworker Study (IFS) to the California Endowment, 2010. Available online at http://indigenous farmworkers.org/IFS%20Full%20Report%20_Jan2010.pdf (accessed Sept. 4, 2010).

Mondavi, Robert. *Harvests of Joy: How the Good Life Became Great Business*. New York: Houghton Mifflin Harcourt, 1999.

Moran, Warren. "The Wine Appellation as Territory in France and California." *Annals of the Association of American Geographers* 83 (1983): 694–717.

Mukhopadhyay, Dripto. "Role of Tourism Sector in Climate Change: A Perspective." November 7, 2008. Available online at www.slideshare.net/indicusanalytics/ role-of-tourism-sector-in-climate-change-indicus-analytics-presentation (accessed Sept. 6, 2010).

Myers, Dennis. "Gold in the Fields—the Very Reserved Napa Valley Reserve." *Colorandaroma.com*, May-June 2008. Available online at http://writingchef.com/ lifestyle_new/Napa_Reserve.pdf (accessed Oct. 20, 2010).

"Napa County General Plan—Circulation." Napa, Calif.: Napa County, 2008.

Napa Valley Vintners website. June 25, 2006. www.napavintners.com (accessed June 25, 2006).

Napa Valley Vintners. "Economic Impact of the Napa Valley Wine Industry." 2005.

Narlock, Lori Lyn. *The Food Lover's Companion to the Napa Valley*. San Francisco: Chronicle Books, 2003.

"New Mexico Drunk Driving Statistics." *United States Department of Transportation (USDOT)*. 2008. http://www.alcoholalert.com/drunk-driving-statistics-new-mexico.html (accessed March 10, 2009).

Nichols, Sandra. *Saints, Peaches and Wine: Mexican Migrants and the Translation of Los Haro and Zacatecas in Napa, California*. PhD diss., University of California, Berkeley, 2002.

Noble, Ann. *The Wine Aroma Wheel Web Portal*. http://www.winearomawheel.com (accessed Nov. 27, 2007).

Nordhoff, Charles. *California for Health, Pleasure and Residence*. New York: Harper and Brothers, Publishers, 1873.

Nossiter, Jonathan, dir. *Mondovino*. Diaphana Films, 2004.

Palmer, Lyman L. *History of Napa and Lake Counties, California*. San Francisco: Slocum, Bowen & Co., 1881.

Parker, Robert. *Inglenook Vineyards*. Rutherford, Calif.: Inglenook Vineyards, 1979.

Passmore, Nick. "World's Most Expensive Wines." *Forbes*. Nov. 19, 2003. Available online at http://www.forbes.com/2003/11/19/cx_np_1119feat.html (accessed March 8, 2009).

Pearce, Philip. "The Relationship between Residents and Tourists." In *Global Tourism,* ed. William Theobald. Burlington, Mass.: Elsevier Science, 2004.

Peters, Gary L. *American Winescapes: The Cultural Landscapes of America's Wine Country.* Boulder, Colo.: Westview Press, 1997.

Petrini, Carlo. *Slow Food: The Case for Taste.* Trans. William McCuaig. New York: Columbia University Press, 2003.

Peynaud, Emile. "Tasting Problems and Errors of Perception." In *The Taste Culture Reader: Experiencing Food and Drink,* ed. Carolyn Korsmeyer. New York: Berg, 2005.

Pietrykowski, Bruce. "You Are What You Eat: The Social Economy of the Slow Food Movement." *Review of Social Economy* 62(3) (2004): 307–21.

Phillips, Rod. *A Short History of Wine.* New York: HarperCollins, 2000.

Pinney, Thomas. *A History of Wine in America from Prohibition to the Present.* Berkeley: University of California Press, 1989.

Pollan, Michael. *The Omnivore's Dilemma.* New York: Penguin, 2007.

———. *In Defense of Food.* New York: Penguin, 2009.

Saunders, Jenan. "Ranchers, Farmers, and Vintners: The White Church and Pioneer Cemetery at Bothe-Napa Valley State Park." Unpublished manuscript, 1997.

Saekel, Karola. "Frog's Leap Wine Comes with a Bit of Whimsy." *San Francisco Chronicle,* May 3, 2009.

Schlosser, Eric. *Fast Food Nation.* New York: Houghton Mifflin, 2001.

Seremetakis, Nadia C. "The Breast of Aphrodite." In *The Taste Culture Reader: Experiencing Food and Drink,* ed. Carolyn Korsmeyer. New York: Berg, 2005.

Shepherd, Gordon M. "Smell Images and the Flavour System in the Human Brain." *Nature* 444 (Nov. 2006): 316–20.

Siler, Julia Flynn. *The House of Mondavi.* New York: Gotham Books, 2007.

Skinner, Angela M. "Napa Valley, California: A Model of Wine Region Development." In *Wine Tourism around the World,* ed. C. Michael Hall et al., 283–96. London: Butterworth-Heinemann, 2002.

Sorenson, Lorin. *Beringer: A Napa Valley Legend.* St. Helena, Calif.: Silverado Publishing Co. 1989.

Stankey, G. H., D. N. Cole, R. C. Lucas, M. E. Petersen, and S. S. Frissell. *The Limits of Acceptable Change (LAC) System for Wilderness Planning.* Ogden, Utah: U.S. Department of Agriculture, Forest Service, Intermountain Forest and Range Experiment Station, 1985. Available online at http://www.fs.fed.us/r8/boone/documents/lac/lacsummary.pdf (accessed Sept. 6, 2010).

Stearns, Robert. "On Certain Aboriginal Implements from Napa County, California." *The American Naturalist* 16(3) (1882): 203–209.

Sterling, Joy. *A Cultivated Life: A Year in a California Vineyard.* New York: Villard Books, 1993.

St. Helena Star. "St. Helena Economy Is Hurting, Worth Healing." Editorial. Aug. 12, 2009.

Stokstad, Marilyn. *Medieval Art*. 2nd ed. Boulder, Colo.: Westview Press, 2004.

Stonebridge Research. *Economic Impact of the Napa Valley Wine Industry: Prepared for the Napa Valley Vintners*. October 2008. Available online at http://www.napa vintners.com/downloads/2008_Economic_Impact_Report.pdf (accessed Oct. 20, 2010.

Street, Henry K. *The History of Wine in New Mexico: 400 Years of Struggle*. Ponderosa, N.Mex.: Ponderosa Valley Vineyards and Winery, n.d.

Strum, Adam M., ed. "Wine Enthusiast Buying Guide." *Wine Enthusiast Magazine* 21(5) (2008): 82.

Sullivan, Charles. *Napa Wine: A History*. 2nd ed. San Francisco: Wine Appreciation Guild, 2008.

———. *American Generations: Who They Are, and How They Live*. 6th ed. New York: New Strategist Publications. 2008.

Sutton, David E. "Synesthesia, Memory, and the Taste of Home." In *The Taste Culture Reader: Experiencing Food and Drink,* ed. Carolyn Korsmeyer. New York: Berg, 2005.

Symons, Michael. "Simmel's Gastronomic Sociology: An Overlooked Essay." *Food and Foodways* 5(4) (1994): 333–51.

Tabor, George M. *In Search of Bacchus: Wanderings in the Wonderful World of Wine Tourism*. New York: Scribner, 2009.

———. *Judgment of Paris: California vs. France and the Historic 1976 Paris Tasting That Revolutionized Wine*. New York: Scribner, 2005.

Terrio, Susan J. "Crafting *Grand Cru* Chocolates in Contemporary France." In *The Cultural Politics of Food and Eating: A Reader,* ed. James L. Watson and Melissa L. Caldwell. Malden, Mass.: Blackwell Publishing, 2005.

Thach, Liz, and Tim Hanni. "Wine Marketing for Diverse Palates." *Vineyard and Winery Management* 34(1) (2008): 30–34.

"Top 20 Small Towns in the West." *Sunset Magazine,* March 2009.

Trubek, Amy B. "Place Matters." In *The Taste Culture Reader: Experiencing Food and Drink,* ed. Carolyn Korsmeyer. New York: Berg, 2005.

———. *The Taste of Place: A Culinary Journey into Terroir*. Berkeley: University of California Press, 2008.

Tuan, Yi-Fu. "Pleasures of the Proximate Senses: Eating, Taste, and Culture." In *The Taste Culture Reader: Experiencing Food and Drink,* ed. Carolyn Korsmeyer. New York: Berg, 2005.

Turgeon, David. "Napa Valley Gets a New Branding Image." *Napa Valley Life Magazine,* August-September 2008.

Vannini, Phillip, Dennis Waskul, and Simon Gottschalk. "Introduction: The Senses as Social Construction." Available online at http://www.sensorystudies .org/?page_id=323 (accessed Sept. 20, 2010).

Vanderbilt, Tom. *Traffic*. New York: Alfred A. Knopf, 2009.

Veblen, Thorstein. *The Theory of the Leisure Class*. 1899. Reprint, London: Oxford University Press, 2008.

Verardo, Denzil, and Jennie Verardo. *Napa Valley: From Golden Fields to Purple Harvest*. Northridge, Calif.: Windsor Publications, 1986.

Vigneron, Franck, and Lester W. Johnson. "A Review and a Conceptual Framework of Prestige-Seeking Consumer Behavior." *Academy of Marketing Science Review* 1999(1): 1–23. Available online at http://www.amsreview.org/articles/vigneron01-1999.pdf (accessed Sept. 5, 2010).

"Vintage Charts." *WineSpectator.com*. http://www.winespectator.com/Wine/Vintage_Charts/ (accessed March 10, 2009).

Walker, Larry. *The Wines of the Napa Valley*. London: Mitchell Beazley, 2005.

Weaver, David, and Laura Lawton. *Tourism Management*. Milton, Queensland: John Wiley and Sons Australia Ltd., 2000.

Weber, Karl, ed. *Food, Inc*. New York: Public Affairs, 2009.

Weber, Lin. *Old Napa Valley: The History to 1900*. St. Helena, Calif.: Wine Ventures Publications, 1998.

———. *Roots of the Present: Napa Valley 1990 to 1950*. St. Helena, Calif.: Wine Ventures Publications, 2001.

Wemyss, Nina, ed. *Soul of the Vine: Wine in Literature*. Oakville, Calif.: Robert Mondavi Winery, 1998.

Wong, Wilfred. "Wine Shopping the Millennial Way." *Vineyard and Winery Management* 33(5) (2007): 10–12.

Williams, George. *Hot Springs of Northern California*. Carson City, Nev.: Tree by the River Publishing, 1997.

Wilson, James E. *Terroir: The Role of Geology, Climate and Culture in the Making of French Wines*. Berkeley: University of California Press, 1999.

Wine Market Council. "2009 Consumer Tracking Study." Available online at http://www.winemarketcouncil.com/research_summary.asp (accessed June 16, 2009).

"World Drinks Less Wine per Capita." *Wine Spectator*, May 18, 2009. Available online at http://www.winespectator.com/webfeature/show/id/World-Drinks-Less-Wine-Per-Capita_4800 (accessed Oct. 20, 2010).

Young, Stanley. *Beautiful Spas and Hot Springs of California*. San Francisco: Chronicle Books, 1998.

Zauner, Phyllis. *Wine Country*. Tahoe Paradise, Calif.: Zanel Publications, 1983.

Ziegler, Rue. "Round Pond: The History of a Napa Valley Estate." Unpublished manuscript. 2006.

Zraly, Kevin. *Kevin Zraly's American Wine Guide*. New York: Sterling Publishing Co., 2008.

———. *Windows on the World: Complete Wine Course*. New York: Sterling Publishing Co., Inc., 2008.

Zwerdling, Daniel. "Shattered Myths." *Gourmet*, August 2004.

INDEX

Page numbers in italics indicate illustrations.

GEORGE GMELCH is Professor of Anthropology at the University of San Francisco and at Union College. He has studied Irish Travellers, English Gypsies, return migrants in Ireland, Newfoundland, and Barbados, commercial fishermen, Alaska natives, Caribbean villagers and tourism workers, and American professional baseball players. Before becoming an academic, he played professional baseball in the Detroit Tigers organization. He is the author of eleven books and many scholarly articles, and has also written widely for general audiences, including the *New York Times, Washington Post, Psychology Today, Society,* and *Natural History.*

SHARON BOHN GMELCH is Professor of Anthropology at the University of San Francisco and Roger Thayer Stone Professor of Anthropology at Union College. She has published seven books, including *Tinkers and Travellers,* winner of Ireland's book of the year award; *Nan: The Life of an Irish Travelling Woman,* which was a finalist for anthropology's Margaret Mead Award; and most recently, *The Tlingit Encounter with Photography.* She is also the co-producer of an ethnographic film, *A Matter of Respect.* Her interests include visual anthropology, gender, interethnic relations, and tourism.